Alpine and Rock Plants

This book is dedicated to my father and to Ernest Ballard. Two men, both now sadly dead, who, in my formative years, imbued in me a love of plants and all the beauties of nature which has endured throughout my life.

'God grows weary of great nations, but never of little flowers'
Rabindranath Tagore

Alpine and Rock Plants

Will Ingwersen V. M. H

Illustrated by Charles Stitt

J. M. Dent & Sons Ltd
London Toronto Melbourne

First published 1983
© Will Ingwersen 1983

Phototypeset in 10½/13pt Linotron Sabon by
Tradespools Ltd, Frome

Printed and made in Great Britain
by Biddles Ltd, Guildford, for
J. M. Dent & Sons Ltd
Aldine House, 33 Welbeck Street, London W1M 8LX

British Library Cataloguing in Publication Data

Ingwersen, Will
    Alpine and rock plants.
    1. Rock plants   2. Alpine garden plants
    I. Title
    635.9'672   SB421

    ISBN 0-460-04386-2

Contents

Acknowledgements

'Miss Martindale worked on and on' by Reginald Arkell from *Green Fingers Again*, reprinted by permission of Herbert Jenkins Ltd, now a part of the Hutchinson Publishing Group.

List of Colour Photographs

Introduction

When I started to write this book I particularly wished to avoid the 'catalogue style' in which so many gardening books appear. To discover a style that is both readable and informative has not been easy, but I hope to have succeeded in offering to lovers of alpine plants what really amounts to a résumé of a life spent in seeking and growing alpine plants from all parts of the temperate world.

Any attempt at an alphabetical arrangement has been cheerfully abandoned—a comprehensive index will enable reference to be made to any particular plant—although some of the more important genera will be found in close association. This is a book to read, not a catalogue to consult. Reginald Farrer, who can be thought of as the patron saint of alpine gardeners, once wrote: 'On every account, and from every moral, intellectual and emotional point of view, it is in the best interests of all mortals to take joy and glory in a rock garden.'

With no intention, or hope, of imitating Farrer's inimitable style of writing I yet have the audacity to believe that this book may fill a gap which has become increasingly apparent since the heydays of Farrer and a few other notable horticultural writers. If it should stimulate the enthusiasm of those hesitating on the brink of an alpine path, while simultaneously providing interesting reading for those well advanced upon the same road, I shall feel that my objective has been achieved.

At one point I seriously toyed with the idea of adopting a geographical arrangement with plants grouped according to their provenance, but plants are so cosmopolitan that I decided to regard all alpines as being stateless—although I shall, of course, indicate their individual origins. Many of the most desirable plants are garden hybrids or selections with their true origins often shrouded in the mists of time.

For the benefit of the beginner I have decided to write a short initial chapter on cultivation, giving the general principles involved, as a guide to those who have not yet advanced to a position where they are able to form their own conclusions and develop their own recipes for success. A belief still exists among those who do not know them well, that alpines are temperamental and difficult to grow. This is quite unfounded and is true of only a minority of the rarest high alpines, which offer a gleefully accepted challenge to those who have passed the initial stages.

The final pages of the book consist of a series of lists of plants for special places and conditions. This again, is for the benefit of the less knowledgeable who may be in doubt as to the most desirable and advantageous positions for plants they have acquired, or wish to obtain.

It is important, I think, to emphasize that the term 'alpine plant' is a very wide, loose, and often indefinite classification and must include a great many plants which do not come from a truly alpine environment but which enjoy, and fittingly adorn, the various situations allotted to them in our gardens. Of one thing there can be no doubt whatsoever: the present, and continually increasing popularity of alpine plants is due, not only to their beauty and immense diversity, but to the fact that a great many of them can be grown in a limited area—a most important consideration in these times of small gardens and costly and scarce experienced labour. It is, *par excellence*, a very personal and do-it-yourself form of gardening.

Everyone and every thing has to have a name and it is not unknown for beginners to be deterred by the fact that plants have names which are derived from Latin or Greek roots. Few alpines have common or vernacular names and even when they do it can be misleading, as the same name may refer to several quite different plants. An example is the bluebell of Scotland which is the harebell of England. Again, the same plant can have several different names according to locality. There are British wild flowers which have at least half a dozen distinct names. This can be very confusing, especially bearing in mind the international implications of horticulture. The only safe way is to adhere to the classical names which are governed by an International Code of Plant Nomenclature.

An additional distraction for the gardener is that botanists occasionally find it necessary to alter a name which has become familiar to us through long usage. It can, for instance, be annoying to discover that the Cheddar Pink, long known as *Dianthus caesius*, is correctly *D.gratianopolitanus* or that our dainty friend *Campanula pusilla* must be addressed by the more cumbersome name *C.cochlearifolia*.

Having, as it were, a foot in both camps, I admit to some sympathy for the botanists, for accurate plant nomenclature is very important, but I am equally sympathetic to those to whom name changes are anathema. In this book I propose to allow myself a considerable amount of latitude and in the case of plants which have become familiar through long usage under a now invalid name I may use the older name but will indicate what it should correctly be called. It seems odd that so many name alterations involve the use of a much more cumbersome alternative to the original. For example, a very precious and rare plant which I knew as *Alstroemeria pygmaea* I now learn is more properly *Scheckendantzia pygmaea*!

Finally, allow me to say that I would like this book to be regarded as a very personal assessment of the plants I have spent my whole life in seeking, growing and loving, both in their native environments and in my own and other peoples' gardens. Alpines are indeed plants which aptly fit the saying that 'small is beautiful'.

1 Cultivation

The one basic necessity for the successful cultivation of alpine plants is the provision of good drainage. Upon this they insist. They enjoy water in plenty when in active growth, but will not tolerate it lingering around their roots. It must pass away rapidly, leaving a residue of moisture in the compost in which the plants are growing.

Plants which are grown in containers of any sort present no problem: it is easy to provide perfect drainage. But conditions in the open garden may not be ideal and it may be necessary to take initial steps to ensure good drainage. On heavy clay soils, for example, especially if the site is on the flat, one might have to dig deep sump holes and fill them with coarse material such as stones, broken brick, clinker, or anything through which water will pass rapidly and without hindrance.

On a sloping site an area can be drained by a narrow channel or channels dug a foot deep, leading downhill, and filled with similar draining material. Should the natural drainage be good these rather laborious operations will not be necessary.

Whatever project one has in mind it is useful to have an ideal at which to aim. An ideal site for a rock garden would be on a gentle slope facing south west, fully in the open and not overhung by trees or shadowed by adjacent tall buildings. I appreciate that these conditions will not always be available, but fortunately there are plenty of compromises. A site to be avoided if possible is one with a due east aspect, but even this can be used if there is no alternative.

When assembling materials it is always preferable to choose a local stone. It will not only fit more appropriately into its surroundings, it will also be much less costly than importing a foreign stone from a long distance. The beautiful, water and wind weathered limestones from the north are very popular, but they are out of place in southern counties and, even in these days of 'clean air', if used in an urban environment, are apt to become a harsh marble-white in colour. Limestones are also inclined to limit one's choice of plants because they are unsuitable for a number of lime-hating plants.

For the commoner and most popular alpines a simple basic soil compost will suffice. It is only when one becomes tempted to accept the challenge of the more difficult high alpines that special mixtures are needed. The main constituent of a basic compost will be loam, or, if genuine loam is not available, one can substitute good field or garden top-spit soil. It is advisable to have this ingredient tested to ascertain if it is acid or alkaline. Inexpensive soil-testing kits are always available from chemists or a good garden centre. The pH testing scale runs from one to fourteen. A pH of seven is neutral, anything below is acid and anything above is alkaline.

A satisfactory compost would consist of two parts of the loam—or whatever substitute is used—one part of fine-grade moss peat and one part of sharp sand or fine grit. Leaf soil or well decayed garden compost can take the place of peat if necessary and the use of yellow builder's sand should be avoided. All parts are by bulk and when the ingredients are assembled and ready for mixing, it will be beneficial to give the heap a generous sprinkling of bonemeal before it is finally mixed.

One can only be rather vague as to the quantity of compost needed for a given tonnage of rock. It will depend to some extent on the type of construction but as a minimum it is wise to provide a cubic yard of compost for each ton of rock. The soil, when used, should be moist (but neither dry nor saturated) and, after building is completed and all pockets filled, allow a period for settlement before planting and have some soil in reserve for 'topping up' where necessary.

The majority of alpines are sun-lovers but for those which seek a modicum of shade positions can usually be found in the shade of a rock, or an adjacent shrub or taller plant. For any quantity of shade-demanding plants a more suitable location will have to be found and regarded as a special area.

At this point I will not bedevil you with complicated recipes for special soil mixtures for rarities. I will indicate where these are desirable when writing of the particular plant or plants in question. By the time the beginner has advanced to the stage of experimenting with rarities he or she will probably have ideas of their own and will be in little need of guidance. There are no hard and fast rules for growing plants, thank goodness, and only too often treatments which Mr. Jones finds successful are a total failure when emulated by Mr. Smith next door. Much of the delight to be found in growing alpines is discovered in the diversity of methods and the importance of developing one's own 'do-it-yourself' techniques.

After-care of plants is largely a matter of common sense and normal gardening practices, but it is well to remember that such plants as *Aubrieta*, *Alyssum*, *Arabis*, *Helianthemum*, many of the genus *Cam-*

panula and some of *Dianthus*, should be clipped quite severely after they have flowered. This encourages new and neat young growth and very often prolongs the life of the plant, preventing it from swamping and possibly destroying less robust neighbours.

2 Daphnes and Primulas in particular

Daphnes are plants for which I have a particular affection, a liking which is, of course, partially due to their beauty and their fragrance—and, possibly, to the intransigence of some which induces a determination to overcome their whims and fancies. Part of my love for the genus, however, is undoubtedly due to the fact that my very first plant hunting expedition, in the mountains of south-east Europe, had, as one of its objects, a sight of *Daphne blagayana* in the wild.

Led by a group of Yugoslavian friends, all fanatical lovers of alpine plants, we eventually came across a strong colony of the daphne, growing in a small wood on an alpine pasture where a thick layer of leaf-mould covered a very stony and sharply drained soil. Gently grasping the stem beneath a cluster of the deep green, glabrous and leathery leaves, I was intrigued to discover that I could gradually extract the woody stem from the leafy soil layer and lead it back to the rooting point more than a yard distant.

At blossoming time, which is usually during March and April, each terminal cluster of leaves envelops a number of cream-white flowers whose fragrance dominates the air for yards around. A confirmed lime-lover, *D.blagayana* is not difficult to grow if one recalls its rambling habit and if the long bare stems are covered by flat stones, or if it can be persuaded to ramble through neighbouring plants, such as dwarf lime-loving heathers like *Erica herbacea (carnea)*. The lengthy, leafless stems do not like to remain fully exposed. Like most daphnes, it will occasionally die with very little warning and it is advisable to keep a small reserve stock against such an unfortunate happening. Cuttings made from soft young shoots in the spring root easily and quickly in a close frame or a mist unit, an aid to rapid propagation with which many amateurs now provide themselves. A small unit is easily and inexpensively installed in a greenhouse.

The supreme aristocrat of alpine daphnes is *D.petraea*, and especially so in its cultivated 'Grandiflora' form. The type is found wild only in an extremely restricted area of the Italian Alps where it inhabits narrow cracks and crannies in awe-inspiring limestone cliffs. Into those crevices plunge the thick and fleshy roots, fortunately almost impossible to extract. From a stout and woody neck rises an intricate mass of small branches clothed in tiny oval, dark green leaves of hard and glossy texture. At flowering time each of the shoots burgeons into a terminal cluster of waxy, rich pink tubular and intensely fragrant flowers. This happens during June and July—sometimes rather earlier in gardens. This precious shrub is very, very slow-growing. In cultivation it is more often than not grafted onto the stock of another daphne, but it can be struck from cuttings. It relishes a spartan diet and, as its habitat suggests, likes to be firmly wedged between pieces of stone. It can be grown out of doors, preferably in a niche reserved for it in a sink or trough garden, but is seen at its best as a specimen plant for the alpine house.

Earlier I said that daphnes are only too likely to die, either wholly or in part. One species which I have found to be less likely than most to behave in this disturbing way is *D.collina*. In the wild it is found in the hills near Naples. In gardens it forms a dense, low bush, usually little more than a foot in height. An aged specimen might be slightly taller with a spread of a yard or more. The red-purple flowers are borne in terminal clusters and are to be seen in great abundance during April and May, but my own experience has always been that there are less bountiful intermittent displays during the summer and into the early autumn months. It is very hardy and easily pleased in any good garden soil, however, it does insist on perfect drainage and is unhappy in soil likely to become waterlogged in winter.

Favouritism is said to be a bad thing, but inevitably one has favourite plants and, next to *D.petraea* I find *D.cneorum* the most desirable. It is a plant which I would not willingly do without. Were I condemned to have but eight plants in my garden, I am sure that one of them would be *D.cneorum*. In the excellent monograph of the genus *Daphne*, written by C. D. Brickell and B. Mathew, is a quotation which I beg leave to copy. It was written in the *Gardeners' Chronicle* of June, 1843 by a correspondent, who said: 'Such a plant on a May morning with the beauty of the flowers and the fragrance they pour forth, drives through the soul a stream of pleasure which is impossible to describe'. As some other, unidentified person, said, 'them's my sentiments exactly'. Few plants give me such pleasure.

Frequent in the European Alps, *D.cneorum* takes kindly to cultivation, especially if provided with steady but not excessive water supply to the roots and frequent mulches of leaf-mould, garden compost or peat. Although in nature it is often found on stony, dry ground, in gardens it seems to prefer a more luxurious life. The mulching also helps to clothe

the stems, which are apt to become bare and leafless in old plants, a condition which, like *D.blagayana*, it resents. Well-established plants may spread over a yard or more and will not exceed a foot or so in height and are unforgettable when covered with myriads of terminal clusters of pink and fragrant flowers. There are several named forms, the best of which I consider to be *D.c.* '*Eximea*', which is robust and has larger flowers of deeper colour than the type. There is also a rare albino, much sought after by plant collectors.

D.arbuscula, originally discovered in the Carpathian Mountains more than a hundred years ago, has long been a favourite among alpine gardeners. It is an aristocratic, very dwarf shrub with woody stems and dark, shining narrow leaves of leathery texture. Reginald Farrer was rude about it for some reason or other—perhaps it would not grow well for him. I have never found it to be a difficult plant. It is another lime-lover and does as well in the open as it does in an alpine house. The low mats are, in spring, plentifully adorned by heads of fragrant flowers. The colour is variable, mostly pink, but some forms are deep rose-red and others almost white. It sets seeds in moderation and can also be increased with ease by making cuttings from soft tips or, preferably, half-ripened shoots from June onwards. Wherever it is grown I have found it prefers having its roots confined. Grown in free soil it is distressingly apt to partially die back. I am confident that much of the trouble which daphnes inflict upon us is due to growing them too fat and too well.

Possibly a little too tall at maturity for small rock gardens, but admissible as a young plant for several years thereafter, *D.retusa* is a useful and decorative dwarf evergreen shrub. A native of China, it has been cultivated for many years. It is a freely branching, compact bush with thick, shining green leaves. The flowers, in terminal clusters, are purple and fragrant and are frequently followed by quite large, fleshy, bright red fruits. Although said by some to be a lime-hater, I have known it grown well on alkaline soil, where it is perfectly happy providing the soil is rich in humus. A fully adult specimen might attain a height of three feet, but it is slow-growing.

One could continue indefinitely in praise of daphnes, but I must content myself with one more, which really completes the tale of those really suited to the alpine garden without becoming involved with one or two truly temperamental species, such as the prostrate form of *D.jasminea* which, delightful though it is, does present some problems. My final choice is *D.striata*, a close relative of *D.cneorum*. This too, does not have a very good reputation, but I have found it amenable enough if given gritty soil rich in humus. I have, in a large stone trough, a plant of it which is now a prostrate foot in diameter and flowers abundantly every year. The small whitish to purple flowers are carried in twos and threes at the ends of the trailing, woody stems in the spring, and sometimes again in the autumn. In its native Greece it is invariably a crevice haunter.

In spite of a foot-loose youth spent visiting many remote areas, I regret never having found my way to Mexico or Guatemala, where, in the craters of extinct volcanoes, *Weldenia candida* grows—a plant for which I have a particular affection. Not a plant to glorify the outdoor garden, it must be grown in pots in the alpine house. The pots must be deep and large to accommodate the robust, fleshy, almost tuberous roots. It is a greedy plant too, and relishes a compost to which has been added good food and it has no objection at all to a hefty dollop of old cow manure over the crocks in the base of the pot. The only species in its genus, with slight variation between the Mexican and Guatamalan forms, it is a plant which is interesting and, when in flower, extremely handsome.

From the lusty roots in late spring, rise great tufts of thick, broad and pointed leaves and from the centre of these rosettes erupt slightly cup-shaped flowers of dazzling whiteness. The blossoms appear a few at a time in a summer-long succession. The characteristic feature which separates the Guatamalan from the Mexican plant is that the former displays tufts of white hairs over the surface of the leaves. It is said to be possible to propagate *Waldenia* from root cuttings; I have never succeeded, but it provides a good crop of seeds—when you can find them!

The apparent flower stems are really extended flower tubes and the sexual parts are at the base of these tubes, at ground level or even just below the surface. When, as autumn approaches, the leaves begin to wither, indicating that *Waldenia* is going to rest for the winter, a slight pull on the tuft will reveal a harvest of seeds. These should be sown as soon as gathered as they seem to lose their fertility if stored for a long period.

As one grows older, memories become increasingly important. In no condition now to engage in active mountain climbing, I can dwell in retrospect upon memories of past events. I remember in particular detail a period of several years which I spent in a valley leading into the Maritime Alps behind the town of Menton. The Gorbio Valley is a narrow channel between steep hills leading into the heart of the high mountains which were, and are, the homes of a great many lovely and exciting alpine plants. With such a field of exploration on my very doorstep and with an unbounded enthusiasm to seek and find and learn, and ample time for exploration, I was able to confirm and elaborate my lifelong love for the jewels of the high places.

Primulas have always ranked high in my esteem and memories of *Primula marginata*, a species almost endemic to the maritime Alps, suggest that here as well as anywhere is the opportunity to consider this invaluable race of plants which, in its innumerable variations, has long glorified our gardens.

There are some plants which not only entice us by the beauty of their flowers, but offer a bonus in the form of handsome foliage, and *Primula marginata* is one of these. It is an infinitely variable plant with flowers ranging from palest lavender to rich purple-blue and foliage which can be lightly or deeply crenulated at the margins, with light or heavy powerings of white farina and varying considerably in shape and size. I would dispute that there is such a thing as a bad *P.marginata* but will by no means deny that some are better than others. It is the good forms that one should select.

This lovely *Primula* is a confirmed lover of narrow crevices, chinks and crannies in which to grow. As it ages it develops quite long, almost woody stems, terminating in rosettes of the handsome leaves. The umbels of flowers are carried on stems well above the foliage and are of good shape and solidity. In its finest manifestation it has been given the clonal name of *P.m.* 'Linda Pope', a form (or possibly a hybrid) of uncertain garden origin. This is a real magnificence displaying all the finest characteristics of the species. Other named variants worth seeking are 'Beamish Variety' and 'Prichard's Variety'.

Few would dispute the right of *P.allionii* to be regarded as the most lovely of all European primulas. It is endemic to the Maritimes and occurs only in a very limited area, where it has dwelt for centuries, to be visited and adored by devotees, but never, please, to be collected. It is firmly established in cultivation and there is no need to decimate the limited wild colonies. It, too, is a variable species, but there are no 'bad eggs'; any of the forms of *P.allionii* are to be cherished. The colour of the almost stemless flowers which adorn the pads of crowded rosettes of softly hairy leaves can range from white, through shades of pink to carmine. This is another plant which should be grown in pots and pans in an alpine house for the best results, although the more daring might insert small plants in holes bored in a tufa rock, preferably so that it is protected by a slight overhang—positions which it seems to prefer in the wild. I have even seen it occupying positive caves where neither rain nor sun could penetrate.

One of the best beloved of the European primulas is *P.auricula*, which is one of the several parents of the garden Auricula. This is another extremely variable species and there are numerous geographical forms, each to be found in its own area of the Alps. The type plant has rather loose rosettes of fleshy leaves, which may or may not be coated with farina. The tubular, yellow, fragrant flowers are carried in heads which may contain few or many blossoms on stems seldom exceeding six inches. Any of the several named forms is desirable, but worthy of special note are those named *albocincta*, *ciliata*, *monacensis*, *moschata* and *obristii*. These are all variations on the same theme, some with heavily farina-coated foliage, others with larger flowers, some with a clear white eye in the throat of the flower. If I were to choose just one of the variants I think I would settle for *albocincta*, which is an especially beautiful form.

The Lilliputian of European primulas is *P.minima*, which is widely distributed in the Alps. It forms clusters of crowded rosettes of small, wedge-shaped leaves, toothed at the ends and the short-stemmed flowers are very large, consisting of five, notched petals of clear pink. Where this species meets others, it cheerfully hybridizes with them and there is a small host of such very desirable bastards. One of the best is *P.bileckii*, a cross between *P.minima* and *P.hirsuta*. *P.minima* itself is apt to be shy-flowering in gardens, but its hybrids will entirely conceal themselves beneath the many large blossoms.

Were I to embark upon describing all the European primulas I should occupy many more pages than this book can spare. I can only suggest to you that you will find pleasure in any of the following: *P.carniolica*, *P.clusiana*, *P.deorum*, *P.glaucescens*, *P.glutinosa*, *P.hirsuta*, *P.integrifolia*, *P.latifolia* (*viscosa*), *P.pedemontana*, *P.spectabilis*, *P.viscosa* and *P.wulfeniana*. There are one or two British species which ought not to be omitted, but do not collect them if you are fortunate enough to see them in the wild, for their natural stations are diminishing. *P.farinosa* is the dainty Bird's-eye Primrose, small and elegant with rosettes of farina covered leaves and short-stemmed heads of small rich pink flowers. It is not long-lived but is easily raised from the seeds which it produces in plenty.

From the far north of Britain comes *P.scotica* a minuteness of no more than an inch or two. The tiny rosettes of farina-covered leaves offer an inch-high stem ending in a cluster of small violet-purple flowers, each with a white or yellow throat. It is sometimes figured in catalogues and should be regarded as a great treasure, of which seeds should be saved and sown, for it does not have a long life.

There are other primulas, from many parts of the world. I ignore all the Asiatic bog-primulas but I dare not omit one special American, from California. This is *P.suffrutescens*, which asks for, and well deserves, alpine house conditions. It is almost shrubby, with short, stiff, branching stems adorned with narrow, leathery, yellow-green leaves. From amidst the terminal leaf clusters appear short stems carrying fragrant flowers of clear pink. It is a most unusual and beautiful plant, best given lime-free, gritty and humus-rich soil.

Not many lilies are dwarf enough, or appropriate for the rock garden, but mention of the Maritime Alps brought back vivid memories of *Lilium pomponium* and of my first discovery of a very charming plant. I knew that it was not a very abundant inhabitant of the region

Primula suffrutescens   *Primula auricula*

and set forth for an expedition which was to last for several days in the more remote regions. Scrambling through thickets on the foothills covered with bushes of *Cornus mas*, already sporting myriads of small yellow flowers, the ground beneath them carpeted with hepaticas, blue, white and pink, I came to the upper rocky regions, but never a sight of the lily.

Becoming more and more dolorous and camping at night with my face open to the stars, I eventually faced a vertical cliff at the head of a valley. My maps promised good hunting on the further side of the forbidding façade, which I began to climb. I finally found myself in a position from which I could not advance, and from which I hesitated to retreat. I traversed a frighteningly narrow ledge and came upon a narrow crack in the rocky walls, through which I literally fell into a hidden valley.

When my footing and breath had been recovered I surveyed the small world in which I found myself and it seemed to be a sort of Shangri-La. A tiny valley, completely surrounded by high cliffs and a level floor of grassy sward in which were two small lakes. Right at my feet, growing from wide crevices in shattered rocks, were many flowering stems of *L.pomponium* and, to my delight, further exploration revealed that it was there literally in hundreds, along with good forms of *Primula marginata*, forms of *Saxifraga lingulata* (now correctly *S.callosa*), great pads of the Cobweb Houseleek, *Sempervivum arachnoideum*, golden-flowered sheets of the grass-leaved buttercup, *Ranunculus gramineus*, and many other delights.

After a night and day spent in this paradise I felt that few other human feet could have trodden its meadows, for I could discover no entrance or exit apart from the one cranny through which I had so fortunately tumbled. A skilled mountaineer might possibly have scaled those sheer cliffs, offering few, if any, hand or footholds, but it was an exercise I had no desire to attempt. During the following two years I returned a few times but that was long ago and I wonder if anyone else has discovered that small valley, visible only from the air? There is a warning here for those who go scrambling in the mountains. I was very much a 'loner' and there were many occasions when it would have been safer to have had a companion. I was fortunate and never had a serious accident—perhaps because of a natural temerity which prevented me from attempting any really dangerous climbs.

Even now in my garden is a colony of *L.pomponium*, seed progeny of the few bulbs I ventured to take from such a plentitude. From their scaly bulbs rise eighteen-inch stems clothed densely in narrow, silver-edged leaves and topped by half a dozen or more brilliantly red Turk's Cap flowers with the characteristic rolled-back segments, each blossom black-spotted in the centre.

A great many good garden plants have been discovered by careful weeders who kept a watchful eye for any seedling that looked interesting. A good example of this exists in a splendid dwarf, shrubby verbascum. Ken Aslet, when he was curator of the rock garden department at the Wisley Gardens, was tidying up the staging in the alpine house when he noticed, between two large pots, one containing *Verbascum dumulosum* and the other *V.spinosum*, a self-sown seedling growing in the gravel. This he carefully potted and it proved to be a natural hybrid between the two species, which he eventually named *V.* × 'Letitia'.

This discovery has provided an excellent hardy dwarf shrub for the rock garden or alpine house. The rigidly upright, woody stems branch freely and carry lobed, softly hairy grey-green leaves and all the tips carry racemes of large, clear yellow flowers in great profusion over a long summer period. Each petal of the flower has a brown spot at the base. The flower racemes eventually become stiff and very spiny and I prefer to cut them off during the winter.

Another accidental discovery was made in a garden in Kent, many years ago. It is assumed to be a hybrid between *Viola pedata* and *V.septentrionalis* and was named *V.*'Delmonden', after the garden in which it occurred. It has proved to be a delightful plant, of good constitution. Amidst and above the deeply cleft leaves are splendid lavender flowers of good size and substance. Here again, each of the parents is worthy of praise. *V.pedata* is an American species, inclined to be temperamental but it can be made happy in light shade and leafy soil. It forms low tufts of divided leaves amidst which appear the flowers, deep violet on the upper petals, much paler on the lower ones. *V.septentrionalis* is also North American and very easily pleased, although it, too, prefers a modicum of shade and humus-rich soil. In such conditions it grows into wide mats of spreading rhizomes with plentiful wide, pointed and toothed leaves and many handsome violet-purple, or sometimes white, flowers, There is confusion in gardens between this species and another North American, *V.cucullata*, which is very similar in general appearance but should have violet flowers with a white throat. A plant sometimes grown under this name has pure white flowers, the petals veined with thin purple lines.

The very thought of violas prompts another jog down memory lane as my thoughts fly back to a plant hunting expedition in the mountains of Canada and North America. One of the highlights of a prolonged and rewarding exploration was a visit to the Olympic Mountains in the State of Washington. One of the objects was to see exquisite *Campanula piperi* growing in its only native habitat, but more of that anon. Another plant endemic to the Olympics is *Viola fletti*, where it inhabits shady crannies in cliffs of dark volcanic rock. Still a rarity in cultivation, it is grown by a few enthusiasts and even makes occasional appearances in specialist catalogues.

A tiny plant, it makes small tufts of rounded, scalloped leaves of firm texture, each tuft displaying a few quite large flowers of reddish-violet, the petals veined with deeper colour and yellow at the base. In cultivation it should be given lime-free soil and is another plant which likes a rather spartan existence, relishing a crevice between small pieces of rock. An easy life in a body of rich soil is not much to its liking.

Some alpine plants have a wide natural distribution and it is possible to encounter old friends in far distant lands. Pretty little *Viola biflora* can be found wild in Europe, through North Asia and into North America. It will be a familiar sight to those who penetrate high into the European Alps for it has an engaging habit of peeping out from cool places beneath and between rocks, often by the very pathside, with the neatest of small, twin, bright yellow violets.

Also small and clear yellow is *V.aetolica*, an Eastern European species. If you seek for it in catalogue it often lurks under the aliases of *V.saxatilis* 'Aetolica' or *V.aetolica* 'Saxatilis'. Like other violas it will sometimes, by the aid of its own secret cosmetics, paint its two upper petals violet. These exquisite flowers are carried on short stems over neat tufts of tiny, toothed leaves. Not very long-lived, it provides plenty of seeds from which a new stock is easily raised.

The mountains of Australia are beginning to yield to British gardens some very attractive small plants but *Viola hederacea* came to our gardens more than a hundred years ago. It has dithered uneasily between two genera and is sometimes listed as *Erpetion reniforme*. It has also proved rather inconstant, for it is not completely hardy and can succumb in the open after a severe winter. It likes a cool position in moisture-retentive soil, where it will make spreading mats of tiny heart-shaped leaves over which flutter white-tipped violet-blue flowers. Its creeping stems root as they go so that it is quite easy to lift and pot a plant or two for winter protection as an insurance against possible loss. It is dainty and likeable enough to justify such a small chore.

The full tale of violas would be a very long one and I must content myself, and you, with just a few of my own special favourites. I would

Viola aetolica

Viola hederacea

consider my garden impoverished if I did not have some colonies of *Viola cornuta*, and especially in its albino form. I have always suspected that this should have specific rank, for it breeds completely true from seed, which a mere colour variant should not do. It flowers continuously through the spring and summer months, with abundant flights of butterfly-like flowers of purest whiteness, carried on six-inch stems. The flowers of the type, which occurs plentifully in the Pyrenees and more sparingly elsewhere in the Alps, are a good rich purple in colour. It has also been instrumental in the parentage of several good tufted pansies, violas and violettas.

There is a trinity of unusual and delightful violas, unfortunately very rare in cultivation and not plentiful in nature. They can almost be classified as minute shrubs, for their thin stems are woody. *V.cazorlensis* is a Spaniard, *V.delphinantha* comes from Greece and Bulgaria, and *V.kosaninii* must be sought in Albania and one or two areas in Macedonia. There is a family similarity between all three. Their slender, woody stems clothed in needle-fine dark green leaves carry pink, twin-spurred flowers. None of them can be described as easy to grow, but, given a sunny crevice with a restricted root run they may be attempted with some confidence—if they can be obtained. *V.cazorlensis* is the only one appearing very occasionally in specialist catalogues and it is high time someone brought some seeds of the others for they are adorable plants which ought to be established in cultivation.

The common viola of alpine meadows is *V.calcarata*, which grows amidst the alpine herbage and displays typically viola-shaped flowers of rich violet. A special favourite of mine is the version of this species from the Eastern Alps, *V.c.* subspecies *zoysii*, which is smaller, neater, with dark foliage and more rounded flowers of clear yellow.

The true *V.gracilis* is unusual because it is, as far as I can trace, extinct in cultivation. All sorts of violas are distributed under its name, but they are all hybrids and none of them equals in beauty the plant which I remember vividly from the days when I was a youthful nuisance on my father's nursery. There is no good reason why it should not be reintroduced from its native haunts in Greece and the Balkans. It would be an immediate success if made available for it has splendid, rich violet flowers, a neat habit and a long flowering season. It is curious that some plants once plentiful in gardens should become rarities, for no obviously apparent reason. Maybe *V.gracilis* was too easily persuaded to hybridize and thus became lost among the host of its children.

Two violas which are sometimes condemned as weeds, will always find a welcome in my garden. One is the purple-leaved form of

V.labradorica and the other a subspecies of our wild violet, *V.tricolor*, which goes under the name *macedonica*. Both seed themselves very freely and I employ them as easy ground cover beneath and between shrubs. They will even flourish in poor soil where little else will grow. *V.labradorica* makes low tufts of small, rounded leaves and its purple flowers are like those of a violet. *V.macedonica* resembles a violetta and is coloured reddish-purple. It flowers without ceasing throughout the summer and will even brave the depths of winter with a few blossoms.

With *V.beckwithii* I have a love–hate relationship. It is a dainty and desirable little North American which I would dearly love to grow, but it has consistently refused to accept any advances from me. It just sniffs disdainfully at whatever I offer it—and dies. The lobed and hairy leaves grow in neat tufts over which hover short-stemmed flowers with upper petals of rich violet and the lower ones a paler shade with a yellow base. I have not seen it in the wild but I am told that it favours rather damp situations although the nearest to success I have ever attained was when I planted it in a rather dry scree in the shade of an adjacent rock.

You have to be courageous and lucky—or skilful—to persuade *V.cenisia* that life is bearable in the lowlands. It is well worth the effort, as anyone who has seen it rambling through the high screes and moraines of the Alps will agree. Its frail underground stems wander here and there, emitting tufts of tiny grey-green leaves and quite large purple flowers, golden-eyed and delicately pencilled black moustaches. Definitely a treasure for the alpine house, it might accept a large but shallow pan filled with soil which is fifty per cent sharp grit. It will grow in alkaline soil, but the finest plants I ever saw in the wild were definitely flourishing in lime-free conditions.

No qualms need be felt about *V.elatior*, which is both European and Asian in origin. Different in habit of growth to most violas, it has erect, leafy stems up to a foot or a little more in height and from spring until early autumn appear large violets of clear lavender colour. Happy in any soil or situation, it is a long-lived delight needing no special care or attention. Much as I enjoy tending and fussing with my plants, it is nice to possess a few which will look after themselves and display no resentment if they are temporarily forgotten while interests are concentrated elsewhere in the garden.

To make up the score of violas, which is all that space permits, but less than such a pleasing genus deserves, I include another of my favourites. *V.nuttallii* from North America, when in leaf alone, far from resembles one's conception of a violet. Clustered in loose tuffets are quite

large, broad and pointed and intensely hairy leaves. It is only recognizable when the four-inch stems emerge from the clustered leaves, each
one displaying a large, clear, golden-headed violet. I have found it to be
happiest in lime-free soil, gritty but rich in humus. It will grow in full
sun, but is by no means averse to a modicum of light shade.

Stepping right out of context, and including a shrub which really has
no place among alpines, I cannot resist the temptation to make some
mention of *Hymenanthera crassifolia*, an Australian shrub which,
surprisingly, belongs in the natural order Violaceae, although no eye but
that of a trained botanist would see the relationship. A semi-evergreen, it
forms a yard-high bush of woody, branching stems with small, leathery
leaves. The flowers are inconspicuous but are followed by attractive,
pure white fruits. It is not too large for a sizeable rock garden and is a
good enough plant to have been deemed worthy of a First Class
Certificate in 1892, although today, against fiercer competition, it might
not receive such an oscar.

When good fortune provided the opportunity to live for some years
in the south of France, with Italy only a stone's throw away, I was able
to pay many visits to Corsica and became well acquainted with its coasts
and valleys and mountains. It has been aptly named the Fragrant Isle, for
as one approaches it from the sea, the warm, aromatic fragrance of the
maquis greets you when the land is still far distant. It was on the heights
of Monte d'Oro that I first came to know *Helichrysum frigidum*, one of
the several good plants which are endemic to the island.

I became increasingly despondent, knowing that the plant had been
recorded as plentiful on that particular mountain, as I climbed higher
and higher, with never a glimpse of the silvery tufts I was eager to find. It
was not until I was nearly at the summit that at last I began to see
colonies tucked into rock crevices and then, suddenly, it surrounded me
in abundance. The thin, frail stems are densely clothed in tiny, intensely
silver leaves and crowd into the neatest of hummocks no more than an
inch or two in height. The small heads of minute flowers are surrounded
by a circlet of silver-grey, papery bracts, looking rather like a daisy
flower. The blossoms have the everlasting quality of many helichrysums
and persist for a long time. It is not a difficult plant to grow, given
somewhat spartan conditions in gritty soil. In the open it does well
planted in a tufa rock but, on the whole, is happier given alpine house
treatment.

As you read on—if you do—there will be many more references to
Corsica and its treasures, but the thought of *H.frigidum* brings to mind a
few other species which no collection of alpine plants should lack. From

the Drakensburg Mountains of Lesotho (formerly Basutoland) comes *H.milfordae*, first introduced to Britain as *H.marginatum*, and still frequently grown under that name. Despite its South African habitat, it is very reasonably hardy if grown in a warm and sunny position, assured of perfect drainage and a soil which is not over rich. The silver-haired leaves are packed into dense rosettes and form flat, spreading pads. From the centre of each rosette will rise a large, conical bud composed of crimson-backed bracts, which expand into large, short-stemmed everlasting flowers of glistening white. A plant displaying both unopened buds and expanded flowers against the argent carpet of its foliage is a quite spectacular sight. Should it rain while the flowers are fully open, they will almost instantly close, exposing the vividly coloured reverse side of the bracts.

The genus *Helichrysum* is widely scattered about the world, and to see *H.coralloides* as a wilding a journey to New Zealand would be required. I first saw this curious and fascinating plant many years ago on what was, I believe, its first public appearance in this country. It was exhibited as one specimen at a Chelsea Flower Show, where it created quite a sensation. For a long time it remained a great rarity because it proved to be very difficult to propagate, but eventually the secret was discovered and it is now reasonably plentiful and much in demand.

The erect, branching stems are clothed in a dense pelt of small, pointed, overlapping leaves which cling tightly to the branches. Their bright green colour is an intriguing foil to the margin of white wool over which they are laid and which can be seen at the edges of the leaves. The final effect is of a dwarf, gnarled bush of silver and green. It is slow-growing and much hardier than has been supposed, especially if pushed into a tight crevice or planted in a hole bored in tufa—it should, in fact, be given austere conditions in the open. It is, of course, a perfectly splendid alpine house plant. Flowers are seldom produced and when they do occasionally appear are little tufts of yellow at the tips of the shoots, making no contribution of beauty to a plant which is sufficiently attractive without the aid of flowers.

Another New Zealander exists in the form of *H.plumeum*, which can be likened to a smaller, less rigid and generally 'fluffier' version of *H.coralloides*. In my own experience, it is less tolerant of outdoor cultivation and should be given at least winter protection under glass, although I have persuaded it to live with reasonable contentment in a tight chink on the corner of a stone sink. A splendid *Helichrysum*, this time from the Balkans, is *H.virgineum*, but this is very definitely an alpine house plant. It forms clusters of wide leaves coated in silver hairs and at the end of its nine-inch stems carries fat buds which are enveloped in shell-pink bracts, opening finally into wide, white everlasting flowers.

You will by now have discovered, and I have already said, that this book is not alphabetically arranged; it, however, seems sensible to gather together in one place the desirable members of some of the larger genera and one which immediately comes to mind is the great and invaluable genus *Campanula*, which has made major contributions to several forms of gardening and, not least, to the rock garden and alpine house. This is yet another group which demands a volume of its own if it were to be described in detail, but there are some which I count among my favourites. There are enough of these to demand a short chapter to themselves, with apologies to all those which are omitted.

3 Campanulas

Probably the most valuable of the several awards which are given to plants by the Committee and Council of the Royal Horticultural Society, from the ordinary gardener's point of view, is the Award of Garden Merit (AGM), for, to receive this award, a plant must be thoroughly garden-worthy. It must grow well in ordinary garden conditions and, possibly more important than anything else, it must be readily available. Such awards as the First Class Certificate and the Award of Merit are highly prized, and rightly so, but they can be given, and sometimes are, to plants which, after a brief appearance to receive their accolade, are either not seen again or may prove very difficult to obtain.

Few of the dwarf species of *Campanula* have received the AGM, but it was given to *C.portenschlagiana* in 1927, and it is as good a plant now as it was then. It is a native of Dalmatia and sometimes seen under the names *muralis* or *bavarica*, both invalid synonyms. I am not sure when it was first introduced to cultivation, however, it must have been a very long time ago, for I have known it and cherished it all my life. It will grow in sun or light shade, it is long-lived and very free-flowering. In fact, I cannot think of anything bad to say about it! Forming nine-inch masses of crowded stems, each of which ends in a tuft of bright green glabrous leaves, it is evergreen, but the whole plant will disappear for weeks on end beneath a wealth of bell shaped flowers carried in many-flowered panicles. One cannot have too much of it, and it is easily increased by dividing the clumps in autumn or early spring.

To really enjoy the much rarer *C.zoysii* it is essential to erect slug-proof barriers, for I know of no plant upon which the slimy gastropods will more gluttonously feast. On a memorable plant hunt through remote regions of Yugoslavia we were led to a valley into which an entire cliff had fallen during some past disaster. *C.zoysii* is normally a saxatile plant, haunting narrow chinks and crannies. The fallen cliff must have been full of it and it had taken root and spread extensively in wide areas of shale and stony debris and was there in such quantity that no shame was felt in lifting a few mats, an operation which would have been impossible had one tried to wrest it from its conventional habitats.

A true Lilliputian, it makes the neatest of tiny tufts of glossy green leaves, over which appear short stems, each bearing a few clear blue flowers of curious shape, the mouth of the narrow, tubular bell being crimped and puckered like the lips of a pouting mouth. You will not find it as easy to buy as *C.portenschlagiana* but it does appear from time to time in specialist catalogues (my good friend Joe Elliott, grows it extremely well and often has young plants available on his nursery at Broadwell, Moreton-in-Marsh, Gloucestershire.) Give it a spartan, gritty, limy mixture, or wedge it into a crevice; it is, however, easier to keep the slugs from it in an alpine house.

The bearded bellflower *C.barbata* grows all through the European Alps, and northward into Scandinavia. It is an easy, but rather short-lived plant and therefore it is advisable to gather a few of the plentiful seeds from time to time to ensure a continuity; it will often self-seed and thus provide its own progeny. Usually found on granitic formations in the wild, it displays no aversion to lime in captivity. For a short-lived plant it makes an extraordinarily deep and stout tap-root from which emerge loose rosettes of narrow and roughly hairy leaves. From the centre of the rosette rise foot-high stems carrying many pendant blue bells, heavily bearded on the inside. Albinos are frequently found among the seedlings. (Illus. see below)

My father was responsible for the introduction of many good plants and it is he we have to thank for *C.poscharskyana*. He was heard to say, some years after he brought it from Eastern Europe in 1933, that it was the only plant he almost regretted having put into our gardens! Lovely though it is, it is assuredly a ramper and will very quickly cover square yards of ground. If the space for a spreader is available it pays a good rent by the profusion of its long sprays of starry, lavender-blue flowers. It combines to perfection with that other rampageous grower, *Alchemilla mollis*. They flower together and the association of the grey leaves and chartreuse flowers of the *Alchemilla* with the soft blue of the *Campanula* is quite enchanting.

Why is it, I wonder, that certain plants do not seem to achieve the popularity which their beauty so well deserves? *C.betulifolia*, which flaunts its handsome flowers from rock crevices in Armenian mountains, although not difficult to grow, is all too seldom seen. Always a staunch defender of the underdog, I like to sing the praises of these Cinderellas of the plant world. Its toothed and wedge-shaped leaves adorn stems which are semi-procumbent and radiate from a common centre, carrying terminally loose clusters of large, bell-shaped flowers which are deep pink on the outer side of the petals and may be white or soft pink on the inner surface. This handsome plant received an Award of Merit in 1937 and is a plant which ought to be in every alpine garden, either in the crevice of a wall or the rock garden, or as a specimen in an alpine house. (Illus. see below)

One of the daintiest and best loved of all the small campanulas is undoubtedly *C.cochlearifolia* (formerly *C.pusilla*), known and cherished in our gardens for more than 150 years. Native to the European Alps, where its frail, thread-like stems and roots thread their way about, forming wide mats of erupting tufts of tiny shining, almost round leaves, modestly toothed on each side. Up to six pendant bells of lavender blue are carried on slender, wiry stems, but the colour is variable through shades of lilac and blue, and there is a lovely albino which is affectionately known where it occurs in the wild as 'The Nun of the Meadows'. It is a joyous inhabitant of a sunny spot in scree or well-drained soil and is as vigorous and contented today as it was when first introduced those long years ago.

My father may have been slightly dubious about *C.poscharskyana* but he cannot have had any qualms concerning the 'Nana' form of *C.herzegovina*, another of his introductions from the country whose name it bears. It is a perfect illustration of the saying that 'small is beautiful'. Even when smothered with its abundant blossoms it is scarcely two inches in height. It mats into dense cushions of thin, wiry stems set with tiny glossy leaves. Each slender, erect stem carries an upturned starry flower of rich lilac. Such a tiny treasure deserves special treatment, so indulge it with a compost of gritty but humus-rich soil and a sunny chink, or grow it in a shallow pan in the alpine house. Like most campanulas it blossoms after the first spring display is over and is invaluable for a continuation of beauty and interest.

Seek where you will in the Northern Hemisphere and you will find a choice of campanulas, for it is a widely distributed genus. From the Olympic Mountains in the State of Washington comes a particular treasure in the form of *C.piperi*, another plant which I store in my treasurehouse of memories, for it was in the black rocky cliffs above Hurricane Ridge that I first saw it, spreading its way through tiny cracks and crevices, a spartan habitat which gives a clue to its treatment in cultivation. The compost should be lime-free if possible, but it will endure some alkalinity if it has to. Its running roots emit small clusters of glossy, tiny, dark green leaves and, on very short stems appear one or two large, star-shaped flowers of deepest purple-blue, their beauty enhanced by protruding scarlet anthers.

There are plants without which no collection of alpine plants could be considered representative, and *C.alpestris* is certainly one of these. It

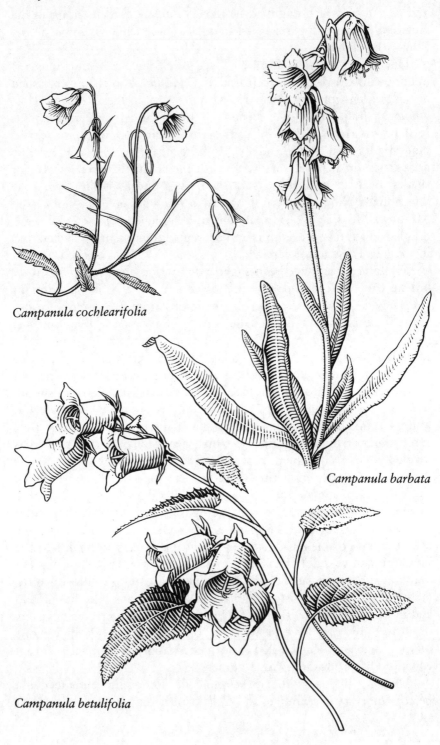

Campanula cochlearifolia

Campanula barbata

Campanula betulifolia

was long known as *C.allionii* and that is the name which invariably trips first off my tongue when speaking of it. I relish it enormously, and try to provide it with the conditions of sun and gritty soil in which it is happiest. Although in nature it is most often found on granitic formations, it is not at all averse to alkaline conditions in cultivation. When encountered in its several localities, it will be seen to vary both in leaf size and shape and in splendour of blossom. The foliage is softly felted with greyish hairs and those plants with the widest leaves commonly display the finest flowers, which are large, usually purple-blue bells, almost resembling small Canterbury Bells borne on short stems. It anchors its main rosette with a deeply-delving root while subsidiary roots go wandering off in all directions, erupting here and there in clusters of foliage and flowers. There are forms with flowers of paler or deeper colour, occasional albinos, and, more rarely, such a one as the deep pink form which, under the clonal name of 'Frank Barker', gained an Award of Merit in 1930. Does this splendour still exist in gardens I wonder?

C.thyrsoides, a rebel in a genus almost universally bearing blue, purple or white flowers, offers short, erect spikes of crowded straw-yellow blossoms which are also sweetly fragrant. A monocarp, it dies after flowering, but is so easily raised from seed that this need be no deterrent. It is perfectly contented in any good garden soil and an open position. I find it amusing to tease friends whose knowledge of plants is limited by telling them that it is indeed a bellflower. My wife tells me that this is a naughtiness of which I should cure myself but it is a game which I persist in playing with a few plants which seem to deny their relationship to others of the same family. You will meet more of them in later pages.

Spain has become a popular holiday resort and, if you care to abandon the overcrowded Costas and climb into the mountains, there are many beautiful plants to be discovered. Among them is one of the neatest and prettiest of campanula in the form of *C.arvatica*. In its home it favours crannies and crevices, yet in cultivation is happily content to grow in a gritty compost, not forgetting that it is definitely calciphilous, or lime-loving. From a central crown it spreads—like the spokes of a tiny wheel—frail, leafy stems, each one carrying several upturned, star-shaped flowers of violet-blue.

At some time prior to 1935 a marriage took place between *C.arvatica* and our native *C.rotundifolia*, resulting in a rather delightful hybrid which has all the ease of cultivation of the native species, combined with the bright and starry flowers of *C.arvatica*, carried on erect, four to six-inch stems. It was considered of sufficient merit to receive the coveted Award of Merit in 1935, and was named C.'Rotarvatica'.

There is a rather special group of campanulas, found under such names as *C.ardonensis*, *C.aucheri*, *C.bellidifolia*, *C.saxifraga* and *C.stenophylla* which all fall under the umbrella of *C.tridentata*. They come mostly from the Caucasus. There is great family similarity between them, although each is a plant in its own right. They all have a deep, almost carrot-like root, from the crown of which a cluster of loose rosettes is formed, with notably broad leaves, sometimes lightly haired and occasionally with gentle marginal toothing. The flowering stems are decumbent and each carries one large, open bell-shaped flower, the colour, according to the particular variant, ranging through shades of violet and purple-blue.

Several of the most spectacular campanulas are monocarpic species from Eastern Europe and Macedonia and one of the most striking is *C.formaneckiana*. I like to grow this handsome bellflower on into pots of increasing size until it has achieved a wide rosette of symmetrically arranged downy-grey, crinkled leaves. When this stage is reached I cease the potting on, and can be confident that the following year will witness an erect, rigid and leafy stem which may well be a foot and a half in height eventually, rising from the centre of the rosette. From the upper leaf axils, on long pedicels, spring splendidly large, rather tubular bells, usually white, but sometimes gently flushed blue or pink. I would like to grow it in the open remembering its magnificence when adorning crevices in high cliffs, but it has no liking for our changeable winters and is best regarded as a highly decorative plant for the alpine house.

C.carpatica, known in our gardens since the late years of the eighteenth century, could well be described as the campanula for everyone. It is never what Reginald Farrer would have described as a 'miff' or a 'mimp' and it is happy in any good garden soil. Small enough for the rock garden, it has sufficient stature to be used grouped in the front of a flower bed or as an edging. I doubt if the original type plant now exists in cultivation—except perhaps in Botanic Gardens—but it persists in a small host of selected forms, cultivars and hybrids in which there is always a strong family resemblance. There is, however, considerable variation in the size and shape of the resplendent blossoms, which are cup-shaped, upturned and vary in colour from pure white through shades of blue to rich purple.

Many campanulas, and especially those which spread modestly by underground roots, are ideal inhabitants of an alpine meadow, or lawn where they delight in the close association and competition with other plants of similar characteristics. Incidentally, such close proximity to other plants is often the key to success with plants which may be dismally unhappy if condemned to a solitary existence in an isolated 'pocket' in the rock garden. I could name several which detest being grown 'on their own'.

Certainly *C.raddeana*, a handsome species from the limestones of Transcaucasia is fond of company, although I have to admit that it grows well enough by itself. From its spreading roots rise tufts of quite long-stemmed, triangular, heart-shaped, dark and glossy green leaves and twelve-inch stems bearing showers of pendant bell-shaped flowers of deep violet-blue. If treated as a meadow plant it can be left alone and will care for itself, but if it grows in solitary state it benefits from occasional division and replanting in fresh soil and a new position.

C.sarmatica which is short-lived, but beautiful, was introduced from behind the iron curtain long before that barrier existed. Its wide clumps of softly downy grey leaves, gently toothed and somewhat crinkled at the margins provide the perfect setting for foot-high stems carrying one-sided racemes of grey-blue bells. Save a few seeds each year as the plants which flower often perish, although it is not a true monocarp. It is more than likely that there will be a few albinos among the seedlings.

The true *C.pulla* seems to have become regrettably scarce in gardens and I treasure the few plants I have which survive from seeds originally collected in the Eastern Alps. It is a dwarf plant and another 'runner' producing a plentitude of four-inch stems on which are pendulous bells of luminous purple. In gardens it married with a form of *C.carpatica* to produce *C.pulloides*, a pleasing and plentiful hybrid, slightly taller than *C.pulla*, and with more upturned and larger flowers of a lighter blue. There I must leave this splendid genus, lamentably eulogising only about a score, but they are the ones without which I would count my garden inadequately inhabited. I know of at least one enthusiastic amateur who is collecting them and one day there may be a splendid book.

4 Corsica

There are places, both parochial and cosmopolitan, with which one seems to have an immediate affinity. They inspire an irresistible urge to return again and again. There are many places which I have visited in a footloose life and to which I would happily return, but I think Corsica has the strongest pull of them all. I wrote in an earlier chapter of my good fortune in spending some years so conveniently situated that I could pay frequent visits to The Fragrant Isle, as Doris Archer named it in her book. Another writer, 'Snaffle' called it 'The Impossible Island' (also the title of his book, published in 1923 by H. F. & G. Wetherby). That, however, is just one of the aspects of Corsica's fascination. It either attracts or repels.

The primary attraction for me, of course, was the fact that it has so many beautiful and interesting plants, but there are other things too: its history and the rugged beauty of the mountains which, on its western side, sweep down to the very shores of the blue Mediterranean Sea. One of my most vivid memories of the island concerns a curious plant—not really a rock garden subject, although it comes from an alpine environment. I knew that *Polygonum equisetiforme* was recorded as a native of Corsica and it was the primary object of one of my many visits.

For several days I climbed and sought without success and, after one long day, I found myself benighted, far from any human habitation, and weary to boot. The discovery of a partially ruined stone hut made me decide to camp for the night and, in the gloaming, I sought for something with which to make myself a bed on the floor of the hut—which, from the pervading odours, had obviously also sheltered goats! Finding some great clumps of rushes, I cut enough of them to make a couch, and slept well. When, in the morning I was able to see more clearly what my bed consisted of, imagine my astonishment to discover that it was the very plant I had been seeking.

This strange polygonum makes tangles of rush-like wiry stems, along the lengths of which are innumerable tiny, pure white flowers. A small bundle of the stems were sent home to England and I still have some of the descendents among a small group of what I call my memory-joggers.

One of the prizes of Corsica is the Corsican Lilly, *Pancratium illyricum*. It is plentiful from sea level and up to the lower mountain slopes and can also be found in Sardinia, Sicily and a few areas in southern Italy. In spite of its resemblance to a lily it really belongs to the Amaryllidaceae and, from a deeply buried vast bulb emits sheaves of sword-shaped glaucous leaves. The strong, rather flattened stems which emerge from the leaves to a height of some eighteen inches, carry an umbel of several large, white, sweetly fragrant flowers. It is hardy enough here to be grown in a warm, sunny position but in very cold and wet gardens it might not succeed.

On one occasion, while struggling to extract from the stony ground two or three of the huge bulbs to take back to my Menton headquarters, I was watched by two characters, well armed with long guns and knives in their belts. I felt sure they must be a pair of Corsica's famed bandits, but they were friendly enough. They spoke a dialect which was sufficiently similar to the sort of French I had learned on the mainland and we were able to converse. All they really wanted to know was—'Was I gathering the bulbs to eat them?' Upon being told that I only wanted to grow them in my garden, they shrugged their shoulders and walked away.

Although it is one of the smallest, I consider exquisite little *Leucojum roseum* (*Acis roseus*), a tiny, dainty bulb which is endemic to Corsica and Sardinia, to be one of the most beautiful flowers to be found there. It is far from plentiful and should never be collected except by gathering perhaps a few seeds—if you can find them, for it flowers in the autumn and is hardly visible when not in flower. It grows in sandy areas which are not infrequently sea-washed. The tiny bulbs emit a few, threadfine leaves and a two-inch stem usually carrying just one pendant, elegantly shaped flower of the purest pink. Because it is so frail it is not really adapted for outdoor cultivation but it makes an exquisite adornment to the alpine house or cold frame.

Knowing full well that the plant I have known and loved for so long as *Helleborous corsicus* is now more correctly addressed as *H.argutifolius*. I cling to the more familar name—as, I am sure, do most gardeners. This is another of the glories of Corsica and it is a thrilling sight to see the vast mounds of its tall stems, clothed in handsome, evergreen dark green leaves, sharply toothed at their margins and surmounted by great terminal clusters of apple-green, cup-shaped flowers, which, in gardens, expand from February onward. It is hardy and long-lived, and, although it will grow in semi-shade, it is more content in fully exposed positions and will happily accept any ordinary garden soil.

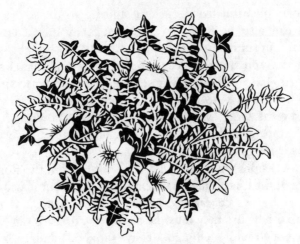

Morisia monantha

An inhabitant of the sea sands of Corsica and Sardinia is the pretty little Crucifer, *Morisia monantha*, long known and liked by alpine gardeners as *M.hypogaea*. Its long, white roots delve deeply into the sand and are topped by prostrate tufts of saw-edged leaves, centred by almost stemless golden flowers. Crevices in the neighbouring rocks, sea-washed at their base, are inhabited by *Erodium corsicum*, another endemic of the two islands. Tuck it into a sunny crevice in a wall or the rock garden and it will be happy enough and make close clusters of softly hairy, lightly scalloped leaves adorned by pink flowers veined with deeper colour. The blossoms vary in shade and forms can be found with red flowers and there is even an occasional albino. In gardens it has recently formed an alliance with *E.reichardii* (*chamaedryoides*) which has resulted in some very attractive hybrids, intermediate between the parents.

Spring in the Corsican woodlands is made beautiful by quantities of *Cyclamen repandum*, with the occasional prize of a pure white flower among the traditional pink ones. Here too, I recall memories both horticultural and domestic, for where else could I take my wife on our honeymoon than to my beloved Corsica? We hired a car on the island and drove hither and thither, my spouse having instructions to shout whenever she saw a white flower, for it was springtime and *C.repandum* was in full resplendent blossom. In the first week her sharp eyes had captured a hundred albinos, of which twenty were carefully lifted and brought home. In these days of much wider travel by the masses and tourists everywhere, I would not collect plants, but in those distant days there were very few visitors to Corsica and those who did go mostly stayed on the coastal fringe without penetrating to the interior.

So many aromatic plants and shrubs grow on Corsica that the summer air is filled with an all pervading fragrance. A plant of modest stature which contributes a not inconsiderable proportion of the aroma is the small *Mentha requienii*. Its frail stems and minute green leaves cling closely to the ground, forming widespread mats, spangled in spring and summer with myriads of small pink flowers. This charming mint has almost taken possession of our nursery paths and seems to thrive on the herbicides used to destroy other and less pleasurable weeds. There is no more charming inhabitant of chinks between paving stones or as ground cover for tiny alpine bulbs, but it does favour a not too hot and dry position.

An easy little alpine which grows in cool places on Corsica's mountains is *Stachys corsica*. In gardens it is not very long-lived but is pretty enough to justify the easy task of occasionally lifting, dividing and replanting plants which have become loose and untidy. When they reach such a condition they may perish if not attended to. Its habit is to make low mats of glistening, emerald-green leaves, upon which rest very short-stemmed flowers of creamy-pink.

Should you be contemplating a visit to this fascinating island, there are many places to be explored: in particular, the Spelunca Gorge. It is near Porto on the west coast and climbs to the small town of Evisa, and is well worth traversing. It is full of good plants and the scenery is wild and superb with a good trail underfoot. Another spot not to be missed is Vizzavona, and two of the highest mountains, Monte Cinto and Monte d'Oro, offer a strenous but not too difficult scramble full of plants and scenic interest all the way.

5 Our Native 'Alpines'

The word Alpines in the above chapter heading is deliberately placed between inverted commas since some of our native plants, although well suited for growing on the rock garden, are not truly alpine. A few of them are relicts from the time when Britain was more alpine in climate than it is now; others are lowland inhabitants, as so many of the plants commonly regarded as rock garden subjects.

One of the memories which writing this book evokes is of walking through a valley in Teesdale and marvelling at the wide colonies of exquisite *Gentiana verna* with myriads of flowers reflecting the blue of the sky above and inter-mingled with the clear pink flowers of our native Bird's-eye Primrose, *Primula farinosa*. Alas, that valley is now a reservoir and all its lovely flowers have been submerged. Both plants can be found elsewhere in the British Isles and, fortunately, are readily available from stock which has long been nursery grown and does not involve robbing the depleting native colonies.

More of a mountaineer is *Dryas octopetala*, the Mountain Avens, which almost qualifies to be thought of as a prostrate shrub, for its spreading stems are woody and clothed in dark green foliage shaped like those of a tiny oak leaf. The large, eight-petalled white flowers remind us of the rose, a family to which it is closely related. Plant it so that it can spread its stems over an adjacent rock and it will flower more freely. It offers a bonus too, for its seed heads are very decorative, consisting of crowded, silvery awns.

We have other native gentians, although one or two of them are annuals and probably more correctly named Gentianella. *Gentiana pneumonanthe* is a rarity to be found growing on some of our heathlands, usually in moist positions. It must never be collected but can sometimes be obtained from a specialist nursery and is well worth having, carrying the erect, tubular blue flowers, several to each nine-inch stem.

In mountainous areas of Scotland, North Wales, in the Lake District and in Ireland, may be found the humped cushions of *Silene acaulis*, another plant with which I have a love–hate relationship. As it can be seen in the wild, with its cushions of congested rosettes concealed

Dryas octopetala

beneath countless stemless pink flowers, it is a sight for the gods, but in gardens it is usually more reluctant to blossom. Spartan treatment in gritty soil and full sun will sometimes persuade it to be more forthcoming. However, even as a cushion plant with few flowers, it is a charmer. There is a continental form named *pedunculata* which carries its flowers on very short stems and is more generous in the display it offers.

Two of our few native species of *Dianthus* are good garden plants in their selected forms, of which there are several. *D.caesius* (which I refuse to recognize by its correct name of *D.gratianopolitanus*) is rare and confined to a few limestone cliffs in the Cheddar Gorge, where it should be left in peace. It is garden-worthy in its own right, bearing good, shapely pink flowers over pads of grey leaves, but is more commonly seen in one or other of the garden-raised forms and hybrids.

Dianthus deltoides is the Maiden Pink—a lowland plant in England and northward to Inverness. Although a pretty enough plant with rose or pink flowers, spotted with deeper colour on the petals, it is best grown in a selected form, one in particular, *D.d.*'Flashing Lights' being especially handsome, carrying rich crimson-red flowers on nine-inch

stems in great profusion. Seeds sown of the type or any form of
D.*deltoides* are likely to produce a range of colours, including some nice
albinos whose white petals are speckled with red spots.

In the same sort of areas in which *Gentiana pneumonanthe* is likely
to grow, you may also expect to see the Grass of Parnassus, *Parnassia
palustris*. It is a pleasing dwarf plant to set in damp soil where it makes
tufts of heart-shaped leaves and, on six-inch stems, bears white flowers
of goodly size, each petal lightly veined with green stripes.

Our native flora abounds in species of willow, and there is a minority
of these which are dwarf and make ideal rock garden shrubs. One of the
nicest of these is *Salix reticulata*, an inhabitant of Scottish mountains. Its
woody stems cling to the stony ground in which it delights to grow and
are adorned by wide, rounded leaves of thick texture which are
conspicuously netted by deep veins. In the spring it displays creamy
catkins on short stems.

S.arbuscula, is rather more robust, and able to form mounds of
entangled woody stems a foot or so in height and with a generous

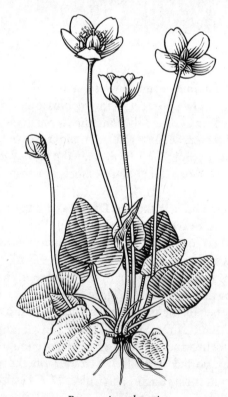

Parnassia palustris

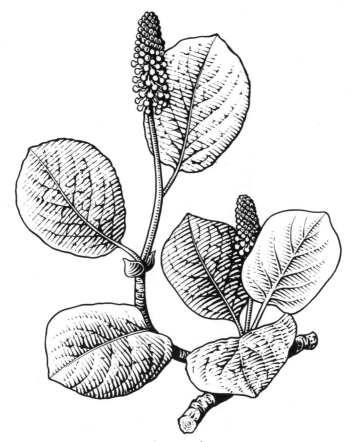

Salix reticulata

spread, while *S.herbacea* is one of the smallest of them all, with tiny
leaves set on the ground-hugging stems to form prostrate mats,
bedecked in spring with small catkins. One of the gems of the genus is
S.boydii, a natural hybrid, probably between *S.reticulata* and *S.lanata*.
Its provenance is slightly obscure, but it was discovered on a Scottish
mountain in the 1880s. From that one original discovery have arisen all
the plants now growing in our gardens. Very slow indeed to increase in
size, it will eventually become an erect cluster of gnarled branches with
rounded, leathery leaves, grey-green and strongly reticulated. The
stubby catkins are large and silver coloured, maturing to cream. A
specimen which I have happily owned for more than twenty years is
even now only a little more than a foot in height.

The keen eyes of the same Mr. Boyd to whom we owe the willow, found for alpine gardeners another treasure in the shape of *Sagina boydii*. It, too, is of obscure origin and has never again been found wild. It must surely be a natural hybrid, but the parentage has never been more than speculative. Its flowers are so small and green as to be ignored, but it grows into fascinating, tight hummocks of congested rosettes of minute, intensely glossy leaves and bears comparison with the choicest high alpine cushion plants. To enjoy it to perfection, grow it in a gritty scree, in a stone sink or trough or in the alpine house.

That most delightful very early-flowering native alpine, *Saxifraga oppositifolia*, has an immensely wide natural distribution and can be found in Britain, throughout Europe, in North America and in the Himalayas. One of its classic stations is on the curious limestone cap which tops Mount Ingleborough in Yorkshire. On its prostrate stems are rows of symmetrical pairs of tiny dark green leaves. The purple-red flowers are produced at the ends of the shoots. It is as variable in appearance as in its distribution and there are numerous selected forms. The one most commonly grown is *S.o.* 'Splendens', in which the flowers are larger and more rounded and of a richer colour than those of the type. It prefers a position which is cool rather than hot, and is capable of opening its flowers as early as February. Some years ago I under-planted a group of it with some corms of an early-flowering yellow crocus and almost always the two flower at the same time and create a highly decorative scene. There is an albino, but it is inferior in flower and is really of interest only to those who collect oddities.

A pleasant little cushiony native is *Minuartia verna*. It has hovered uneasily between several genera and has been named *Alsine verna* and *Arenaria verna* but seems finally to have come to rest as *Minuartia*. It can be found, but must never be collected from, the debris heaps of old lead mines in the west and north of Britain and it also occurs in Wales, Scotland and Ireland. The threadfine stems and tiny, thin green leaves are compacted into tight domes, over which flutter innumerable white flowers on frail stems. It is a dainty little plant, for which a friend of mine once coined the adjective 'plim'. It likes very gritty soil and, although a sun-lover, does not appreciate being scorched.

Now almost extinct as a native, the Lady's Slipper Orchid, *Cypripedium calceolus* has one or two hallowed sanctuaries in the north of England, sites which are closely guarded secrets. I have vivid memories of a night spent in a Yorkshire village, en route to Scotland. In the cool of the evening my father and I took a stroll through the village street, and encountered a small girl carrying a bunch of wild flowers, among which were at least a dozen flowers of the *Cypripedium*. The child was

Saxifraga oppositifolia

unable to remember where she had plucked the flowers and a search next morning on the high fells behind the village was completely unsuccessful. Fortunately the plant is still quite widely distributed on the Continent and it is fortunately among the species which are officially protected. Another memory is of being taken to a copse not one hundred miles from Munich and shown it growing literally in hundreds—a wonderful sight to see those countless yellow and brown pouched flowers adance in a gentle breeze. (Illus. see below)

It is not only in the north of Britain that *Loiseleuria procumbens* exists. It extends into Scandinavia and Iceland. You could find it in North America and far away in Japan. What an aggravating little plant it is in gardens! Closely related to rhododendron (it was at one time known as *Azalea procumbens*), it is a lime-hater and reluctant to establish. If it can be made content in a peat bed it will very slowly spread into a flat pad of interlaced stems but only very rarely in gardens will it offer more than a meagre spattering of its small pink flowers. My nursery staff became so annoyed with its behaviour that they finally rechristened it and named it 'Lousy Laura'!

Cypripedium calceolus

Should you have a small saturated area, or if you can provide shallow pans filled with soggy sphagnum moss, you might be able to delight in *Pinguicula grandiflora*. It comes from Irish bogs and has flat rosettes of wide, sticky leaves, from which spring four-inch stems each bearing a large, rich blue flower rather like that of a violet. It is insectivorous and traps small insects by means of the glands on the leaves. The prey is slowly digested and provides the *Pinguicula* with the nitrogenous food which its normal watery habitation denies.

It is amusing and rewarding to assemble a collection of these native plants, most of which are available from nursery grown stock. Their native stands must never be depleted. Even gathering their flowers can be harmful since some of them, and notably our lovely primrose, can only spread by means of seed. If the flowers are plucked, there will be no seeds.

6 Early Flowers and Oddities

Plants which endear themselves—especially to those who find joy and pleasure in their gardens—are the ones which brave the elements and blossom very early in the year, heralding the spring we all look forward to with impatience. *Hacquetia* (*Dondia*) *epipactis* delights me every year. From its prostrate clusters of three-foliate leaves (rather like those of a tiny *Astrantia*) spring neat heads of tiny golden flowers set on a little platter of green leaves. The only species in its genus, it can be found here and there in the Alps of Europe. I grow it with snowdrops and snowflakes in a corner of the garden devoted to pre-spring flowers—a cool place and lightly shaded, where it never fails to perform.

Here too, grow several of the delightful hepaticas which relish similar conditions and are eager to burst into flower as soon as winter begins to recede. *Hepatica nobilis*, is still familiar to we older gardeners as *H.triloba*. (The genus has had an uneasy taxonomic existence. All hepaticas were once included in the genus *Anemone*.) This particular and exquisite harbinger of spring has an immensely wide natural distribution and can be found in Europe, Asia and America in slightly varying forms. The characteristic flower colour is blue, but there are variants with white or pink blossoms and some are fully double, but these are rarities. How well I remember as a young man admiring paths in cottage gardens edged with great clumps of white, pink or blue hepaticas. One old lady in particular told me that every time she had a teapot to empty she gave the tea leaves to the hepaticas and they were without doubt the best I ever saw.

H.transsilvanica (*angulosa*) is rather more robust and with larger flowers, and a magnificent hybrid between the two species, raised by the late Ernest Ballard of Michaelmas Daisy fame, is *H.* × *media* 'Ballardii'. In 1938 it was given the Award of Merit and also won the Cory Cup, which is awarded to the best deliberate hybrid between two species exhibited in the current year.

Very little will be written in this book about bulbs, which are a complete and separate subject, but there must be an occasional mention of some species of bulb which falls into a particular context. Thinking of the area devoted to very early flowers, I cannot avoid mentioning *Scilla*

Hepatica nobilis

tubergeniana (which is correctly named *S.mischtschenkoana*—drat those botanists). This treasure from Iran and the Caucasus is so eager to blossom that the flowers are already expanding as they emerge from the soil. The petals are soft blue with a stripe of darker colour down each segment. There are many flowers to each lax raceme and the stems gradually elongate so that eventually the spike is some four to six inches tall. It is a splendid colonizer and a few bulbs planted two inches deep will quickly spread into a handsome group, each year offering more and more of the delectable flowers.

One of the first hedgerow plants which signals the arrival of spring is *Arum maculatum*, known to the non-botanical observer as Preacher in the Pulpit, or Cuckoo Pint, or Lords and Ladies. It is not a garden-worthy plant, but *A.creticum*, a related species from Crete, is a gem to be sought, and treasured if obtained. Unlike our own wildling, its wide leaves are not mottled but the spathe and spadix are both clear yellow in colour. It relishes a warm and sunny position and, given reasonable weather, can be in blossom in late February.

The arums belong to a group of plants known collectively as aroids. They are plants for which I have always had a particular liking. Some are beautiful, others are less comely, but compensate by their curious and interesting shape and colour, and I find them quite irresistible. Every garden in which there are children should cultivate a colony of the

Mouse-tail plant, *Arisarum proboscideum*. From the small, tuberous rhizomes rise (in the spring) many green, spear-shaped leaves, among which are the innumerable curious flowers of olive-green and white, with a long, tail-like appendage, giving the impression of a horde of long-tailed mice plunging into the dense foliage. Believe it or not, I once tried to persuade the nursery cat that these really were mice, to be reproached by the sort of disdainful look after an exploratory sniff that only a cat can give.

An aroid which is both interesting and extremely beautiful, is *Arisaema candidissimum*, which came to our gardens from West China in 1924 and quickly became a sought-after favourite. From large, rather flat tubers arise, (sometimes as late in the year as early June) bold, three-foliate leaves, quickly followed by the 'flower', which is a wide, white, pink and green striped hood sheltering the phallic spadix typical of the aroides. I have planted it in various positions out of doors and found it to be comfortably hardy if given a warm exposure in any good, well-drained soil. It is an ideal occupant of one of those narrow beds against a house wall which can harbour so many plants which appreciate just that little extra warmth.

A similar plant, regrettably rare but to be eagerly sought for is the Japanese *Arisaema sikokianum*. In this case the bold hood is purple in colour, and striped in a spectacular pattern of white and green. It, too, will relish the same sort of conditions accorded to *A.candidissimum*.

Lacking any floral beauty, but a source of never failing interest, is tiny *Pinellia ternata* (*tuberifera*). Native to China and Japan, it forms very small tubers, from which ascend segmented green leaves and green 'flowers' with a curved-over tip. They look for all the world like small hooded cobras about to 'strike'. My wife has an aversion to snakes and will not have the plant in the garden, but I like it as an oddity and would not happily be without it. *P.ternata* has the added curiosity of producing on its stems little snail-like bulbils which can be detached and grown on as separate plants.

There is a small genus of plants which look as if they ought to be included among the aroids, but which actually belong to the *Aristolochia* family. There are the species of *Asarum*; again plants which make no floral display but are interesting and have very definite garden value in certain situations. *A.europaeum* is a European but has naturalized in a few British stations. It makes low mats of glossy green, kidney-shaped leaves. The flowers are small, tubular and dull greeny-brown and are, perhaps fortunately, semi-concealed among the foliage, which is the plant's greatest virtue. As a ground cover in cool places it is useful for the sake of its quite decorative leaves. There are three other species, two from California and one from eastern North America, which are similar in appearance although perhaps a little more robust. These are *A.caudatum*, *A.canadense* and *A.hartwegii*, but they are usually less readily available than *A.europaeum*.

Plants, and perhaps particularly alpines, have always seemed to me to possess some of the characteristics of children, who, however much we may love them, can be aggravating in the extreme. *Aquilegia jonesii* has exasperated me for many years. I first made its intimate acquaintance when I came upon a huge colony of it growing high up in the Rocky Mountains of North America. It was a joyous occasion at the end of a day which had been filled with excitement as more and more treasures of the alpine flora were discovered. I had grown it for many years before but only very occasionally did it condescend to offer me its lovely blossoms.

It was, therefore, with special interest that I was able to observe that, although it was growing literally in thousands, only a percentage of the plants carried flowers. It would seem that it is a shy flowerer even in nature. From the neatest of tiny tufts of silvery-grey foliage emerge short stems, usually only one to a rosette, carrying a large flower of soft lavender-blue. I was able to revisit the site later in the year and gather seeds but, although these were obviously from flowering plants, the young plants which I eventually grew were as reluctant as ever to blossom and this has been my constant experience in subsequent years. Some seem to be more fortunate. I read in W. H. A. Preece's excellent book on North American rock plants that it flowers freely for him!

The plateau on which the *Aquilegia jonesii* grew in such profusion was on a gentle slope leading to higher mountains behind and was bisected by numerous small streams of running water, by the sides of which grew *Mimulus lewisii*, flowering in such abundance that the entire area was mantled in a haze of pink. Perhaps a trifle tall for the average rock garden (carrying its blossoms on eighteen-inch stems) it is an admirable subject for planting at pond or stream sides, especially in places where there is no objection to a considerable amount of self-colonization. I like it, but am even more fond of its less common albino, which is dwarfer, with flowers of pure white. After enjoying it for many years I have lost it and, if anyone has it, or knows of a source, I would be extremely grateful for information as to the whereabouts of *M.lewisii* 'Albus'.

Although alpine plants are usually accepted as being Lilliputians there are Brobdingnagians among them. Growing along with the

Mimulus and the *Aquilegia* in that alpine meadow were great tussocks of Bear Grass, *Xerophyllum tenax*, with which I immediately fell in love, and for which I retain much affection although it is another plant which has caused me much irritation. From the tussocks of crowded, narrow leaves—rather like a miniature Pampas Grass—rise bold stems to a height of three feet or more, crowned with kniphofia-like heads of white flowers. Of this handsome giant also, I was able to collect liberal quantities of seed, none of which germinated. I have been sent subsequent supplies year after year, through the offices of good American friends, but it was not until two years ago that success arrived. I now have a fine colony of sturdy young plants, one of which flowered in 1981 for the first time—in the herbaceous border; it is too massive for the rock garden unless this, too, is of Brobdingnagian proportions.

It is always pleasant to meet old friends in unexpected places and I was delighted, on a later spur of the same expedition which took me almost into Arctic regions, to encounter *Silene acaulis*, already written of in the chapter devoted to some British alpines. It appeared to be identical in form to the European colonies and, although its flowering time was past, the quantity of seed pods in evidence indicated that it had been very floriferous indeed. It was accompanied by another old friend, *Salix reticulata*. There, too, was *Cornus suecica*, which creeps underground, emitting short, woody stems clothed in oval leaves of solid texture. The tiny white flowers are surrounded by conspicuous white bracts and, later, there are globose berries of glistening red. It is far from easy to cultivate, but may be essayed with some optimism in a bed of acid peat and a cool situation. On our northern mountain moors it is occasionally to be found, usually sheltering with, and beneath, heathers and bilberry.

Another inhabitant of sub-arctic North America is the aggravating little *Cassiope hypnoides*—not a British native, but to be found plentifully in Scandinavia. I believe the first attempts to persuade it to accept garden conditions were made in the last years of the eighteenth century. Ever since then gardeners who delight in accepting the challenge of a 'difficult' plant have tried to grow it, but there have been no resounding successes, although a few have discovered, if not how to grow it well, at least how to keep it alive. My own repeated efforts have been dismal failures but I would dearly like to gloat over healthy pads of its entangled, prostrate stems, forming almost moss-like pads and solitary, white, bell-shaped flowers carried on slender red stems. The only hope is to give it acid peat and protection from heat. Fortunately there are other cassiopes which are more amenable and I shall have something to say about them on later pages, for I plan a chapter devoted to plants for the peat garden.

Having given *Aquilegia jonesii* a rather bad name it is only right that I should lavish some praise on one or two other American species about whose flowering there need be no qualms. One which never fails to give me pleasure is *A.saximontana*. The short-spurred blue and white flowers are borne on four to six-inch stems. An even greater favourite is *A.scopulorum* which bears some resemblance to *A.jonesii* but is taller and more robust and carries its large blue blossoms above tufts of very blue-grey foliage. Each of them should be given fairly spartan treatment in gritty soil for they tend to grow rather taller in cultivation than they do in the wild, especially if too generously fed.

Pyxidanthera barbulata, yet another American, flourishes in the Pine Barrens of New Jersey as it has never been persuaded to do in gardens. Pixy Moss, as it is known, is a most exasperating little cuss. It belongs to Diapensiaceae, a family notorious for containing some tricky subjects. Perhaps I should not tantalize those eager to 'have a go', for it is not in commercial cultivation in this country and is only likely to exist in botanic gardens or the treasure house of a few avid collectors. Even there I would wager that survival is very dubious.

To see it in the wild is to be immediately seduced as one kneels to worship the pads of tiny russet leaves, hidden at blossoming time by the profusion or rounded, pearl-white flowers which rest almost stemlessly on the cushions. The only route to even moderate success seems to be to give it a compost composed of peat and/or leafsoil with plenty of gritty sand, and to ensure a constant supply of moisture underneath. I once kept it alive for three years by growing it in such a compost in a shallow pan standing in a saucer of water. Reginald Farrer, in his *magnum opus* The *English Rock Garden*, actually describes it as a *Diapensia*.

7 Invaders

Together with other writers, I have at times been called to task for lavishing praise on plants which, when acquired, have flourished only too well; but I an unrepentant, for there is a place in most gardens for 'spreaders' and I do always give a warning of what to expect. This chapter should, therfore, be read with such a warning in mind as it deals exclusively with plants which will be eager to usurp surrounding territory.

Many gardeners nowadays take full advantage of ground-cover plants, primarily perhaps to reduce labour but also realizing that it is better to clothe the soil with decorative plants than to leave it bare and have the chore of keeping it clear of weeds. Such plantings generally occur in areas beneath and between trees and shrubs, positions for which few alpines are suited but there is no reason why certain alpines should not serve the same purpose in a proper environment. There are places on rock gardens where it is desirable to provide a ground cover for bulbs and there is no lack of appropriate plants for such purposes.

Another area for which these alpine invaders are useful is in the cracks and crevices between the paving slabs which are, in many gardens, replacing the conventional lawn; and not only the spreaders, for such situations provide just the conditions which alpines prefer. Their roots are in cool, moist soil, their heads in the light and they do not have their stems surrounded in winter with cold and often saturated soil. Lacking a conventional rock garden a host of rock plants can be accommodated in such places.

To return, however, to the invaders. One which is not seen as often as I would like it to be is *Phuopsis* (*Crucianella*) *stylosa*. The only species in its genus, it came originally from the Caucasus. Not a true alpine, it is yet very suitable as a carpeter in a sunny spot in the rock garden. The mats of thin stems and slender green leaves are decorated in summer by many heads of small pink flowers, but it should not be planted near to less vigorous plants, which it will be only too ready to overwhelm. It has a curious characteristic: after a shower of rain, it emits a strange musky scent, pleasing to some but repellent to others. I have never been able to make up my mind one way or the other and have to return to it again and again, usually compromising by describing it as an 'interesting scent'.

Between acaenas and myself there has always existed a sort of love-hate relationship. At times, and in the right place, I adored them, but there have been occasions when, having stupidly misplaced them, or when they have insiduously invaded areas where they were very definitely *persona non grata*, I have ripped out their spreading mats of entangled, creeping stems and adhesive burrs and consigned them to the bonfire.

Those kinds commonly grown in Britain come from New Zealand, where most of them are natives, although there are one or two outliers of the genus in South America and in Polynesia. There have been times when, hearing New Zealanders inveighing against the European bramble, I have retaliated by some less than kind comments concerning acaenas.

To be seen at their best they must have space. They are quite definitely not plants to be used in confined areas, or adjacent to less vigorous neighbours, over whom they will sweep with all the enthusiasm and vigour of an All Black rugby team. I remember seeing them employed with immense advantage in the garden of Mr. Harold Hillier at 'Jermyns', in Hampshire. Wide drifts of intermingled varieties had been planted on a gently sloping bank in what appeared to be poorish soil and they had spread into a colourful carpet of grey, bronze and crimson foliage sprinkled with the brightly coloured burr-like inflorescences of *A.microphylla*.

Such an effect as this would not be either possible or desirable in a very small garden—unless, of course, you happen to be a reluctant gardener and only too happy to cover the entire area with something demanding little or no attention and reasonably decorative at all times! Even in small gardens, however, if employed with caution, they have their uses. I allow the most prostrate and smaller-leaved kinds to ramble along the cracks between paving stones, and some of the more rampagious ones are permitted to spread as ground cover for colchicums and other strong-growing bulbs, corms and tubers.

Remember then, that if you plant them too close to more precious and less invasive plants, before you can say *Saxifraga infundibuliformis*, the smaller plants will be totally submerged. An experiment I once made of using them as component parts of an alpine lawn in which campanulas, dianthuses, antennarias, *Dryas octopetala*, cushion phloxes, sedums and other plants eager to ramble were closely planted, was initially successful but ultimately disastrous. In three years there was nothing but a solid *Acaena* lawn.

A dozen or more species are cultivated and easily obtained, and among the most attractive from which to choose are *A.buchananii*, *A.glauca*, *A.microphylla* and its variety *inermis*, *A.novae-zealandae* and *A.sanguisorbae*. They, too, are very desirable as plants for paved areas, which benefit so materially from plant life to break the monotony of stretches of bare stone.

Much to the annoyance of neighbouring farmers, the lovely but fiendish *Veronica filiformis* has swept through our boundary fences and is steadily advancing across adjacent fields which are kept to permanent grass and used for grazing cattle. There are times, when the *Veronica* is flowering, that the green fields change to a gentle and pervasive blue. The cows do not appear to object but the farmers become very indignant and even resort to herbicides, upon which *V.filiformis* seems to thrive! Less than an inch in height, it spreads by rooting as it goes and it also seeds prolifically, so do beware. I grow it because I like it, but I am very careful where I allow it to persist. It makes pleasant, sometimes green, sometimes blue carpets in places where little else will grow.

The few permissible species of *Cotula* (native of the Southern Hemisphere) are to be esteemed only for their foliage. They compare with the acaenas and are useful in similar situations, making dense carpets of creeping stems dressed with deeply-fretted and cut leaves. They are invasive but controllable and any of the three species *C.potentillina*, *C.reptans* and *C.squalida*, if used with caution, will give pleasure and serve a useful purpose.

A delightful little nuisance to which I give full licence is *Erigeron mucronatus* (now, alas, more correctly named *E.karwinskianus* and it has also been known as *Vitadenia triloba*). A pretty weed from Mexico, it has many virtues to offset its less pleasing qualities. An inveterate seeder, it places itself in all sorts of nooks and crannies but never to the point of becoming totally unacceptable. I have particular affection for a plant which blossoms from early spring until late in the autumn. There have been years in which I have been able to discover flowers on *E.mucronatus* during every month. From a woody, persistent root it sprays out thin, wiry and leafy stems and constant showers of daisy-shaped flowers which open white and alter as they age to shades of pink to almost crimson.

It has been said that no one in his senses would plant *Sedum album* in the garden but I learned a lesson from William Robinson which I have not forgotten. I knew him well as a young man and often visited his famous garden at Gravetye Manor in Sussex. Although he was one of the foremost exponents of natural gardening and, along with Gertrude

Jekyll, helped to break the tradition of formal bedding, just outside the rear door of his house he had a very formal garden divided into regular beds in which grew *Clematis* trained up branched poles, and roses. Some of the rose beds were carpeted with *Sedum*. I know that rose growers in general do not approve of ground-cover in rose beds, but this association was extremely effective and, in the confines of the stone-edged beds, *S.album* was kept under control, forming even carpets of succulent foliage, at times sheeted with the white flowers.

Having tried, on several occasions, to eradicate *Sedum acre* from places where it had taken over, I have finally decided that this is one plant I will never willingly introduce to my garden. A native species, commonly known as Wall Pepper—its fleshy leaves have a hot taste—it becomes such a pest that even its sheets of golden flowers do not offer sufficient compensation. If it is weeded out it is so brittle that it breaks to pieces and every tiny scrap that is left will quickly root and start another colony. Fortunately it has several variants which are more trustworthy, notably *S.a.*'Aureum' with golden leaves and *S.a.*'Elegans' whose shoots are silver-tipped and, best of all, *S.a.*'Major', also known as 'Maweanus', larger and more robust than the type, but not at all invasive.

Although it is by no means an invader, as this is a chapter of warnings, I should perhaps include a plant which is its own worst enemy. *Crepis aurea*, a European alpine, carries flowers which are a replica of those of the dandelion but bronzy-orange in colour. Unfortunately its foliage too, is like that of the dandelion. I well remember setting a student gardener to weed a rock garden, who came to me with a large trug basket filled with uprooted plants of *C.aurea*, saying how surprised he was that a weed had been allowed to grow in such hallowed surroundings! Of course it has always been agreed that, if the common dandelion were more rare, it would be a treasured garden plant. With no little surprise and excitement I have recently been told of the discovery of a dandelion with snow-white flowers. If this is true and if it ever gets into cultivation it will create a considerable excitement.

Beware when you read, or are told, that a plant spreads by means of underground running roots. I ignored this warning when I first introduced *Eomecon chionanthum* into a semi-shaded bed amongst hellebores, primroses of various kinds, and some highly treasured doubles and other choice plants. The genus contains only this one species which inhabits cool mountain woodlands in China and belongs to the poppy family. Here and there along the length of its far-spreading roots it emits a few rather fleshy, wide, grey-green leaves and twelve-inch stems carrying loose panicles of very handsome snow-white flowers. Although it has, to all intents and purpose, taken possession of the entire bed, I haven't the heart to uproot it entirely for it really is very beautiful and it does not seem to harm the plants among which it spreads so lustily.

It would be well to be equally cautious about another monotypic plant, *Houttuynia cordata*, from East Asia. It has an identical manner of growth, greedily reaching out with underground stems in all directions and emitting tufts of broad, pointed leaves on erect, foot-high stems which end in a head of small white flowers. There is also a form with double flowers, which I prefer. I planted it at the same time and in the same position as the *Eomecon* and they are now inextricably tangled. As the white roots are indistinguishable when the plants are dormant, it is no easy matter to sort them out. It may also deter you to know that the leaves of *Houttuynia* when roughly handled give out a most disgusting smell. In nature the plant is said to be semi-aquatic but in gardens it seems more than happy in dry conditions, although it does appreciate shade.

On an earlier page I gave full credit to *Campanula poscharskyana* for its ability to spread, but it should be mentioned among the invaders, for it will smother any plant within a yard of it as it throws out its vigorous, leafy stems; it must always have a position allotted that will permit it scope to fulfil its rumbustious and disorderly habits. Given sufficient space one ought not to be deterred by such behaviour for it pays a very handsome rent for every inch that it occupies; it is an unruly but lovable scamp.

Among the plants which invade by means of underground roots or seeding one should include a few which, although rising from a single crown, grow to such proportions that neighbouring plants are endangered. A good example of such behaviour is found in *Anthemis cupaniana*. I planted just one of these on top of a wall—an excellent position for it—and in one year it had developed a spread of three feet, making an eighteen inch high mound of silvery foliage over which, on elegant stems, was a host of large, white, yellow-centred daises. If cut over after the first early summer flush of blossom fades, it will continue to produce flowers well into the autumn. It is a commoner, but none the less beautiful for that.

Artemisia stelleriana is another good example for a similar position and having similar habits. It has no flowers worth retaining—I always remove the flower stems before they develop fully—but the sprawling stems are clothed in luscious and intensely silver leaves.

Invaders which are valuable for clothing the ground in shady places, especially between shrubs and under trees, are the forms of the Periwinkle, *Vinca minor*. They all spread from a central root with long, ground-hugging stems and are evergreen, making dense mats of green leaves of thickish texture. The flowers of the type are blue, but there are named forms which carry white, purple or burgundy-red flowers, and of all of them there are variants with double flowers. The double white, however, is now extremely rare and if anyone knows of its whereabouts I would be immensely grateful to be told: I have been seeking it for a long time. Another of their advantages is that they will prolong their flowering into the winter months.

A neat little wanderer of which I am extremely fond is *Scutellaria hastata scordiifolia*. In a sunny place and given gritty, sharply drained soil, it spreads into quite wide colonies by means of white, macaroni-like underground roots, along the lengths of which rise erect, nine-inch stems dressed with narrow, deckle-edged leaves and innumerable tubular flowers of indigo blue. It came originally from Korea but is now an old and valued garden inhabitant. One has only to bear in mind its ability to travel when choosing its position. Even so, it is neither a thug nor a smotherer and will mingle harmlessly with its neighbours. Plants with flowers which are of an impeccable blue are not so common that one can afford to ignore such a charmer.

Another very mobile, but much dwarfer plant, which is a pleasant inhabitant of a gritty scree is *Cymbalaria* (*Linaria*) *hepaticifolia*. It can also make its number very effectively if allowed to wander along the narrow cracks between paving stones. It has no height at all and carries amidst the greyish, kidney-shaped leaves, lavender, dark-tipped flowers during all the summer months. It might well have been included in the Corsican chapter, for it is yet another inhabitant of that mountainous island, where I belatedly remember it as a plant to be encountered with much pleasure. I recall seeing it creeping among the rough stones of the trail through the Spelunca Gorge, and taking particular care not to tread upon it too harshly.

Any plant which will blossom valiantly through the autumn months is worthy of a place of honour and I always reserve several places in which *Polygonum vaccinifolium* can luxuriantly spread its wide mats of thin, woody stems, clothed in tiny, leathery, pointed leaves which, as a bonus, adopt fine autumn tints of bronze and gold. The small, heather-pink flowers are crowded on slender, erect racemes. It has all the virtues expected from a good garden plant: it is completely hardy, it flourishes in any ordinary soil as long as there is good drainage, it will grow and flower in sun or light shade—but it does demand a full yard over which to spread and is too overpowering for small neighbours.

Looking from my window as I write in mid-December, I can see a sprawling mat of *Geranium wallichianum* 'Buxton's Variety' and it is still displaying a few of its wide flowers, coloured in nemesia-blue with an attractive white centre to each blossom. It has been in flower since early summer without ceasing. Once again, it is essential to realize that one plant will handsomely cover more than a square yard, to the detriment of anything less vigorous within reach of its wide-flung and leafy stems. Here it is growing in the partial shade of an ancient specimen of the mountain pine, *Pinus mugo* and it is happier in such a situation than when in full sun. *G.wallichianum* itself came to us from the Himalayas and, good plant though it is, the flowers are less beautiful than this form ('Buxton's Variety'), which originated many years ago as a chance seedling in the garden of Charles Buxton at Betws-y-Coed.

Anyone who unwarily plants the Cypress Spurge, *Euphorbia cyparissias* in a position where a rampant spreader would prove unwelcome,

Polygonum vaccinifolium

Geranium wallichianum

is in for trouble, for this rampageous spurge is an inveterate rambler and not easy to eradicate once firmly established. I have great affection for all the euphorbias but admit to definite reservations about this particular species. Set in informal surroundings, with plenty of space, it is highly decorative. It runs beneath the ground, emitting countless foot-high, erect and leafy stems, crowned with heads of greenish yellow flowers and bracts. The foliage takes on colourful autumn tints so that it is handsome from the moment when its stems first appear above ground until it finally goes to rest late in the autumn.

The tiny *Rubus arcticus* which creeps through peaty soil in many parts of the Northern Hemisphere and far away in Arctic regions is a nomad to which I have no objection. There could be no nicer inhabitant of the peat garden than this bramble, which threads its way harmlessly among its companions, popping up here and there with a neat tuft of small, trifoliate leaves which are accompanied by short-stemmed and quite large rich pink flowers. Although it does not fruit freely, it does produce a few clusters of amber coloured drupes, which are edible and sweet. It is an asset to any area of peaty, lime-free soil and is never a nuisance.

Rubus arcticus

For a similar situation and slightly more robust as a wanderer, but permissible where there is space for it to colonize, is *Leucopogon (Cyathodes) fraseri*. An Australasian, it is a dwarf, heath-like shrublet whose thin, woody stems are thickly beset with tiny, pointed leaves, in the axils of which (during the summer) appear cream-white, bell-shaped fragrant flowers. It does run about—some of its growths emerging a foot or more away from the original plant—but it has never, in my own long enjoyment of it, proved an objectionable companion to other peat garden plants.

Should you ever allow *Ranunculus ficaria*, our native Lesser Celandine, to obtain a firm roothold in your garden, you will surely live to regret it, for it is almost impossible to rid the garden of it. It makes a mass of tiny bulblets underground and every one of these, if left, will quickly grow into a healthy invader. Lovely though it is, and one of the first heralds of approaching Spring, it must be left to please us in the wild. Having unfortunately introduced it to my own garden accidentally, it was four years before I could say with confidence that it was no longer there.

Even those who have suffered, and toiled to rid themselves of a pest, may take comfort in the fact that there are some selected varieties of *R.ficaria* which are as beautiful as they are trustworthy. In particular, *R.f.*'Aurantiaca' is unlikely ever to outgrow its welcome and will reward you for your courage in planting it in a cool corner by a long springtime display of flowers which are a rich copper-orange in colour. It does increase, by means of similar tiny bulbets, but never to the extent of becoming unwelcome. There are several other forms, all originally found among the wildings which can be planted with confidence, some with cream or white flowers, some fully double and all quite enchanting in pre-spring days. However, one to be avoided, unless it can be given a place in a wild garden, is the 'Major' form, which is the type magnified to a foot-high giant, with large, glistening yellow flowers and very leafy.

Curiously belonging to the potato family, Solanaceae, *Nierembergia repens* (*rivularis*) is yet another insidious spreader by means of far-travelling underground roots, but in this case one can be grateful for its readiness to spread because it is not utterly hardy and can suffer in very wet and cold winters. It comes from South America and emits, from the running roots, broad, blunt green leaves and very short-stemmed, bell-shaped white flowers, often tinted yellow in the throat. It is more likely to be lost if it is grown in rich soil. A colony, which I planted in a narrow bed beside a gravel path, died out in the soil but spread happily and permanently into the adjacent gravel.

There is another species, *N.caerulea* (*hippomanica*) from the Argen-

Nierembergia repens

tine, which is also slightly suspect for hardiness. It is a stay-at-home, with leafy, foot-high stems and profusions of violet-blue flowers during the summer and on into the autumn. Nice enough, but not really a rock garden plant.

A state of continual disagreement exists between my wife and myself concerning the Triquestrous Garlic, *Allium triquetrum*. Now accepted as a British native, although originally an escapee from gardens which has naturalized in many places (especially in the western counties), it is a common inhabitant of Cornish hedgebottoms. I do not deny that it can become a weed, but I am so fond of it that I gladly forgive its misdeeds for the sake of the enjoyment I receive when it hangs out its drooping white flowers, sketched with lines of soft green. It is bulbous and seeds with abandon and I have to fiercely protect the small colonies which are allowed to exist. There is no mistaking the fact that it is an onion, for the family odour is very evident when it is handled. If you keep it within bounds in a semi-wild place, I know that you will become fond of it—even the naughtiest children have redeeming characteristics!

For a similar dismissal to less formal parts of the garden is another bulbous onion, *Allium moly*. A native of south-east Europe, it really can become a nuisance in the wrong place. It is an avid sun-lover—as opposed to *A.triquetrum*, which is happier in light shade—and sheds golden light from the clusters of rich yellow flowers borne on nine to twelve-inch stems. I have not dared to introduce it into my own small garden—a domestic war embracing two species of *Allium* would be too much to endure— but I relish it in parts of the nursery where it can spread to its hearts content, and it does.

So, be warned but not discouraged. Even the most inveterate invaders can play their valuable part in gardens. Used judicially and with full knowledge of their capabilities, there is no good reason to deny oneself their beauty. Even if some of them do become pests they are better than the common weeds and pay a more generous rent for the space they occupy.

8 Aristocrats

Without at least one chapter devoted to the aristocrats of the alpine world surely this book would be incomplete. Undoubtedly many plants in other chapters could justly lay claim to nobility, but here will be the *crème de la crème*—bejewelled treasures which are the enchantment of high mountain regions as they nestle between the rocks and lend their loveliness to soften the austerity of their environment. My own taste in plants is catholic, but it is to these precious alpines that my greatest love is given.

That they are not every gardeners choice I know well, but once bitten by the alpine bug you will inevitably arrive at a condition of knowledge and skill which will insist that you accept their challenge and do your best to accustom them to our very different climate. Some of them are difficult to grow but the reward of success is so great that no effort is grudged and failures come to be accepted as just steps on the road to ultimate triumph.

Here then, is an unalphabetical medley of a chosen selection of plants which I unhesitatingly classify as aristocrats.

The fact that there is really only one species of *Anchusa* suitable for the rock garden has always saddened me, for the flowers of these, mostly tall, border plants are of an incomparable blue, and flowers of genuine blue are by no means plentiful.

From the heights of Cretan mountains comes the pygmy *A.caespitosa*, and it is a treasure indeed. Soon after its original introduction, by some mishap, a much taller plant began to be distributed under its name. This proved to be another species, by name *A.angustissima* and it took a few years to get the confusion sorted out. Many gardeners were puzzled and disappointed when, having sown seeds, reputedly of *A.caespitosa*, and happily expecting a tiny tuffet of narrow, dark green rugose leaves with undulating margins, and gentian-blue flowers resting almost stemlessly among the leaves, they were presented with a plant throwing erect stems up to eighteen inches in height. The flowers were blue enough, but this was by no means the choice alpine plant they had expected.

Like almost everyone else given the opportunity to experiment with this precious new introduction I gave it V.I.P. treatment in an alpine house, growing it in pots deep enough to accommodate its long and fleshy roots. It grew reasonably well, but was not the success that had been hoped for. It was clever Bill Bishop, then in charge of the parks and gardens in Harrogate, who boldly planted it out on a sunny limestone scree, where it quickly gave evidence that this was the treatment it preferred, and grew into wide mats. How well I remember, on an occasion when I was admiring it enviously in his company, that he fetched a spade and chopped pieces off and gave them to me—and they all throve when given similar treatment in my Sussex nursery after an initial period in pots to get over the shock of such ruthless treatment. It just goes to prove that we can be too fussy and cautious, and that some plants are killed by kindness.

To see *Calceolaria darwinii* in its native habitat you would have to make the long journey to the Straits of Magellan. It is said to have been discovered by Charles Darwin (after whom it is named) on his famous voyage in rl.M.S. Beagle. Although it comes from an utterly un-alpine environment, it has been happily adopted by alpine enthusiasts and is one of their annual excitements when it displays its astonishing flowers, which are certainly not 'beautiful' in the accepted sense; they are, however, curious and arresting and never fail to arouse interest and admiration. From small, branching rhizomes rise tufts of toothed, dark green leaves and four-inch stems, each carrying one pouched, yellow-brown blossom with a vivid bar of pure white across the broadest part of the pouch.

If grown under glass it is vulnerable to attack by red spider mites, against which precautions should be taken by using an appropriate insecticide. It can be grown successfully out of doors, but I have always been surprised to discover that, although it comes from what I am told is one of the windiest spots on the globe, it is definitely averse to exposure to cold winds here. From Patagonia and the Falkland Islands comes the rather similar *C.fothergillii* and there now exists an interesting race of garden-raised intermediate hybrids between the two.

Of absolutely top rank among the aristocrats must be placed *Paraquilegia anemonoides* (erstwhile *P.grandiflora* or *Isopyrum grandiflorum*), which is claimed by some to be the most beautiful of all alpine plants. I have several contenders for the same distinction, but when confronted by a flowering plant of this exquisiteness from Kashmir and eastward through the Himalayas, I would not argue. Its delicate tufts of ferny, silver-grey foliage form the perfect setting for the rounded, rich lavender flowers, carried singly on slender four to six-inch stems. I remember surrendering all my own contenders to a junior status when I worshipped at the shrine of a marvellous specimen exhibited at the Harrogate Spring Flower Show a year or two ago. Filling a nine-inch pan it proudly displayed more than one hundred flowers and was unanimously awarded the special medal reserved for the best plant in the show.

In the south of England it is usually given alpine house treatment, but in the more humid north it succeeds in the open air, although it asks for, and deserves wherever it is grown, the special care accorded to such rare and breath-taking beauty. You may have to seek through many specialized catalogues before finding it offered for sale, but it is worth any effort to obtain and cherish.

There are several androsaces of the Aretian section which certainly rank as aristocrats, but I find it impossible to select just one of them to include here and they will be found in a later chapter among others of this invaluable and highly appreciated genus (see pp. 77–97). There have been times, when they are blossoming in the spring, when I could only quote from the *Beggar's Opera*: 'How happy I could be with either, were t'other dear charmer away.'

The woods and mountains of Japan are full of treasures, many of which have become firm favourites in our gardens. No garden which can provide an area of lime-free, peaty soil should be without *Shortia uniflora* in its 'grandiflora' form. Growing as low mats of thin, woody stems which bear rounded, leathery and lightly toothed leaves—in themselves attractive—it bursts into its full loveliness when carrying (singly on short, naked stems) the large pink flowers, each petal delicately frilled at the edge. It can sulk for a while after planting, but will eventually establish and may even self-seed.

An exciting plant to discover in the wild, and to grow, is *Kelseya uniflora*, curiously related to the spiraeas, a relationship which would never be guessed by an unbotanical eye. It is confined to a few scattered localities in the states of Montana, Wyoming and Idaho, where it inhabits sheer limestone cliffs, choosing the narrowest of cracks and crannies in which to develope into wide hummocks of compressed tiny stems and grey-green leaves. It is very, very slow growing, and specimens which can be seen in its mountain fastnesses may be as much as six feet across, and are surely hundreds of years old. Its flowers are not spectacular, but they are produced in such abundance that the whole cushion takes on a canopy of pink when the myriads of stemless blossoms appear. I have grown it successfully in a hole drilled in tufa rock, but it is probably best as a specimen plant in the alpine house, in a compost which assures it a gritty and spartan diet.

If only tiny *Oxalis lobata* would be a trifle less irritating in its habits it would be everybody's darling. It comes from Chile, and exists in the form of minute bulbs, tunicked with soft brown hairs. From these miniscule bulbs early in the spring arise neat tufts of bright green leaves, and those who do not know how it behaves are delighted. Quite soon their delight turn to chagrin, for the leaves fade away and the plant is apparently moribund. It is not unknown for nurserymen to receive indignant letters stating that the plant has died, and can they have a replacement! It then has to be explained to them that if they will wait until September the leaves will reappear, but this time they will be accompanied by a galaxy of short-stemmed richly golden flowers. *O.lobata* has a double dormant period. When it finally dies down it should be kept dry until late February or early March, when it may be expected to produce those tantalizing leaves once again.

It may already have been noticed that I take particular pleasure in plants whose flowers are of a true blue colour and this is one of the reasons why I take great delight in *Cyananthus lobatus*, a *Campanula* cousin from Asia. From a deeply delving root it radiates many leafy stems at ground level, each one terminating in an astonishingly large, round flower of deep blue. It is hardy and long lived and a sun lover.

In 1913 Reginald Farrer wrote briefly of the genus *Dionysia*, saying that it was: 'A race never found in either list or garden, but well deserving to be cherished in both if it would accept of such observance.' Since that time explorations in the mountains of the Middle East and southern U.S.S.R. have resulted in the introduction of a number of species of this exciting family, related to the primrose but vastly different in appearance from primulas as we know them. The greatest concentration of species is to be found in the mountains of Iran and Afghanistan.

At the time Farrer wrote the above words, a score of species had been recorded, although none was in cultivation then. The number of identified species has now grown to thirty-five, several of which are being very successfully grown, especially by the enthusiastic and skilled members of the Alpine Garden Society, to whom the exquisite beauty and undeniable intractability of these alpine gems offers a challenge not to be rebuffed. They will never be plants for the open garden, but they demand and deserve the more intimate worship that can be given to them when grown as specimens in an alpine house.

In nature the species jealously confine themselves to very restricted localities and seldom if ever cohabit with other species. Some go to the extreme of confining themselves to just one mountain. Nearly always they grow on limestone, in chinks and crannies of partially shaded rocks

Oxalis lobata

Cyananthus lobatus

and cliffs. In some instances they occur in regions where the rainfall is extremely limited, relying for moisture on night precipitations or from low clouds. One particular species actually occupies an upside-down position in caves!

The most cherished species are those which adopt a tight, hummocky habit, crowding their tiny rosettes of small, usually hairy leaves in domes and buns, which they decorate with countless short-stemmed and often fragrant flowers. The first to be successfully cultivated was *D.curviflora*, which came to our gardens in 1932 and is one of the least difficult to grow, delighting us with its abundance of long-tubed pink flowers. It was not until about 1960 that *D.aretioides* arrived. Not only is it one of the most lovely but it has a kindly disposition, growing into massive domes of grey rosettes, hidden in the spring beneath myriads of primrose-scented golden flowers.

Some of my most cherished memories of periods spent in Iran during recent years are of journeys into the mountains, now, alas, so inaccessible during the troubled period through which Iran and Afghanistan are passing. We can be thankful that a good deal of plant hunting was done before the political upheaval. I treasure the recollections of what I was able to see and do, and hope that peace will eventually be restored to those ill-fated countries.

From the Aleutian Islands to Japan is the home of *Cassiope lycopodioides*, just one of a family of heath-like plants which inhabit many mountainous and Arctic regions of the Northern Hemisphere. They are all counted among the most desirable residents of peat gardens, or other positions where they can be assured of lime-free and cool conditions. Given these—with the one exception of *C.hypnoides*, which obstinately refuses all blandishments and will not thrive in gardens—they are easily grown and very rewarding plants.

C.lycopodioides is one of my own special favourites and I treasure wide mats of its entangled stems, dressed with tiny, overlapping leaves and adorned in season with white fairy bells carried on inch-high red stems and backed by a crimson calyx. It is small, but astonishingly beautiful and I class it high among those amiable, long-lived and hardy plants which add so much to a gardener's pleasure.

Another of the gems of the race, this time from Tibet, is *C.wardii*. Not quite so accommodating as *C.lycopodioides* it is, nevertheless, a charmer. Its erect stems attain a height of some nine inches or so and are clothed with the characteristic, scale-like, overlapping leaves, from among which gleam large white bell-shaped flowers. You might have to give it a little more loving care and attention to make it really happy.

Cassiope lycopodioides

There are nice North American species, such as *C.tetragona* and *C.mertensiana*, all built upon a similar pattern. I have seen and admired them growing in great colonies in western North America and they are great memory joggers whenever I encounter them in gardens. In cultivation a number of good hybrids have happened or been induced, all of sterling worth.

This then, eulogizes a few of the aristocrats. There are more, many of which will be written about in following pages in the context of their particular families, but it would not be fitting to conclude this chapter without mention of *Eritrichium nanum*, the incomparable alpine Forget-me-not which refuses to descend from its Olympian heights to adorn our gardens. To offer it the worship it commands you must ascend to the mountain fastnesses where it dwells and there fall upon your knees to render homage. Maybe it is only right and proper that at least one alpine plant should spurn all our blandishments and mourn to the point of extinction the pure air and sanctity of the environment from which it has been snatched. The moments of triumph which have attended my own infrequent attempts—I cannot call them successes, but something less than absolute failures—have no comparison with the sublime peace and contentment which have attended my various encounters with *Eritrichium* in the solitude and purity of the mountains.

Just why this jewel of high places in Europe should be so capricious has never been discovered, although there is undoubtedly a warning to those with experience in such matters who will note the frail, softly hairy leaves, gathered into compact tufts and surely ill-adapted to endure an average British winter without the protective covering of snow beneath which it sleeps through the long winter months. This is definitely one of the plants which should be attempted only by highly skilled fanatics, for it will never offer its utter serene loveliness in any garden. Go, then, to the mountains and worship at its shrine and drink in the perfection of its azure, yellow-eyed flowers which reflect the sheer blue of the skies above. I admit that I still make occasional attempts to please this capricious child of the hills, but always with a feeling of guilt, doubting my right to destroy such perfection.

9 North American and Canadian Alpines

It has been my great good fortune to spend some time in the vast mountainous areas of western North America and Canada, where many delectable alpine plants have their habitat, and most of them are agreeably willing to adapt themselves to European conditions and make a major contribution to any representative collection of alpines. They are so numerous that anything like a comprehensive enumeration would be impossible if this is not to become a multi-volume book. This imposes a limitation, which I admit to be welcome, of writing only of those which are my own particular favourites. It must be obvious to anyone who has had the patience to read so far that this is a very personal selection—a selection from which I find it more difficult to exclude than to include.

For the sake of convenience, I shall write of all plants in this chapter, whether they come from America or Canadian mountains, as 'American'. I think there can be no doubt that the genus of American plants which has become overwhelmingly popular with alpine gardeners is *Lewisia*, a family which has taken very kindly to our conditions—so much so, in fact, that many of my American friends who visit me admit with no little chagrin that lewisias grow better here than they do in American gardens.

This handsome genus is named in honour of Captain Meriwether Lewis, leader of the joint Lewis and Clark expedition, the first coast-to-coast crossing of the American Continent which preceded the construction of the Canadian Pacific Railway. Fortunately for gardeners throughout the temperate world, both men were plant lovers as well as surveyors and engineers. Each is now remembered by a particular genus: Captain William Clark gave his name to the annual *Clarkia* which so brightly emblazons our flower borders.

With a few exceptions lewisias are amoral plants, only too eager to wed with any other species within wind or bee range. This has resulted in a number of hybrids and strains which have largely replaced the original introductions. In the past there were such names as *L.cotyledon*, *L.heckneri*, *L.howellii*, *L.finchii*, *L.purdyi* and *L.mariana*, but these have mostly been submerged in the various named strains, which I have to admit, rather unwillingly as a purist enamoured of true species, are superior in garden value.

There was a time when lewisias were always given lime-free soil, but it is now recognized that they will tolerate alkaline conditions as long as their well-drained soil is well supplied with humus in the form of peat or leafsoil. They dislike being grown on the flat and prefer positions where they can emerge from narrow crevices or grow on a sloping site. They also appreciate a drying-off period after they have flowered.

L.tweedyi, universally acclaimed as the most beautiful of all *Lewisia*, is one of the exceptions which has never, to my knowledge, hybridized with any other species. Together with others I used to grow it in rich soil and moist conditions, but when I saw it growing wild in the Wenatchee Mountains of the State of Washington, I learned my lesson. Plants which I grew under the accepted conditions made vast, lush specimens which all too often collapsed during the winter. In nature it is subjected to intense heat and dryness after it has flowered. This glory of the genus will form massive but loose clumps of large leaves, fleshy in texture, amid which spring many stems carrying large, wide-petalled flowers of a colour most difficult to describe, being a suffusion of yellow, apricot and pink—a tint which has defeated every colour chart upon which I have attempted to match it. The seeds which it provides with modest liberality are easily raised and may give plants bearing flowers of clear, rich rose colour and even an occasional pure albino.

An absolute startler is *L.rediviva*, named Bitter Root by the American Indians. I was once taken to a place where it was known to grow in profusion but it was too early in the season and nothing was to be seen—it is a deciduous species, dying back to rest in a thick, fleshy root—and was told that we should come back later, preferably after a warm spring rain. This we did, and I shall never forget the sight of literally acres of sub-alpine turf sheeted with thousands of the short-stemmed very large flowers of intense rose-red. The appearance above ground of *L.rediviva* is brief, for the narrow, fleshy leaves begin to wither as the blossoms fade and it soon retires for its long dormancy. It too is variable and there are one or two distinct forms which have been given clonal names, but it is strictly moral and does not, as the Quakers would say, 'marry-out' and form marital relationships with other species.

One of the criticisms which is sometimes aimed at lewisias is that their flowering season is short and confined to early spring, but there is a hybrid, raised by my nursery foreman (and named 'George Henley' in his honour) which carries on nine-inch stems, from May until October,

Lewisia tweedyi

showers of small, cerise-red blossoms. Admittedly the colour is not everyone's choice, but there is much to be said in favour of a plant which gives so generously of its flowers over so long a period. Another which makes only a short appearance above ground is *L.brachycalyx*. It is seen at first as a cluster of narrow, fleshy green leaves which develop into a loose rosette, centred by bunches of almost stemless large, pure white flowers, sitting among the leaves like a Victorian posy.

One of the first of all *Lewisia* hybrids to appear in cultivation was from the garden of Dr. Paul Giuseppi, a famous alpine gardener who lived in Felixstowe. It is named *L.*'Trevosia' and is an elegant plant offering long sprays of salmon-red flowers. It is sterile, and has to be propagated vegetatively, but has retained all its vigour and is a universally popular plant.

Paul Giuseppi was one of the founders of the Alpine Garden Society and travelled the world over in search of plants. He was responsible, together with my father, who was his frequent travelling companion, for the introduction of many good plants, notably from Greece and the Balkans, and from the vast ranges of the Caucasus mountains. It was they who first firmly established in our gardens that most lovely of all dwarf geraniums, *Geranium subcaulescens*, whose crimson-red, dark-eyed flowers outsmart those of the Pyrenean *G.cinerium*, of which it is botanically a subspecies.

There are certain plants for whose first appearance above ground one looks with special fervour. I just cannot wait in the spring to see the first folded leaves of the Canadian Bloodroot, *Sanguinaria canadensis*, thrusting through the soil. As the wide, scalloped grey-green leaves unfold it is seen that they had in their protective clasp pearl-white buds, which expand into cup-shaped flowers of purest white. The individual life of the flowers is brief, they endure for only a day, but there is a cherished variant with fully double flowers which are more enduring. This, too, is a plant giving pleasure which can be savoured only briefly, for it dies back into the thick, fleshy, red-blooded roots quite soon after it has finished flowering. Give it peaty or leafy soil in a cool place—it is an ideal peat-garden plant—and mark its position carefully so that subsequent excavations do not damage its roots.

Taxonomically, the genus *Douglasia* has always hovered uneasily between the genera *Primula*, *Gregoria*, *Aretia* and *Androsace*, and there are indications that modern botanists wish to include it in yet another genus, *Vitaliana*, but I stubbornly adhere to common usage and insist upon knowing the several species as douglasias. There is one very desirable European species of which I shall have something to say on later pages, and two or three Americans which might well resent not having been included in the chapter devoted to aristocrats.

D.laevigata is one of which I have pleasant memories—I recall seeing it growing in the gorges of the Fraser River in British Columbia. It qualifies to be associated with the best of the alpine cushion plants, making neat tufts of short, pointed, deep green leaves, over which stand many clusters of rose-red flowers on erect inch-high stems. It is fairly widely distributed in North America and Canada and each region seems to have its own particular variant, those from the Fraser River and Columbia River bearing the most richly coloured flowers. On the whole it is happiest in lime-free soil, but is reasonably tolerant and is by no means difficult to please.

In the Cascade Mountains of North America you may find *D.dentata* which is of similar habit but has rosettes of ash-grey leaves and flowers which are violet rather than pink. With me it has always been a little more fussy than *D.laevigata*, demanding more care and attention, but by no means being what Farrer would have called a 'miff' or a 'mimp',— two words he coined to describe plants he considered difficult, and which have been widely accepted in the alpine gardener's vocabulary.

When I consider the family of *Sisyrinchium* I am irresistibly reminded of the verse about the little girl who, 'when she was good, was very, very good, but when she was bad, she was horrid'. For there are good and bad sisyrinchiums. They are all garden-worthy from the point of view of offering pretty flowers, but some are so eager to seed themselves that they can become a proper nuisance. I have known gardeners consign the entire genus to the devil after struggling to eliminate thousands of self-sown *S.angustifolium*; but were they to do so they would deprive themselves of some very desirable and well-behaved plants.

All the species are native of North or South America and there are two of the North Americans upon which I can unhesitatingly lavish praise. *S.douglasii* (*grandiflorum*), erupts very early in the spring from dormant roots into clusters of narrow, grass-like leaves from which rise nine-inch stems carrying pendant wine-red bells. It is another plant which dies down very soon after flowering and whose position should be carefully marked. If you raise it from seed there may well be some nice albino forms.

Several years ago a good friend in America sent me a box containing some tiny plants labelled *S.macounianum*. These entranced me when they eventually produced their large, snow-white flowers rising from clusters of sword-shaped leaves, but I have since discovered that the type species carries blue flowers and the plants I have are the albino variant. I now have younglings of the type, but in the meantime am well content with *S.macounianum* 'Album'. It is easily grown but very well behaved. Another, with the slightly dubious name *S.brachypus*, has golden flowers. It is invasive, but not unduly so.

I hesitated to mention *S.macrocarpum* because I have not been at all sure that it is really hardy. My doubts have been confirmed—all my plants perished during the winter of 1981–2, except for a few which had been given protection. However, as one of the most handsome species it deserves mention. If it is grown in the alpine house it will survive the coldest winter. Although it was first described in 1881, there are very few references to it in literature and it has only recently become more widely distributed. It is a native of Patagonia and Argentina. Its grey-green leaves are arranged in flat, erect fans and the flowers are flat, wide-petalled and large. Their colour is deep yellow and there is a conspicuous brown mark at the base of each petal. It was exhibited in London in 1977 and given an Award of Merit.

My first sight of *Synthyris pinnatifida* 'Tomentosa' was on the Hurricane Ridge in the Olympic Mountains of Washington and I knew immediately that here was a plant that I just had to grow. That was many years ago and I am still struggling to persuade this wilful creature that a comfortable home in Sussex need not induce the homesickness it displays. It grows, and flowers too, but with obvious reluctance. In the Olympics it grew among black volcanic rocks which formed a spectacular background to its tufts of deeply cut, intensely silver leaves, over which hovered short, erect stems bearing heads of blue flowers protruding from large silvery calyces. It is so resentful of captivity that it refuses to set seeds, but I am able to obtain occasional supplies from good friends in America which enable me to continue my efforts to discover what it really asks for. It has been given every possible sort of compost and exposure, none of which have been more than partially satisfactory. The best results have been when I grew it in deep pots in the alpine house, in a very gritty, lime-free mixture of loam, peat and sand. I am always reluctant to overfeed alpines but have found that an occasional feed with Maxicrop has met with some approval. It never fails to arouse interest and a desire to grow it, but it does demand V.I.P. treatment and a certain amount of optimism.

Another species (they are all American) is *S.reniformis* (*rotundifolia*) which, although perhaps not such an aristocrat, is of an amiable disposition and well worth growing. Its clumps of bluntly-toothed green, rather leathery leaves form a base for short racemes of purple-blue flowers. It is very hardy and asks for no more than a fairly cool position in any good soil.

Comparable to the silver-leaved *Synthyris* for contrariness is lovely *Phacelia sericea*, which was the sensation of a period spent near Lakes O'Hara and McArthur in the Canadian Rockies. It grew on steep slopes covered with rocks and debris from high cliffs above. I remember how difficult it was to decide which demanded the most attention; the superb grandeur of the mighty mountains which towered on all sides, or the enticing plants which grew at our feet. While trying to take in all this scenic beauty I finally stumbled and fell, to find myself face to face with *Phacelia sericea*, a plant so handsome and so utterly desirable that I was immediately jerked back to reality. Even when not in flower the plant is exceptionally beautiful; loose rosettes of deeply-cleft silver-grey foliage make it well worth growing even without the bonus of bold spikes or reddish purple flowers, from the tubular throats of which protrude bright orange stigmas. To have any hope of success, give this charmer the same treatment recommended for the *Synthyris* and be prepared for disappointment. If it can be persuaded to flourish any effort can be counted as well spent.

It was here that I first made the acquaintance—later to become a lasting friendship—with tiny *Erigeron aureus*, and what a gem this is. From the neatest of congested tufts of grey-haired, spoon-shaped leaves rise innumerable three-inch stems, each carrying one inch-wide golden-yellow flower. You need have no qualms about this dainty composite. It flourishes in any sunny spot in sharply drained soil and has the additional virtue of blossoming on and on throughout the summer. I have recorded flowers on my plants during nine months of the year.

On that same expedition I was able to collect seeds of another American species, *E.flettii*, which resembles *E.aureus* in some respects, but is slightly larger in all its parts and the flowers are pure white. At home I grew the two more or less side by side and, after a few years, among seedlings of *E.aureus* there appeared an obvious hybrid between the two. It was christened 'Birch Hybrid', a rather unimaginative name which identifies a really worthwhile plant, intermediate between its parents in appearance and with flowers of softly cream-yellow colour.

The Olympic Mountains in the State of Washington, to which my thoughts constantly return as I dip into my rag-bag of memories, are notable for the number of endemic species to be found there and nowhere else. One of the nicest of these is *Petrophytum hendersonii*. The few plants in this genus were included in *Spiraea* but, for once I agree with the botanists who decided that their characteristics were so distinct that they deserved a genus of their own. A crevice dweller by choice, it makes tidy hummocks of dark green, sometimes slightly bronzed leaves of thickish texture, over which hover short, fluffy spikes crowded with myriads of tiny white flowers. It is a happy and rewarding plant to grow, either in an outdoor crevice, or as a specimen in the alpine house.

Conscious of the fact that I lavish praise on a number of plants which are both difficult to obtain and not easy to grow, I was amused while browsing through the pages of one of the Alpine Garden Society's invaluable Bulletins, to come across some lines, paraphrased by Paul Rosenheim from Lewis Carroll; they express so exactly the feelings of those of us who are enthusiastic enough to contend with the idiosyncrasies of the more temperamental children of the hills:

> The time has come
> The Walrus said
> To speak of many ills,

> Of miffs and mimps and treasure plants,
> Wee children of the hills,
> And if the dear will die on me
> And whether rehash kills?

Many exciting plants are to be found on mighty Mount Rainier, whose often snow-capped head towers 14,000 feet into the skies of Washington. I was overjoyed to see there in flower tiny *Lupinus lyallii*. I am told that it is more correctly *L.lepidus* 'Lobbii', but I shall save that for times when I am conversing with savants. This small member of the lupin tribe does not exceed a modest four inches in height, forming tidy rosettes of silvered and filigree foliage and displaying on very short stems its clusters of bright blue flowers. There are several miniature lupins to be found in America. *L.ornatus* comes from California and I have not been so fortunate as to see it in the wild, but I grow it from time to time, when it makes its spasmodic appearance in gardens. Rather taller than *L.lyallii*, it has equally silver leaves and short spikes of intensely blue flowers carried on nine-inch stems. Both are hardy and good plants for a sunny scree, but neither is very long lived so that some seeds should be saved and sown.

Another of Rainier's treasures is a tiny cousin of the lewisias, which Americans call 'Pussy-paws'. Botanically it is *Spraguea multiceps*, or, if you wish to be pedantic, *Calyptridium umbellatum*, but here again I adhere to the name I grew up with. From its rosettes of small, fleshy leaves radiate prostrate stems terminating in a head of fluffy pink papery bracts enclosing tiny flowers. Like its related lewisias it prefers lime-free soil. It is a long time since I climbed Mount Rainier but even then it was a tourist's paradise and it was distressing to see the lovely Avalanche Lilies, *Erythronium montanum*, growing and blossoming as thickly as bluebells in an English wood, being trampled underfoot by surging multitudes of trippers. What it must be like today I shudder to think.

A dainty *Primula* which lingers only in my memory, for I lost it long ago and am doubtful if it is even in cultivation in this country now, is *P.mistassinica*. To all intents and purposes it is a miniature version of our native Bird's-eye Primrose, *P.farinosa*, and enjoys similar moist conditions. Over the tiny rosettes of crinkled leaves stand short, erect stems supporting a terminal umbel of pink flowers. Although it looks so frail, and is certainly not a long-lived plant, it is not difficult to grow and it is surprising that it has not secured a firmer root in cultivation.

Mrs. Rae Berry, who created a wonderful garden in Portland, Oregon, and was one of America's leading authorities on the genus *Primula*, was always distressed that *P.mistassinica* would not linger with me, and regularly sent me supplies of seed with which to 'have another go'. Alas, she died some years ago at a great age and her garden is now being cared for by a trust. Although stone-deaf from birth she had reduced lip-reading to a fine art and was an intrepid traveller and was still actively seeking plants in the mountains when she was well over eighty years old. I believe it was she was found the first rare albino of *Campanula piperi*.

Gentians are universally loved, and there will be a chapter devoted to them, but I must include *G.calycosa* in this chapter of American alpines. It is found on several of the higher mountains of western North America, usually growing in moist alpine meadows. Its erect, foot-high stems carry pairs of leaves, the topmost two encircling the base of the solitary flower, which is a bell-shaped, clear blue blossom, about one and a half inches long, the exterior of the flower segments shaded to a tint of purple-mahogany. It has been grown, off and on, in this country for many years, but is now a rarity, which is a pity for it is a handsome species and would be a worthy addition to any collection of alpine plants.

Perhaps it is stretching it a little to classify trilliums as alpines. They inhabit North American and Oriental woodlands and find acceptable accommodation in other parts of the garden than the rock garden, but most alpine gardeners have an affection for them and I would be less than content if this book did not lavish upon them a little of the praise they deserve.

The most commonly grown species is *Trillium grandiflorum* and it is one of the best. Like all of the genus it may sulk for a while after being planted but will eventually settle down and grow into sturdy clumps, with deeply delving, almost tuberous roots. It heralds our uncertain springs with broad, three-parted leaves and large, snow-white flowers on erect, foot-high stems. There is also a rare but very lovely form with fully double flowers.

Those for whom small is beautiful, and rarity is a virtue, will seek *T.rivale*, a Californian miniature no more than a few inches in height. The flowers may be white or faintly pink and there is an even more rare version which has been—or will be—given the clonal name 'Verne Ahiers' which has rather cup-shaped blossoms of clear shell-pink. Both are greeted with acclamation when they make their occasional appearances on the show benches of the Alpine Garden Society's exhibitions, but neither is likely to be obtainable from commercial sources so rely for distribution upon the usual generosity of gardeners who are always willing to share their treasures with fellow enthusiasts.

The boldly handsome *T.erectum* is one for which I have much affection. From a circlet of three wide leaflets atop a foot-high stem, rise large, richly red-purple flowers. There are forms with white or faintly yellowish flowers which I find less admirable. *T.undulatum* is extremely dainty and elegant. On its short stems are the usual three-petalled blossoms, each white segment painted with a rose-red smudge at its base. Another, strong-growing species with richly coloured flowers is *T.sessile* whose large blossoms are deep mahogany-red.

It was about 1935 that *Kalmiopsis leachiana* made its debut into British gardens, where it is now firmly established. The only species in its genus it was at first treated with great respect. My own early experiences with it were not encouraging. As it belonged to Ericaceae I assumed that it would probably be a lime-hater but none of the blandishments I showered upon it persuaded it to do more than grudgingly exist. Finally, and in despair, I planted it in a limestone scree, where, although it certainly did not 'spread itself like a green bay tree', it did at least grow and flower. Ridicule was heaped upon me when I broadcast my partial success and eventually those particular plants did depart to whatever nirvana is sought by plants which give up the ghost. I certainly do not recommend a limy diet for *Kalmiopsis*. Young plants subsequently raised from seed and cuttings took more kindly to cultivation and this very good dwarf shrub is now firmly rooted in cultivation.

There is only this one species in the genus from western North America, but it occurs in different localities in slightly varying forms. The particular variant from the region of the Lepiniac River seems to be the most vigorous. A mature plant will attain almost a foot in height and be of similar diameter, forming a hummocky, rounded bush of wiry, woody stems clothed in small, dark green leaves of thick texture. The bell-shaped flowers are carried in short terminal racemes, usually from March until May.

Although I accept and find pleasure in many natural hybrids, I do not myself try to improve upon nature, but I admit to being a little surprised that there have not yet been recorded, as far as I know, any hybrids between *Kalmiopsis* and other members of Ericaceae sufficiently akin to make possible a marriage. (Several such intergeneric hybrids have been recorded since this paragraph was written.) That such unions can produce good garden plants is evident in such plants as *Phyllothamnus erectus*, which resulted when a species of *Phyllodoce* mated with *Rhodothamnus chamaecistus*—and the latter, by way of interest, is one of the very few lime-loving Ericaceae.

10 Ericaceous Plants

It has often been said that a wise gardener will restrict his choice of plants to those which it is reasonably certain will adapt themselves readily to the particular environment he has to offer. If this is true I have met very few wise gardeners. Quite the reverse, in fact, for most of us seem to have an irresistible urge to grow the very plants which would seem to be unsuited to whatever soil or climate we can provide.

As a young man I lived in an area where the soil was definitely alkaline and special preparation had to be made for any of the lime-haters. Of course I developed an intense interest in these particular plants—perhaps because of the very challenge they offered—but it was a constant struggle, with many disappointments and frustrations and I admit to an abiding joy when I moved to the Weald of Sussex, midway between the North and the South Downs and found myself on soil that was just on the acid side of neutral. This provided me with the best of both worlds, for I could grow all the lime-intolerant plants and also the much more tolerant lime-lovers, most of which would succeed; it is a happy fact that nearly all calciphilous plants will succeed in even slightly acid soil, whereas the califuges are quite intolerant. I do have problems however with the common *Aubrieta*, for example, which is a confirmed lime-lover and does not give of its colourful best without it.

If, therefore, you inhabit an area and do your gardening where there is a definite lime-content to the soil, you will have to take steps to provide a special environment should you wish to grow any of the plants described in this chapter; meanwhile, I gloat because I can attempt any of them with confidence and every hope of success—apart from any individual quirks they may possess.

At this point it may not be inappropriate to give some thought to the problems of those who do their gardening on soil which is definitely alkaline and are yet determined to provide conditions which will be found tolerable by the lime-haters. I know of one unfortunate gentleman who takes a deep interest in dwarf rhododendrons and heathers, to say nothing of vacciniums, gaultherias and all the other delights to whom the mere smell of lime is abhorrent. His garden consists of a few inches of soil over hundreds of feet of solid chalk, but his determination was such that he has made a series of peat beds at the top of his sloping site in which he has achieved a very fair measure of success.

When he first consulted me as to what he could do, after a careful inspection of his garden, my advice to him was that he should move. This was a step too extreme for him to contemplate and I have been astonished by the way in which he has triumphed over adversity. Even *Gentiana sino-ornata*, whose leaves will turn yellow at the merest suspicion of lime, is growing and flowering—not perhaps quite as luxuriantly as it might on acid soil, but well enough to give him no little delight.

To accommodate a few special treasures it is possible to excavate a hole perhaps two feet deep, line it with polythene sheeting, punching a few small holes in the base so that surplus water can drain away and then filling with lime-free compost. Without the protective lining it will only be a question of time before lime-impregnated moisture seeps upward by capillary action.

A more ambitious project, offering a much wider scope, would be to secure a supply of peat blocks and with them to build a peat garden by constructing a series of walls, eighteen inches to two feet high, filling in behind them with a peaty compost. The peat blocks are used just as one would employ bricks when building a wall, making sure that the blocks in each course overlap the joints in the course below. It is also wise to ensure that the blocks are very thoroughly saturated before they are used. The blocks in the lowest course should be sunk about an inch into the ground. If this is not done there is a danger of the wall bulging outward and finally collapsing. Even here a protective lining is advisable to guard against capillary seepage. Should the garden be on a sloping site, one would, of course, create any such sanctuary at the top so that the lime-impregnated water does not flow down and fatally infiltrate the compost.

Should neither of these alternatives be feasible, it is, of course, possible to grow the lime-haters in pots, pans or even boxes of special soil, being careful not to water them with tap water, which will probably be too hard, and is in any case chlorinated and not acceptable. A tank conveniently placed to catch rain water will serve, or it may be possible to provide water which has passed through a water-softening process.

It will now be obvious that to ensure favourable conditions in an unfavourable environment involves a good deal of labour and care. If, therefore, you have lime in your soil, and are not possessed by an irresistible urge to grow such plants, you should leave this chapter unread beyond this point, contenting yourself with the thought that the vast majority of plants are lime tolerant.

As these calicifuges are counted among my own particular favourites, I shall now enthuse about some of my special pets. Many of the handsome andromedas are not only too large for rock gardens, but many of them have now been placed in other genera, although *A.polifolia* remains. A native plant (now becoming rare in England but still fairly common in Ireland), it makes a pleasant low, humped bush of entangled woody stems, adorned with narrow, leathery leaves and displaying, during late spring and early summer, terminal clusters of pink, pitcher-shaped flowers. Of its several named varieties the one named 'Compacta' is especially desirable. It is no more than three inches high and particularly free-flowering.

Among the many enticing plants which have come to our gardens from Japan is tiny *Arcterica nana*, a monotypic genus. Never more than two or three inches tall, it spreads around modestly by underground stems, creating a mat of short, woody stems and tiny, glossy, dark green leaves over which can be admired the clusters of cream-coloured, urn-shaped flowers of waxy texture. It has special value when planted between the blocks of a peat wall, as its running stems bind the blocks together and guard against erosion. Even when I have planted it on the flat bed I notice that it gravitates naturally to the edge and spreads along the face of the wall.

I have already written of cassiopes in a previous chapter, and here in the peat garden is their ideal situation. Another Japanese monotypic plant which relishes all that a peat bed offers is *Tanakaea radicans*—but it can be grown elsewhere. I remember seeing great tufts of it flourishing in a north-facing sandstone wall in a Yorkshire garden. It spreads by woody rhizomes which give forth many short, running stems carrying leathery, evergreen heart-shaped leaves, toothed at the margins. It erupts rather late in the spring into loose cymes of small, pure white flowers. Actually it has no right to be included in this chapter, as it belongs to Saxifragaceae, but it is such an ideal peat-garden plant and associates so well with genuine Ericaceae that I break the rules and place it in its most fitting context; after all this is not a botanical treatise, but a book about plants, and memories of plants, places and people.

Immediately offending once more I must include the creeping cornel, *Cornus canadensis*, for which there is no more appropriate place than the peat bed or garden. It will, admittedly grow elsewhere but it is a good companion to all the plants we are now considering. I have vivid memories of walking over literally acres of this creeping shrublet in mountain woodlands of North America and Canada. It was interesting to note that, where it grew between and under trees, it would adventurously scramble a few feet up the tree trunks, clinging to and even penetrating any bark that was loose. Remember that it is capable of colonizing a considerable area by means of its far spreading underground runners but it should not be grudged any territory that it desires to conquer. It is so different from other species of *Cornus* that botanists have created for it the separate genus *Chamaepericlymenum*, a distinction which I imagine is likely to be ignored by most gardeners—it is so well known and loved under its older, even if improper name.

The six-inch woody stems are renewed annually from the creeping roots and carry rounded, leathery dark green leaves, which often take on rich autumn tints. The groups of small, inconspicuous flowers are surrounded by four large white petal-like bracts. The berries which follow the flowers are as red as those of the holly.

Deciding what to exclude has been one of the problems encountered in writing this book, and one of which I am acutely conscious at this moment when contemplating the genus *Gaultheria*, which offers what amounts to an embarrassment of riches, for there are more than two hundred of these desirable, peat-loving evergreen shrubs distributed over a tremendously wide area; they are to be found in North America, the Magellan region, the Himalayas, East Asia, Australia, Tasmania and New Zealand. Rather curiously, at the beginning of the present century only two species, *G.shallon* and *G.procumbens*, were in general cultivation. Since that time there has been a great influx of others, although too few of them are easily available. I must, as I have done with other major genera, restrict myself to a few special favourites. Those with a particular interest in gaultherias can find very full information in Hilliers' magnificent *Manual of Trees and Shrubs* and in the new, four-volume edition of Bean's *Trees and Shrubs hardy in the British Isles*.

We have Japan to thank for *G.micqueliana* whose neat bushes may attain a height of one foot. The pure white, urn-shaped flowers are followed by white or soft pink berries which, incidentally, taste exactly like toothpaste! Rather similar in general appearance, *G.pyroloides* has thicker leaves, the surface noticeably netted with deep veins, and the fruits which follow the pink blossoms are blue-black.

There have been times when I became so disgusted with our rare native *Loiseluria* (*Azalea*) *procumbens*, that I almost decided to abandon it—but always eventually relented, for I am genuinely fond of it in spite of its reluctance to flower in cultivation.

Were I compelled to choose my favourite *Gaultheria*, which Heaven forbid, I think it would have to be *G.tricophylla*, a tiny gem from China and the Himalayas. Its four-inch pads of smooth green leaves do not

Gaultheria micqueliana

offer anything conspicuous by way of blossom, but the small white—or occasionally pink bells—are followed by turquoise-blue berries. It is not one of the easiest to obtain but is worth any effort in search of a source of supply.

One of the commonest and easiest, and well qualified to hold top rank, is the Partridge Berry of North America, *G.procumbens*. It is a creeper, by means of underground stems, forming wide mats of rounded, glossy green leaves, amidst which gleam the white, sometimes pink-flushed bell-shaped flowers and these are followed in the late autumn by berries as glisteningly red as the holly. I remember regretting having to trample it underfoot when walking through North American woodlands where it grew in unbounded profusion.

An enticing species is the Chinese *G.cuneata*, very dwarf and very compact. Its nodding, white, urn-shaped flowers are carried in small axillary racemes and the fruits are enclosed in a shining white fleshy calyx.

To give cursory treatment to the vast family of heathers and to attempt to make a selection from the innumerable callunas and ericas is such an impossibility that I include only one, which might be regarded as a pseudo-heather. *Bruckenthalia spiculifolia*, the only species in its genus. It is native to south-east Europe and Asia Minor and demands the lime-free soil expected by all plants in this chapter. Its particular virtue is that on its neat, nine-inch bushes it carries crowded racemes of bell-shaped pink flowers from May to July, thus bridging the gap between the flowering times of the true heathers.

It seems inevitable that a general interest in any subject will diversify into special curiosities and thus we become 'collectors'. I can remember a period when I sought after every monotypic plant that I could find, finding a fascination in those genera which confined themselves to just one species. One ericaceous plant which has always intrigued me is *Tsusiophyllum tanakae*, a Japanese shrublet of which some authorities speak rather disparagingly and with whom I find myself in disagreement. It has been in our gardens since 1915 and was first introduced by that great plant collector, Ernest Henry Wilson, to whose explorations we owe so many good garden plants. This engaging little plant forms a loosely twiggy bush up to a foot or a little more in height. It is partially evergreen with narrow, hairy, dark green leaves having slightly recurved margins. The snow-white flowers are admittedly small, but display themselves well against the dark foliage in early summer.

Another prime favourite from my collection of monotypes is *Chiogenes hispidula*. Primarily Japanese, it does also occur in North America. It is a frail tiny thing and should be planted in the front of a peat bed in a position where it is not overshadowed by more robust plants. It is evergreen, of creeping habit and the small, ovate leaves are backed by rusty hairs and are gently aromatic. Borne singly in the leaf axils are solitary, bell-shaped white flowers which are followed by berries of glistening white.

In eastern North America there is a treasured native called 'May Flower'. Botanically it is *Epigaea repens* and is regarded by the many who have failed to establish it as a tricky customer. Given light shade or a cool north aspect and acid soil it is always worth a try, being forewarned that it will probably take some time to decide whether it likes you or not. If it really takes a grouch against what you have to offer, it might be wise, unless you are very persistent, to admit defeat and have a go at its Japanese cousin, *E.asiatica*, which is usually better tempered. Both are mat-forming evergreens with rounded leaves of leathery texture and terminal or axillary clusters of bell-shaped white or soft pink flowers.

The glory of this race, which used to be *Orphanidesia gaultherioides*, but is now included in *Epigaea*, represents a real challenge, which is worth accepting for it is a supremely beautiful plant. Confined in nature to one or two small localities in the Black Sea area, it has the typical *Epigaea* leathery leaves but the flowers, carried in few-flowered racemes, are very large, saucer-shaped and coloured a pure soft pink.

On a memorable, if brief venture into Kamtschatca, I remember being much impressed by tiny, evergreen, mat-forming *Bryanthus gmelinii*—it used to be known and is more familiar to the older generation as *B.musciformis*. One of the smallest of all Ericaceae, it has very thin but wiry stems which interlace into dense pads with very small leaves overlaid by short racemes of pink, bell-shaped flowers in the spring and early summer. This, too, is a treasure which should be placed well to the forefront of a peat bed. For such a frail looking plant it is surprisingly tough and, given peaty soil and a cool or shady position, presents no problems; after all, it has survived our attentions since it was first introduced in 1834.

It is surprising how many monotypic genera there are in the natural order Ericaceae. One which has long been a high favourite on my peat bed is *Leiophyllum buxifolium*; also another old-timer as far as British gardens are concerned, for it was first discovered in eastern North America and introduced by Peter Collinson in 1736. It is a dwarf shrub of tidy habit, forming rounded, compact bushlets adorned in May and June with clusters of pink buds and white flowers. Like many good plants it had to wait a long time before its merits were officially recognized, for it did not receive its well-deserved Award of Merit until 1955. It has two variants: *L.b.hugeri* is rather similar to the type, differing only in having leaves rather longer than the species, but *L.b.prostratum* spreads its branches horizontally to make a most attractive dwarf plant. Surprisingly it received its accolade ten years before the type.

Fond as I am of pernettyas, I should like them even more if they would be more sexually consistent. Some are unisexual and others hermaphrodite and one never quite knows whether there will be a crop of splendid berries or not. Anyway, most of them are too tall for the rock garden, but I must include *P.tasmanica* for which I have a whole-hearted admiration. Its slender, fragile leafy stems tangle into dense mats no more than an inch or two in height. The flowers are so small as to be inconspicuous, but they are followed by fat red fruits, scattered over the intricately tangled network of interlaced stems, as though some eastern potentate had strewn a handful of unwanted rubies.

As these words are written we are emerging from one of the most severe winters known for a great many years and birds, desperate for food and moisture, have taken every berry from the taller pernettyas, but have not taken a single fruit from *P.tasmanica*, even though one or two well-berried plants were free from snow covering and would seem to have been an obvious meal.

When Linnaeus brought order into the chaos of plant nomenclature, he pleasingly named several genera of Ericaceae after mythological nymphs and goddesses, one of which was *Phyllodoce*, named after a sea-nymph. It is a desirable group of evergreen, heath-like plants, distributed throughout the northern hemisphere. One of them, *P.caerulea*, is a rare British native. In spite of its specific name, the flowers—urn-shaped and carried in terminal clusters—are only by courtesy blue, tending much more to a dark purple. I find the Japanese species, *P.nipponica*, more pleasing. It is dwarfer, and of neater habit and its bell-shaped flowers are white, or gently pink. In some catalogues and books you may still find *P.nipponica* listed as *P.tsugaefolia*, so named because of a supposed resemblance of the leaves to those of the *Tsuga*, a genus of conifers.

As with the gaultherias, there are some species of *Vaccinium* which are much too tall-growing for any rock garden, but this genus too, offers several dwarfs which are quite indispensable for the peat bed. We can count three of them as true British natives. The bilberry, or whortleberry is *V.myrtillus*, the cranberry, whose red fruits make the jelly associated with venison, is *V.oxycoccus*, and *V.vitis-idaea*, probably the most garden-worthy of the three, inhabits our northern moorlands. I grow all of them, and enjoy them, although, to make my favourite blueberry pie, I choose the tall-growing cultivated kinds whose berries are much larger and less tedious to gather.

V.vitis-idaea is found widely distributed in North America and Asia as well as in several European localities. I am especially fond of its carpets of box-like leaves, which glisten as though recently polished. The bell-shaped flowers are white, often flushed with pink, and the globular berries are as bright as those of the holly.

From far Ecuador we gratefully received *V.floribundum* (which I still think of as *V.mortinia*, under which it received its Award of Merit in 1935, another delayed accolade, since it was first introduced in 1840). It has so many attractive features that any peat garden lacking it would be incomplete. Neat and dwarf and evergreen, its young growths are red and the glossy leaves, densely clothing the spraying stems are purplish-red, later becoming dark green. In June there are short, crowded racemes of cylindrical flowers, rose-pink in colour and the red berries which follow are sweet and edible—what more could one ask of any plant? Although its birthplace is so close to the equator, I have never known it to be distressed, however harsh the winter.

Just one more *Vaccinium* must be praised, even though I know it to be a rarity and not easy to obtain. I first made its acquaintance through the kindness of a Japanese friend, who sent me a tiny scrap of *V.praestans*, polythene wrapped in an ordinary envelope. It survived and now occupies an honoured position at the edge of a peat bed. Creeping and quite prostrate, it erupts from the running roots into short shoots adorned with rather rounded leaves. The white or pink flowers are borne singly or in small clusters and its following berries are glossy red, fragrant, and pleasant to taste. It has the additional virtue of richly tinted foliage in the autumn.

So much for ericaceous plants—with one or two interlopers. Others will doubtless be found on subsequent pages but these are just a few of the *crème de la crème*. As I write I am continually beset by thoughts of plants which I have omitted from their appropriate chapters, but comfort myself with the intention to enthuse about them in due course. A plant which I unforgivably left out of the chapter on aristocrats is reproaching me whenever I look at my one surviving specimen. *Jankaea heldreichii*, which dwells among the Gods on Mount Olympus, only occasionally making rather disdainful appearances in gardens, definitely deserves a few paragraphs, even if only to tempt you to a rarely attainable desire.

11 Stone Sinks and Troughs

It must have been about 1925 when Clarence Elliot wrote an article in the weekly journal *The Garden*, in which he drew attention to the advantages of growing the smaller alpine plants in old stone sinks and pig troughs. An immediate interest was created and the search began throughout the country for examples. In the early days of this new and fascinating cult, one could pick up sinks and trought for the proverbial song, but they have now become collector's pieces and are not easy to discover.

Tales are told of remarkable discoveries. One lady, famous in the alpine world, was driving her car when a cat ran from a builder's yard in front of her car and was killed. Anxious to make reparation she carried the corpse into the yard and was confronted by a great pile of splendid stone sinks which had been taken out of old kitchens being modernized. Having pacified the owner of the cat she negotiated for the sinks, and was able to buy them at a bargain price.

When visiting Leeds many years ago, at the time when some of the slums were being demolished and replaced by great blocks of flats, I saw a great many sinks among the rubbish from demolished houses—almost every one of which had a sink in the kitchen or scullery. This resulted in a fine lorry-load travelling to Sussex; the demolishers had said that they proposed to break them up to use as rubble for road making and infilling.

On another very memorable day my father and I, having spent the night in a small Yorkshire village en route to Scotland, took a morning stroll through the village before resuming our journey. On our way we passed a cottage with a most attractive front garden full of obviously loved and carefully tended plants. We entered the garden and made our way up a long path to the front door, walking over what appeared to be large rectangular paving stones, and asked if we might look at the garden. A charming and friendly lady of uncertain age said that she felt honoured by the request and showed us all her treasures. Having become rather suspicious about those paving slabs, I asked the good lady what they were. She said that they were old stone sinks, which no one seemed to want and that she had set them upside down to make the path! We asked if we could offer to replace them by old York paving, a suggestion to which she willingly agreed, and so another load eventually made its way to the south.

Of course it soon became known that there was a demand and now such discoveries are well nigh impossible, and fancy prices are asked and paid for genuine old stone sinks and troughs. Nearly all alpine gardeners are alert and eagerly seek for treasure. Inevitably, with their increasing rarity, some form of substitute became necessary and one can now obtain sinks made from reconstituted stone, or from a 'hypertufa' mixture of sand, cement and peat. These are quite acceptable and will, in time, weather so that they have all the appearance of genuine stone. They also have the additional merit of several drainage holes in the base instead of the one found in the originals. Some of the old sinks were very shallow, whereas the substitutes have a greater depth, which is an advantage.

Miniature gardens such as these provide the opportunity to grow a great many plants which are too small or too refined to be attempted on a conventional rock garden and yet do not fall completely within the category of alpine house plants. It is surprising how well some which are definitely difficult elsewhere, will register absolute contentment in a trough. They are well placed on paved areas near to the house and offer the very definite advantage—to those who find kneeling or stooping not as easy as it once was—of being at a convenient height, for they can be raised to any desired height on bricks or blocks of stone.

One of the lists of plants for special purposes at the end of this book will consist of good sink and trough plants, but I cannot pass over them in such a cavalier manner and will suggest, in this chapter, a selected few which I myself grow in sinks and troughs. Their mere names may be duplicated in the list, together with many more, some of which may not have been mentioned in the body of this book.

My interest in and love for sempervivums was fostered by my father, who was an authority on the genus and, together with his close friend Dr. Roy Wale, introduced some order into their chaotic nomenclature. Few of them would cause any traffic jams when in flower, but there is a bewildering and beautiful variation in the shapes of the rosettes and the colouring of their fleshy leaves. Authorities have decided that there are some which have such distinct characteristics that they deserve a genus to themselves, and these are now known as *Jovibarba*, but I take comfort from the fact that this is not a book in which the strict order of botany is observed and shall refer to them all as *Sempervivum*. (Those of you who are, or may become, more deeply interested in the family may

like to know that there is a Sempervivum Society—11, Wingle Tye
Road, Burgess Hill, Sussex RH15 9HR.)

Any or all of the sempervivums are well adapted for growing in
sinks and troughs. They tuck into tight corners and are unchangingly
attractive throughout the year. If I could be said to have a favourite in a
family, all of whose members are dear to me, I think it would probably
be the Cobweb Houseleek, *S.arachnoideum*. It is the perfect inhabitant
of a crevice between the small pieces of rock which you will undoubtedly
use to create the miniature mountainscape. It has been cultivated since
the early years of the seventeenth century and has never lost its
popularity. Its green and pink leaves are formed into neat rosettes which
crowd together and every rosette is netted by a web of white hairs. It is
one of the best for flower effect, carrying the bright red blossoms on
short, erect spikes. There is a form with white flowers which does not
cause me any heart-stirring apart from its rarity.

There are so many plants I want to tell you about in this chapter that
I must limit myself to only two sempervivums. My second choice is
S.heuffelii, and this is now one of those which should be named
Jovibarba. It forsakes the conventional family method of producing new
rosettes on short stolons and multiplies by dividing the actual rosette
into several distinct units. The rosettes are larger than those of
S.arachnoideum and the wide, acutely pointed fleshy leaves may be
bronze-green or a shade of delicate jade, according to the particular
form, of which there are several.

All kinds of natural stone can be employed to make the small
outcrops which add so much to the attraction of sink gardens and I
especially like to use the soft tufa rock, into which holes can be drilled
and small plants inserted. Tufa is so porous and permeable that the roots
of plants will actually grow into it and it is in such positions as this that a
great many of the high alpine cushion plants are ideally situated. Even
the Aretian androsaces, which are seldom seen in gardens outside an
alpine house, will succeed. A select quartet with which it is well worth
experimenting would consist of *Androsace pyrenaica*, *A.pubescens*,
A.vandellii and *A.cylindrica*. They can all be found in the Pyrenees and
are almost invariably haunters of narrow crevices and crannies on cliff
faces. They all compact their rosettes of tiny grey-green leaves into tight
domes and hummocks, which they beautify with almost stemless white
flowers, often in such profusion as to completely conceal the entire
plant. Incidentally, should you seek in catalogues for *A.vandellii* you
might find it listed under one or other of its synonyms, *A.argentea* or
A.imbricata.

Sempervivum arachnoideum

Yet another advantage of tufa is that it can be said to be 'all things to all plants'. Although it contains lime, it is in a form which does not lock up iron and even notorious lime-haters show no distaste for it. I have not yet dared to take such an extreme step, but one day I am going to set some plants of *Gentiana sino-ornata* in tufa holes. It is about the most convinced lime-hater that I know and, in normal garden conditions, its leaves will turn yellow with horror at the faintest suspicion of lime in soil or water.

When my daughter was a child she was a bold and sure-footed climber and often accompanied me in scrambles on the maritime cliffs in Cornwall, where it was one of our particular delights to take our ease on occasional, more or less level, grassy areas, the rocks around us glowing with the rich colour of the masses of Sea Pink, *Armeria maritima* which clothed them. With such beauty at hand, and the prospect over the blue sea, with nothing between us and America, we asked for nothing more to complete our feelings of contentment—although I have a suspicion that Karen was not unmindful of the cream tea awaiting us in our holiday home.

Several named clones of *A.maritima* exist, but they are too robust for these miniature gardens, where their place is well taken by the Spanish species, *A.juniperifolia* (*caespitosa*) which can be relied upon to remain as a tightly compressed huddle of narrow, dark green leaves over which are dispersed many short-stemmed heads of rich pink flowers. A more richly coloured form, discovered in the wild by Dr. R. Bevan, is identified as *A.j.* 'Bevan's Variety' and there is also an albino. Another, *A.j.* 'Beechwood', is of more obscure origin but is probably a hybrid between *A.juniperifolia* and *A.maritima*. It verges upon being too large for a trough, but given austere conditions is a possible. The heads of glowing deep pink flowers are borne on six-inch stems.

A highly treasured feature in our nursery is a huge block of tufa rock, measuring about four feet in height and the same in length and two feet through. It has been punctured by innumerable holes in which exist many plants, including a specimen of *Helichrysum coralloides* which was set in its small cavity as a tiny plant about fifteen years ago. It is now massive and has been unharmed by very severe winters. Just beneath it, on a vertical face, is a silvery-grey hummock of *Saxifraga cochlearis* which is iron-hard to the touch and produces every early summer innumerable elegant sprays of white flowers on arching stems. It is so contented with its position that it has self-sown on the rugged face of the

Armeria juniperifolia (*caespitosa*)

rock and is now surrounded by a progeny of little silver buttons.

The all American genus *Phlox* (there is one exception, but, as far as I can discover, it is not in cultivation) provides a lot of admirable trough plants. Most of the *P.subulata* forms are a trifle over-vigorous, although they can be used in moderation when set to tumble over the edges. The most desirable are the species and the forms of *P.douglasii*. There was an occasion which I remember with glee. I was staying at the time in Calgary, the city in Alberta whose Parks and Public Gardens were at that time in the capable charge of Frank Reader. He had told me that the rare *P.hoodii* grew in great quantity on Calgary golf course, so forth we went, to discover many golfers already enjoying their games. We also discovered great sheets of the phlox, already out of flower but in seed. To the consternation of the players we went on our knees to gather the tiny seeds. We were in the line of fire between two tees and soon had a gathering of initially irate players, who became so interested in what we were doing that they eventually joined us and helped to fill our seed bags. The story also has a sequel. Years later when a party of Canadians visited my nursery they found plants of *P.hoodii* growing in a trough. One of them said to me: 'I come from Calgary, and have been told of a crazy gang of Englishmen who once held up an important match on the golf course whilst they collected seeds.' It gave me much pleasure to inform him that I was the leader of that group!

There was a non-event later in the same expedition which also had an amusing sequel. I had a date to meet Ed Lohbrunner, the owner of a famous alpine nursery in British Columbia. We were to meet on Vancouver Island and he would accompany me on a visit to the Forbidden Plateau. He did not arrive and I was unable to communicate with him before I had to return to England. Three years later he walked into my office in Sussex, saying 'Sorry I'm a bit late for our appointment'.

Unfortunately *P.hoodii* is still a rarity but it does appear every now and then in a specialist catalogue and should be immediately secured. Its flat tufts of needle-fine leaves, starred with white, or occasionally soft lavender flowers, make it an ideal inhabitant of a sink or trough.

With very few exceptions we value gentians because their flowers are so splendidly blue. Some will produce the occasional albino and there is, of course, the stately European *Gentiana lutea*, too large for most rock gardens, but a statuesque and handsome large-leaved plant with spires of straw-yellow blossoms. From topsy-turvy New Zealand comes *G.saxosa*, whose small tufts of very dark leaves produce equally dark stems upon which are pure white flowers. Although inclined to be short-lived (but easily raised from seeds), it is an excellent trough plant, where I often grow it, together with its slightly more robust, but otherwise similar counterpart, *G.bellidifolia.* These two, with Antipodean contrariness have forsaken the family tradition of having blue flowers.

Already described on an earlier page, *Geranium subcaulescens* is a necessity for any well-planned trough. It flowers the whole summer through with a brave display of its carmine-red, dark-centred blossoms, and might well be companioned by *G.argenteum,* which even when not displaying its wide, pink flowers, pleases with the silvery, deeply-cleft foliage. To complete a trinity of neat and lovely geraniums, why not *G.farreri?* They are even smaller, with rounded leaves and short sprays of cup-shaped soft pink flowers, and their charm is enhanced by a central cluster of sooty anthers.

Another *Saxifraga,* very different from *S.cochlearis,* that I like to tuck into a corner of a trough garden, is *S.moschata* 'Cloth of Gold'. It is one of the 'Mossy' section, which are usually considered to prefer a not-too-hot position. This little creature, however, gives of its best when grown in full sun, so that the tufts of soft, cleft leaves are able to adopt their full richness of gold. The flowers are unimportant, small and white; it is the colourful foliage which makes it so likeable. It, too, has a good companion in another cushion-forming 'Mossy' named *S.* 'Bob Hawkins'. The leaves are deeply divided and variegated in silver and green, contrasting pleasantly with the crimson tints of the older leaves. This too, is to be cherished for its foliage rather than the insignificant flowers.

If you should journey into the high European mountains when spring is nigh, there will be water rushing past you on every side as the melting snows send down their contribution to the lakes and streams below. One of the first alpine flowers you will see may well be one of the soldanellas. They will often thrust their stems through a last thin layer of snow and hang forth their nodding, fringed bells to delight you. It has been proved that a growing plant actually generates heat and you will see that the soldanella blossoms each rise from a tiny, round hole which the warmth generated by its growth has created.

The five species most commonly encountered are *Soldanella alpina, S.minima, S.montana, S.pusilla* and *S.villosa.* There is a considerable similarity between these species. They all have leathery, rounded, kidney-shaped leaves and carry their dainty, fringed, lavender-blue bells on short erect stems. They are not difficult to grow, in gritty soil well drained but rich in humus and prefer a cool north aspect, but they have a reputation for being shy-flowering in gardens. I have a strong suspicion

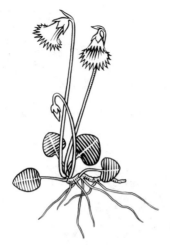

Soldanella minima

that this is not altogether deserved as I have observed that they often form their flower buds in the autumn and winter, the buds resting at ground level beneath the leaves, where they are often devoured by slugs. I do not know if *S.villosa* buds are less tasty but it always flowers freely.

Were I to be asked to name the three most widely grown and popular garden plants I think that I would settle for roses, dahlias and chrysanthemums. For all three families I shamelessly confess to having admiration but no love. There are, however, just a few dwarf species of *Chrysanthemum*, vastly different from the popular autumn-flowering kinds, which are irresistible to any lover of alpine plants. One in particular, which is suited *par excellence* for trough gardens, is tiny *C.alpinum*, to be found in the Alps of Europe. I have a sort of love–hate relationship with it for it is all too apt to die on me for no apparent reason; but it is such a charmer that when this happens I dry my tears and sow the seeds it always bequeaths me. At its best it makes the neatest of tufts of small, deeply cut leaves and offers surprisingly large, pure white, golden-eyed daisy flowers on short stems. My greatest successes with it have been when it was grown in a trough, but it will also do quite well in a sunny, very gritty scree. It should never be grown in rich soil, in which it will overfeed, grow fat and collapse. (Illus. see below)

Buttercups of all kinds have always fascinated me. There is a great diversity of them scattered through the temperate world, many so garden-worthy that they amply compensate for the species of *Ranunculus* which are pernicious weeds. There will be more about the best of

Chrysanthemum alpinum

them in a later chapter, but inclusion here is demanded by delicate little *R.alpestris*, such an admirable little trough plant. No more than an inch or two in height, it has clusters of small, green, rounded and lobed leaves, toothed at the edges. Its flowers are inch-wide rounded saucers of purest white. Should you not be able to obtain *R.alpestris* you could be equally contented with *R.crenatus*, which is rather similar and just as appropriate. Both of them are sweet tempered and well behaved and present no problem, apart from the fact that slugs seem inordinately fond of their young leaves. The fact that all buttercups are poisonous appears not to deter them. I wonder if whatever eats slugs can be harmed by the poison in them after they have made such a toxic meal?

I hesitate over *Ranunculus parnassifolius*, but it is such a splendid plant—if a good form can be obtained—that it would be inexcusable to omit it. Even in the wild it varies. There are forms with small or malformed petals which are not worth garden room, but at its best it is a very beautiful species. Its distinct leaves—heart-shaped and acutely pointed—are of a thick, almost leathery texture and the pure white flowers should be large, with wide, overlapping petals.

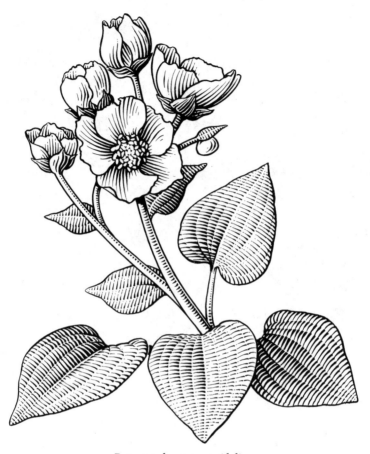

Ranunculus parnassifolius

The miniature landscape contrived in a sink or trough can be put nicely into scale by using one or two really dwarf shrubs. One which is ideal for the purpose, is the Noah's Ark Juniper, *Juniperus communis* 'Compressa'. This dark green columnar conifer is shaped like a candle-flame and is very slow growing and unlikely to outgrow its position. I know of thirty-year-old specimens which have not topped eighteen inches in height. One has to be very cautious when using dwarf conifers in such positions, some so named are far from dwarf after a few years. Apart from the Juniper, choice should be restricted to the very compact forms of *Chamaecyparis obtusa*, which are bun-shaped and very slow.

A pygmy in a race of giants, *Thalictrum kiusianum*, from Japan (whence have come so many enticing miniature plants) is neat and small enough for a trough. Spreading slowly by underground stems, it erupts

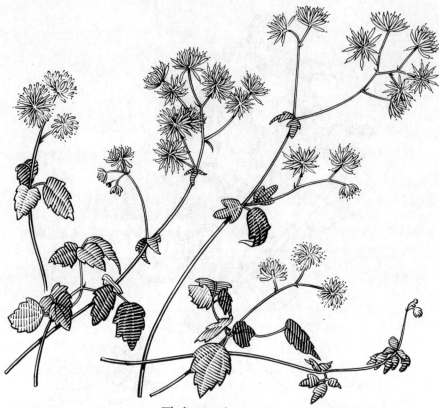

Thalictrum kiusianum

into many erect, six-inch stems on which are loose heads of tiny purple flowers, set off handsomely by the dainty, adiantum-like foliage.

T.orientale, which is even more beautiful, is a rarity hard to come by and its provenance is obscure. *Flora Europaea* says that it comes from Greece and Asia Minor and has white flowers, whereas Farrer states that it comes from the Caucasus. Whatever the rights of the case may be it is a delight and of similar stature to *T.kiusianum* but with individually large flowers of glowing pink.

One always reserves a special place in one's heart for plants which blossom in the early spring to assure us that winter has passed and among these can be counted the Kabschia saxifrages, of which I shall have much more to write on later pages, but for sinks and troughs *Saxifraga burserana* must have priority. Widely distributed, mostly in the Eastern Alps, it varies in each of its locations. Typically it is a hard cushion of small, grey-green spiky leaves over which, on reddish stems no more than three inches high, are rounded, pure white flowers. Some of the best of the variants have been given distinct names and good ones to seek are 'Gloria', 'His Majesty' and 'Crenata'. There is one with yellow flowers, *S.b* 'Lutea', which is almost certainly a hybrid but of uncertain parentage. (Ilus., p. 101)

A pleasant *Sedum* to set in a crevice from which its pendant stems can fall, or to place at the edge of the trough, is *S.cauticolum*. It has the advantage of flowering in late summer and autumn, thus prolonging the interest. The red blossoms are densely packed in terminal heads.

Although it is regarded by some as rather a joke, I would always find room for *Viola verecunda* 'Yakushimana', not that it will occupy much space, for it is the smallest of all the violas, overshadowed by its label if the name is written out in full! Another Japanese Lilliput, it is seen as a tiny tuft of minute leaves, amidst which rest very small white violets, with purple lines on the tiny petals. It will self-sow modestly, never becoming a nuisance. It comes from the Japanese island of Yakushima, noted for its miniature plants. I am told, although I have not yet seen or acquired it, that it harbours a bamboo no more than three inches tall.

To provide colour after the flush of spring blossoms, there are few more useful trough plants than some of the smallest *Dianthus*, and one of the best is *D.alpinus*. Huge, rounded flowers of rose-crimson, on very short stems, rest on flat carpets of narrow green leaves. It has a reputation for being short-lived but this is largely due to the fact that it is apt to be attacked by the Carnation Fly, *Hylemia brunnescens*. Some crystals of paradichlorbenzene scattered round the base of the plant in March and again in August will repel the egg-laying flies.

There are plants which are accepted as being almost legendary examples of what an alpine plant should be, and I would certainly class *Phyteuma comosum* among these. The dratted botanists have decreed that it must now be known as *Physoplexis comosa*, but I cling to the name it has borne ever since I first fell in love with it as a schoolboy. A cliff-dweller by inclination it should be tucked into a tight crevice where it will make a tuft of kidney-shaped leaves and heads of long-tubed, claw-shaped blue flowers. It was well described by a member of the Alpine Garden Society as being both distinctly odd and remarkably beautiful.

12 Saxifrages

'This huge race is the backbone of the rock garden'

Those words were written by Reginald Farrer sixty years ago and are as true today as they were then—perhaps to an even greater degree, for there have been many additions to the clan since Farrer produced his monumental work entitled *The English Rock Garden*, still the rock gardener's bible, and some may well consider that, by present standards, the case is by no means overstated.

Before embarking upon my modest enumeration of plants contained in this family, a few words concerning the genus as a whole may not come amiss; they will be brief, for, as must already be abundantly clear, this is not a botanical treatise. I gladly refer those of you who desire to make a closer study of this invaluable family to a masterly guide written by Winton Harding and published as one of the monographs issued by the Alpine Garden Society, from which I have shamelessly cribbed to supplement my own incomplete knowledge of a genus whose nomenclature is involved, to say the least.

Without species of *Saxifraga*, *Campanula* or *Dianthus*, the rock garden and its accompanying accessories would be the poorer. They literally form the backbone of any comprehensive planting, providing a wealth of flowers and interest from the earliest days of spring right on into the autumn.

Throughout alpine areas in northern and southern Europe, in Asia and North America, rarely in South America, there are saxifrages to be found, but they appear to be entirely absent from Australasia and South Africa. More than three hundred species have been identified. Additionally there are more hybrids, forms and cultivars than I dare begin to count. In gardens they are basically lime-loving although there are exceptions and very few could be described as 'miffs' or 'mimps'. In their infinite variety they are well adapted for all kinds of situations and conditions. Being only too well aware that those which appear on the following pages can only be regarded as an indispensable minority, I apologize to the many which have been omitted.

Vivid memories return to me of my first sight of *S.mutata* in the wild. It was on the occasion of my first visit to the wonderful Schachen Garden maintained by the Munich Botanical Garden high in the adjacent mountains. This alpine sanctuary originated in the fertile mind of Wilhelm Schacht, whose name is famed in the annals of modern alpine history and whose son has now taken over the care of the Schachen Garden during the months when it is accessible.

It was at the time that BBC Radio was broadcasting an excellent series of gardening programmes under the leadership of Roy Hay. To introduce an international flavour to the programme it was decided to send a small party to visit notable gardens in Switzerland, Germany and Austria. I was privileged to be a member of this group and, in addition to the gardens we included in a memorable series, we also found our way to a number of mountain areas to see and describe alpine plants in their native habitats.

The Schachen Garden lies almost on the frontier between Germany and Austria and, after a start so early in the morning that Schacht dragged us from our beds in Munich long before dawn, we travelled to a point where we could be picked up by the frontier guards in the jeep in which they negotiated the terrifying track which led to the garden. How well I remember the many times when, on seemingly impossible hairpin bends, the jeep was backed so that its rear wheels hung over the edge of sheer falls of hundreds of feet. Roy Hay was valiantly trying to record our progress on tape, to the accompaniment of cries of alarm when it seemed impossible that we could avoid being somersaulted into the depths below. Our driver and his colleagues were quite unmoved by our concern, and assured us that no one, as yet, had 'gone over the edge'!

Our route to the meeting place had been through a narrow gorge between high cliffs, and packed into rocky crevices were hundreds of plants of *Saxifraga mutata*, which we stayed to admire and photograph. From its rosettes of strap-shaped leaves rise erect, foot-high stems bearing showers of coppery-orange flowers. Although not officially monocarpic, it is my experience that, in cultivation, it seldom produces side-rosettes, and the flowering rosette dies; in the wild they seemed plentiful. Fortunately it produces abundant seeds, from which new plants can easily be raised.

Early mention must be made of what is perhaps the most spectacular and beautiful *Saxifraga* of them all. A hybrid claiming as one parent *S.longifolia* (whose symmetrical rosettes of narrow, silvered leaves and plumes of white flowers so magnificently adorn cliffs in the Pyrenees), it was introduced by Captain Symons-Jeune, and named by him

S.l. 'Tumbling Waters'. The other parent is supposed to be a form of *S.callosa* (*lingulata*) and the child of this fortunate marriage is a splendour with wide rosettes, sometimes a foot in diameter, from which erupts an arching stem carrying hundreds upon hundreds of white flowers. The actual flowering rosette always perishes, but there are usually a few side-rosettes which can be used as cuttings. It is fertile, but the seeds will produce plants which, although they may be garden worthy, seldom match the splendour of the parent.

Right at the back end of the *Saxifraga* season comes *S.fortunei*, a native of China, Japan, Korea and Manchuria. It is a handsome plant and invaluable for providing a brave display in the autumn. If grown in the open it should be given a cool, possibly lightly shaded position where it will develop bold clumps of large, rounded and lobed leaves, green on the upper surface but reddish-bronze beneath. The elegant branching stems, more than a foot-high, carry a profusion of panicles of white flowers, of which the lower petals are much longer than those above. On the whole I treat it as a lime-hater, although I have known it to tolerate conditions of mild alkalinity.

Excitement always abounds when the silver rosettes of *S.grisebachii* feel the urge of spring and begin to thrust upwards a column of scarlet leaflike bracts, contrasting so handsomely with the argent leaves. These croziers slowly elongate, to become arching crimson spikes, the small flowers concealed between the colourful bracts. The finest manifestation of this splendid Grecian plant is seen in the cultivar named 'Wisley', a selection made in that famous garden many years ago. The type is desirable enough, but is surpassed in beauty by this excellent form.

During the time that I lived on the foothills of the Maritime Alps, I seized every opportunity to make a pilgrimage to the limited area, almost astride the French-Italian frontiers where the almost mythical *S.florulenta* grew. It is a relict species and was, I believe, first recorded as a fossil until a small remnant population, desperately clinging to its final refuge, was discovered. My only excuse for including it here is its historical interest, for it is far from being an easy plant to grow. It is so ancient that it retains little urge to live and it can only be a matter of a few more decades before it finally becomes extinct. On the sheer cliffs that it inhabits I have seen as many dead specimens as live ones.

This is probably due in part to the fact that it is monocarpic, seldom, if ever, making side rosettes. It thus relies entirely upon seedlings for perpetuity and I was always unhappily conscious of the dismal fact that there were few young plants to be seen. Apparently it takes many years to decide that the time has come for it to blossom. The rosettes of

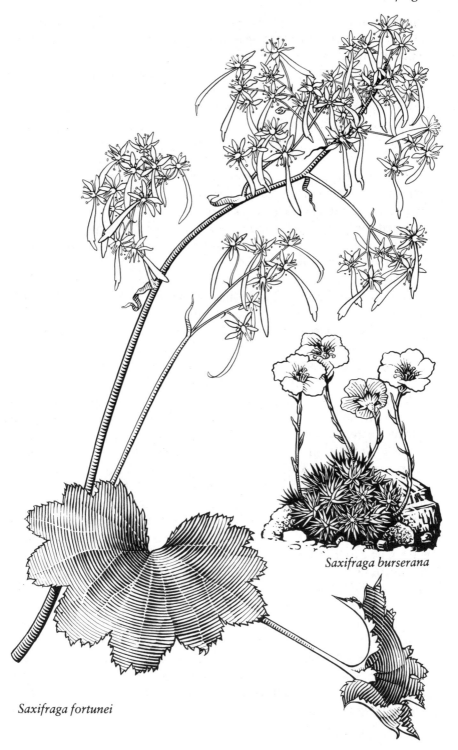

Saxifraga burserana

Saxifraga fortunei

symmetrically arranged green leaves are, in their younger stages very attractive, but as the plant ages it develops into a sort of elongated cylinder with a flat rosette of leaves at the top.

The flowers, when they are eventually and reluctantly produced, will rouse no encomiums in praise of their beauty. They are carried on a slender panicle, a foot or more in length and are of a rather muddy, dingy pink colour. Belonging as it does to an aristocracy of the ancient past, it is understandable that it is seldom cultivated. There is always a flurry of excitement when a specimen appears on a show bench and applause for the skill of whoever has been bold enough to accept its challenge. My own very occasional successes have been achieved when I set a seedling into a V-shape broken in the rim of a pot or pan so that it occupied the vertical position it obviously prefers. It deeply resents any moisture resting between the leaves of the rosettes and equally dislikes continuous damp round its roots.

This is, I feel sure, a genuine if regrettable case of the gradual extinction of a species too old to survive. Doubtless those of us who find gratification in efforts to tame the untamable will continue to endeavour to grow it, as long as a few seeds may be gathered to provide material for our experiments. It may even be that it will eventually survive only in the gardens of a few skilled cultivators.

There is a trinity of tiny species which are so condensed that they grow in the Alps of Europe as lichen-like scabs on cliffs. They are, *S.caesia*, *S.diapensioides* and *S.squarrosa*. They are all disinclined to take too readily to cultivation, but are not so difficult that they should be avoided. Grow them in very gritty soil and provide an existence that is austere rather than luxurious and they will usually delight you with their dense pads of grey-green rosettes of tiny leaves and short-stemmed white flowers. (They did not appear in the chapter devoted to sink and trough plants although they are ideally suited to such an environment.)

Our native *S.granulata* is a pleasant inhabitant of moist pastures and is not unworthy of a place in the garden, but it is the form with fully double, pure white flowers that is more often grown. Apart from being a British native it has an immense distribution throughout northern and southern Europe and extends into North America and Asia. It is a deciduous plant and rests during its dormant period in tiny bulbils; the leaves which arise in the spring are rounded and crenulated and the blossoms are displayed in elegant sprays on nine-inch stems.

Almost rivalling *S.longifolia* for beauty, the silver encrusted *S.callosa* (*lingulata*) makes joyous a journey through any of the several valleys leading from the Italian coast up into the Maritime Alps. It is a variable species and each of its localities appears to offer a slightly different form. In any of its manifestations it is a very handsome *Saxifraga*, with huddled rosettes of narrow, silvered leaves and gracefully arched plumes of white flowers. Of its variants I am especially fond of *S.c.lantoscana*, perhaps because I saw it so often when on my way to the higher mountains beyond San Dalmazzo. There was a train, but I usually travelled on foot, the better to observe and appreciate the many good plants to be seen on either side. Nothing is more frustrating than to glimpse from the window of a train some enticing plant and to be unable to halt for a closer examination. In nurserymen's catalogues you may find the following varieties offered, all are well worth acquiring: *S.c.albertii, australis, bellardii* and *lantoscana*.

It would grieve me to totally exclude *S.paniculata* (*aizoon*) from these pages, although annoyance over the recent change of name might have induced me to do so, but it is such an involved and confused group that any sort of classification would be impossible. Widely distributed throughout southern and central Europe, and on into Arctic regions, it is infinitely variable and I challenge anyone to select one particular plant and say 'this is typical *S.paniculata*'. It is best regarded as an umbrella name, covering a host of useful plants, of which some are admittedly better than others. Choose then, from catalogues or nursery beds the ones which tickle your fancy. I offer here only a few which I believe to have special merit. It is possible that even one or two of these may be of hybrid origin. Two which are quite essential are *S.p.rosea* and *S.p.lutea*. Each is lovely in its own right and they also make good companions, creating an attractive feature with mingled blossoms of pink and soft yellow. These are just two of the several kinds of plants which I often plant in close association.

The smallest of all the group is *S.p.minutifolia*, sometimes listed as *S.p.baldensis*. Its tiny leaves are closely packed into dense, flat pads and the white flowers are borne on very short stems. Another distinct and desirable one is *S.p.*'Rex'. Obviously a hybrid although of unknown parentage, it has neat rosettes and six-inch stems carrying loose clusters of white flowers, the petals heavily speckled with red. Similarly marked, but rather taller in stem, is one which Clarence Elliott amusingly named 'Canis Dalmatica'.

Into the welter of names contained in the section familiarly known as 'Mossy' Saxifrages, I refuse to delve, with the exception of one distinct form which has already been described in the chapter on Sinks and Troughs. They are legion and any good alpine plant catalogue will supply all the information that is needed to make a selection. Suffice it to say that they are easily grown and very showy, with flowers ranging from white, through shades of pink and red to deep crimson. On the whole they are happier when shielded from the hottest sunshine.

An easy and early flowering mat-former is *S. × apiculata*. A hybrid raised a great many years ago, it must have a magnificent constitution, for I have known and liked it all my life and it remains full of vigour in spite of so many generations of vegetative propagation—a process which only too often will gradually weaken the stock and may even lead to its total disappearance. It is a plant for everyone and will flourish in any good soil and full sun, smothering its mats of green rosettes with primrose-yellow flowers. I plan a later chapter in which I shall describe what might be called *hoi polloi* of alpine plants, among which this *Saxifraga* would undoubtedly have appeared had I not included it among its relations.

The plant which is affectionately known as London Pride, and has been since time immemorable called *S.umbrosa,* has been proven a hybrid and is properly named *S. × urbium.* It is dear to our hearts in all of its several forms, and is too well known to need any description from me, but I must lavish praise on one of its miniature manifestations which has crept into cultivation under two clonal names. It is a diminished form of *S.umbrosa primuloides* and was discovered almost simultaneously by my father, and his close friend Clarence Elliott. Each staunchly maintained that his particular pet was the smaller and that its pink flowers were brighter than the other. Thus there came into circulation *S.u.primuloides* 'Clarence Elliott' and *S.u.primuloides* 'Walter Ingwersen'. No one else has ever been able to detect the slightest difference between them and I assure you that whichever you obtain it will prove to be identical with the other. The pink flowers, tiny, but so numerous as to be very noticeable, are carried on six-inch stems in the neatest manner and it flourishes in light shade or modest sunlight. In this section there is also *S.u.primuloides* 'Variegata', whose green leaves are flecked with gold. The larger type too, has a variegated form.

In the Sinks and Troughs chapter I described a valuable trinity of minute saxifrages but it should really have been a quartet, for I unforgivably omitted *S.tombeanensis*, a species found very locally in the Italian Alps and notably on the Cima Tombea, whence it gained its specific name. It grows into hard, tight domes of congested rosettes of tiny grey leaves and on two-inch stems displays surprisingly large white flowers of solid substance. I suppose it could really be a quintet, for the hybrid between *S.caesia* and *S.squarrosa,* known as *S. × tyrolensis,* well deserves to dwell among such august companions. Intermediate in appearance between its parents and, filled with hybrid vigour, it is usually more amenable than either.

Whenever I look at a tuffet of *S.tolmei* my thoughts go straight back to Hurricane Ridge in the Olympics, where I saw it growing on stony slopes in compact cushions. Unfortunately it has gained a reputation for being difficult in gardens, but I believe this is largely due to the fact that it has been given too easy a life in rich soil. Treated with austerity and grown in fifty per cent sharp lime-free grit, it will retain its neat habit and willingly offer white or pale yellow flowers.

Belonging in the same small section as *S.oppositifolia* (see p. 38) are *S.biflora* and *S.retusa*. The former is a high alpine plant and not likely to raise the adrenalin flow in any but a collector of rarities. The small, oval, rather scale-like leaves are set on the prostrate stems like those of *S.oppositifolia* but in a much looser formation. The flowers are reddish-purple, or occasionally a rather dismal white. *S.retusa* is the better plant of the two. It has been said of it that it did not thrive in the open garden and was better regarded as an alpine house plant, but I have had it happily situated in a stone sink, and on an open scree for many years. It is not excitingly beautiful but has a certain charm when the mats of dark leaves are decorated by clusters of small rose-red flowers.

A friend of my father's who used to visit the nursery frequently was the vicar of a parish in the East End of London. Many of his parishioners were rather tough customers, given to expressing themselves forcibly, a habit which our friend had also acquired, and which he found rather embarrassing at times. He was overjoyed on one of his visits to discover *Saxifraga erioblasta*. That, he said, would enable him to let off steam without provoking displeasure. I remember that he returned not infrequently, saying 'my erioBLASTA doesn't like London and has died on me, can I have another one please'. The plant is an unusual 'Mossy' *Saxifraga* from southern Spain, where it inhabits hot hillsides. In the heat of summer its small rosettes become tight, dormant buds, known to the Spanish as Virgin's Pearls. If they are crushed a tiny green spark of life can be discovered. When in growth it is a neat tuft of soft green leaves over which, on short stems, are rounded, pure white flowers.

Although *S.hartii* can lay no claim to outstanding beauty, it is an interesting plant, confined in nature to the sea cliffs of Arranmore Island off the north-west coast of Ireland. It, too, is a cushiony plant with closely packed rosettes of green, hairy and slightly sticky leaves. Its quite good white flowers are carried in small, compact heads on three-inch stems.

Another of our own native species is *S.aizoides*, a lover of wet places and with an enormous distribution throughout Europe, into North America and even Asia. It always gives me pleasure to discover its loose mats of narrow, fresh green leaves, spangled with the yellow flowers which are spotted with red. It has hybridized with *S.urbium*, the child of this union being known as *S.* × 'Primulaize'. It exists in several variations, some having red flowers, while others are carmine or salmon in colour. It, too, prefers a slightly moist situation or a cool north aspect.

The greatest claim to fame that *S.lilacina* can make is that it has been concerned in the parentage of so many delightful early-flowering hybrids, of which, to name but a few, 'Myra', 'Iris Prichard', 'Irvingii', 'Jenkinsae', 'Arco-Valleyi' and 'Riverslea' are good examples. The species itself is inclined to be fractious. It came from the Himalayas a long, long time ago and consistently avoids being a really happy plant. To persuade it to form its totally flat pads of tiny leaves, arranged in quadrangular fashion, and to star the cushions with stemless lilac flowers, you have to give it gritty, but humus-rich soil and a little shade.

Among the many good plants collected by my father and Dr. Giuseppi in Greece and the Balkans, were some fine forms of the *Saxifraga* that we knew then, and recognized until recently as *S.thessalica*, but which must now be addressed as *S.sempervivum*. The species belongs to the same group as handsome *S.grisebachii* but does not make the same rosettes of immaculately arranged silver leaves. It gathers its spiny, silver-grey small leaves into dense mats, from which rise short, slightly arching stems, the upper third of which is thickly set with pink flowers, each one enclosed in an inflated purple calyx.

A feature of this genus which I find pleasing and exciting, is the immense diversity displayed by its members, both in appearance and in the situations best suited to their needs. I admire *S.aquatica* (too seldom grown now) as a handsome plant for a moist position, or adjacent to water into which it can sink its roots. It is a robust native of the Pyrenees, growing into masses of shiny, divided leaves of solid substance. From these billowing mats of foliage rise sturdy stems, up to two feet in height, bearing panicles of large, star-shaped white flowers on their upper third. It is no choice gem to be admired at eye-level, but a handsome stalwart, best seen *en masse*.

A neater, smaller species in the same section as *S.aquatica* is the Spanish *S.cebenensis*, found in the wild only in the Cevennes of southern France. Its domed cushions are formed by crowded rosettes of green, three-cleft tiny leaves which are definitely sticky to the touch. On each three-inch stem are two or three nicely rounded white flowers of solid substance. It is dubiously happy in the open but makes a very attractive pan specimen for the alpine house.

I have a feeling that *S.hirculus* is not an 'everybody's plant', but it will please and interest those who have a liking for our native flora. It is an occasional inhabitant of boggy areas and will respond to a compost of sandy peat kept nicely moist. It has a loose, not over tidy habit and the yellow flowers are prettily red-spotted. Certainly not sensational, but well worth having.

In its wide geographical distribution *S.cotyledon*, a valuable and variable species, generally grows on granitic rock, but I have never known any of its forms to display any serious aversion to alkaline conditions in gardens. A cosmopolitan plant, it is to be found throughout the European Alps and extends far away into North America. In whichever form you acquire it you will find it admirable. Habitually it makes flat rosettes of wide leaves of thick texture, and, should it be desired to achieve a really spectacular result, the side rosettes which form can be removed so that the main rosette grows larger and larger. When it eventually flowers it will display an arching, pyramidal inflorescence of white flowers, although one or two of the variants will spatter the petals with red spots. This is especially noticeable in the cultivar named 'Southside Seedling', which is so heavily freckled as to appear pink at a short distance. As the flowering rosette dies, some of the side rosettes which are removed should be treated as cuttings to ensure continuity. Although some authorities regard 'Southside Seedling' as a hybrid, I dispute this. My nursery was the first to distribute it and I know that the good gardener in whose collection it first appeared was confident that it was a sport from the type species. Whatever the truth may be there is no dispute as to its quality.

Of the several varieties, whether they be hybrids or variants, I would be happy with any of the following: 'Caterhamensis' (although this has really been superseded by 'Southside Seedling'), 'Montavonensis', 'Norvegica' and 'Pyramidalis', the last named having the most imposing inflorescence of any, as it branches from the very base of the flowering stem to make a broad and handsome pyramid of blossom.

Reluctantly withstanding the urge to fill more pages with names and praises of the many which clamour for inclusion, I must turn away and given attention to the innumerable memory provoking alpines which demand space on my rapidly decreasing pages, knowing that this has been no more than a brief introduction to a noble genus of plants.

13 Primulas

Favouritism is as common among gardeners as it is in other walks of life and we all have groups of plants for which we have a special liking. I am no exception and find room in my universal love of plants for a very special corner reserved for the genus *Primula*. It has to be a rather spacious corner, for there are more than 500 known species, distributed throughout the Northern Hemisphere and spreading with some outliers into North America, North Africa and even into tropical Java. Added to these are innumerable hybrids, cultivars and selections. Needless to say I must restrict myself to a limited selection of my own particular pets, leaving unsung the praises of the many others which I would so happily eulogize. There are books, written by experts and devoted wholly to primulas, in which can be sought information concerning the many I have omitted.

A great many of my most felicitous memories of days spent in the mountains are evoked by primulas. I lived for some years on the frontiers of southern France and northern Italy, within easy reach of the area in the Maritime Alps where that gem of gems, *P.allionii*, occupied the crevices and crannies of sheer cliffs. In those days the frontier ran actually through those same cliffs, not far from the station on the railway on which one journeyed from Ventimiglia. On a number of occasions I leapt from the train, crossed the tracks and assumed a strategic position on the rocks, knowing that, before long I would be hauled off by one or other of the frontier guards and conducted to the local lock-up. This happened so often that, eventually, I was more often than not left in peace and regarded as some sort of lunatic.

It is extraordinary that *P.allionii*, with hundreds of square miles of apparently exactly similar territory surrounding it, should have confined itself to this small corner of the Maritime Alps, of which it so obviously approves. It grows into great tufts and hummocks of crowded, sticky-leaved rosettes, always in the narrowest and tightest of crevices; a truly saxatile and rock-loving plant.

There were other great *Primula* days too, spent in various parts of the European Alps. The great excitements were to visit areas where two or more species met, and seek for the beautiful hybrids which frequently occur between them. In the Pyrenees long walks up the mountain paths leading to the cirque above Gavarnie would be enlivened and made less wearisome by wide pads of crowded tiny rosettes of *P.integrifolia*, almost hidden beneath galaxies of short-stemmed rose-red flowers. Even the thoughts of cliffs full of *Saxifraga longifolia* and *Ramonda myconi* high above failed to prevent a certain lingering along the way.

My own particular affection for the genus may also perhaps be attributed to the fact that it provokes one of my very earliest garden memories, when my playground was my father's nursery in Croydon, where I would make a considerable nuisance of myself and where plants began to assume the importance which was to continue and increase throughout my life. To encourage my budding interest, and, possibly, to curtail my interference with the nursery workers, my father had set aside a small area in which I could do my own gardening.

Standing one day in the potting shed I watched a batch of seedlings of *Primula frondosa* being pricked out into boxes. When what was thought to be a sufficient stock had been achieved, the remainder was consigned to the rubbish heap. This unwanted residue I collected and took to my own domain where they were planted in neat rows. Later in the season I heard my father bemoaning the fact that *P.frondosa* was 'sold out' and that existing orders could not be fulfilled. My commercial instincts must have been developing, for I immediately offered to provide one hundred plants, but wanted one penny each! To my gratification the offer was accepted and, as my pocket money amounted to six-pence per week, the 8/4d. which I received seemed vast wealth. I remember that I invested it in packets of seeds and was thus embarked upon a career as a professional nurseryman.

My affection for *P.frondosa* remains, for it is a rewarding plant, resembling a more robust version of our own delightful Bird's-eye Primrose, *P.farinosa*, already praised in Chapter Five. Its clusters of broad leaves rest close to the ground and are heavily coated with white farina on their undersides and the rich rose-red flowers, carried in compact heads on six-inch stems, have each a yellow eye.

Without delving into cytology, a subject about which I know very little, it is obvious that the chromosome count of many European primulas must be compatible, for, wherever one species meets another in their natural distribution, you are sure to find natural hybrids. There have also been several deliberate garden hybridizations, adding to the number of extremely beautiful plants. Generally speaking, my affection goes more readily to pure species than to hybrids, but I make an unreserved exception in the case of primulas and have eagerly gathered together as many of them as possible, and did, at one time, now alas no longer, possess every known natural hybrid.

Tiny and lovely *P.minima*, already described, has been a very prolific source of hybrids and has figured in the parentage of many of the most desirable. Its marriages with *P.glutinosa* and *P.hirsuta* produced respectively *P.* × *biflora* and *P.* × *bileckii*. The latter has already been eulogized, but the former is equally desirable; its habit of growth resembles *P.minima* but it bears two large clear rose flowers on each short stem. Where *P.minima* meets *P.wulfeniana*, hybridization has been prolific, and produced no less than three distinct hybrids: *P.* × *deschmannii*, *P.* × *serrata* and *P.* × *vochinensis*. All three are regrettably apt to be shy-flowering, but rewarding when they do produce their rather tubular pink flowers.

Because of its restricted locality, *P.allionii*, justly acclaimed to be the most exquisite European primula, meets very few potential spouses. We owe, however, several splendid man-made hybrids to Mr. Wooster, who adds materially to the interest of many spring shows of the Royal Horticultural Society in London with his magnificent display of superbly grown pans of *P.allionii* and hybrids therefrom; two, in particular, reputedly crosses between *P.allionii* and *P.marginata* 'Linda Pope' are respectively named 'Fairy Rose' and 'Joan Hughes'. While admitting to some personal and unsubstantiated doubts as to the parentage, I do not deny their beauty.

Individual descriptions of the many natural hybrids would be pointless, but any of the following which you might be able to obtain would be found rewarding. Before listing their names I must rectify two omissions from the *P.allionii* hybrids: 'Barbara Barker', reputedly *P.allionii* × *P.hirsuta*, and 'Beatrice Wooster', *P.allionii* × *P.marginata* 'Linda Pope' again are extremely desirable. Seek, therefore, for any of the following: *P.* × 'Alpina' (*P.auricula* × *P.latifolia*), *P.* × 'Berninae', (*P.hirsuta* × *P.latifolia*), *P.* × 'Ethel Barker' (*P.allionii* × *P.hirsuta*), *P.* × *forsteri*, (*P.minima* × *P.hirsuta*), *P.* × *heeri*, (*P.hirsuta* × *P.integrifolia*), *P.* × *juribella*, (*P.minima* × *P.tyrolensis*), *P.* × 'Marven', (*P.marginata* ×*P.venusta*). There are others, for this is a prolific field, none of which is to be ignored.

Our native Primrose, *P.vulgaris*, is a universal favourite and it, too, has some pleasing geographical variants. When I was able to visit the mountains of Iran, I was delighted to make the acquaintance of their own version of our primrose, *P.heterochroma*. In general appearance it is pure primrose, but the flowers range in colour from white, through shades of pink to almost red. There is also a primrose with large, pure white, yellow-eyed flowers which was discovered by my father and named 'Walter Ingwersen'. One of which I think highly is *P.v.sibthorpii*, whose blossoms are clear pink. This may still be listed in some catalogues as *P.altaica*, an invalid synonym.

Some of the very old hybrid primroses and perhaps the greenhouse auriculas, worn out by generations of vegetative propagation, benefit from liberal doses of really old and well-decayed farmyard manure, but my own experience with the species and hybrids with which we are now concerned is that they should not be overfed. In particular I have found it desirable to replace the use of leaf-mould in their compost with moss peat. The use of leaf-mould very often induced serious attacks of root aphis, a nuisance which has not occurred since the change was made.

One of the delights to be savoured when sampling the rich alpine flora of the Pyrenees, is dainty *P.integrifolia*, which can be seen, often in dense colonies, by the very pathside. It has other localities and occurs on both granite and limestone formations. Its leaves are narrow, strap-shaped and of thick texture in closely packed rosettes. The reddish-lilac flowers are abundantly produced on very short stems. It displays no resentment to a lowland environment and is one of the easiest and prettiest of the European primulas.

There is a lot of confusion, both in gardens and in nature, between *P.latifolia* (*viscosa*) and *P.hirsuta* (*rubra*). Both are variable and confusion has not been lessened by their change of name. Good forms of either are desirable and *P.hirsuta* can be identified by its broad, often toothed leaves which are felted with fine red hairs. The leaves of *P.latifolia* are longer and broader and distinctly sticky to the touch. Each carries its rather funnel-shaped blossoms in many-flowered umbels; those of *P.latifolia* are purple or deep violet in colour and the blossoms of *P.hirsuta* are pink or red—but there are less desirable forms of the latter with dingy pink blossoms of poor shape.

Very soon after its introduction from the Caucasus Mountains many years ago, *P.juliae* became both accidentally and deliberately hybridized with various primulas of the *vulgaris* persuasion. These intermarriages resulted in a race of hybrids once collectively gathered under the banner name *P.juliana*. To the regret of many, botanists have now decreed that this should be *P. × pruhoniciana*. Typical *P.juliae*, rather sadly, is now a rarity and well worth obtaining if true stock can be found. It covers its mats of short, leafy rhizomes with short-stemmed bright purple flowers.

Among the wealth of hybrids and selections are a great many very good rock garden plants, of which our old friend *P.*'Wanda' is a good example. The colour range is extensive, varying from pure white, through cream and yellow to rich reds and purples. To list their many names would be pointless. I will only say that any within what I loosely term the 'Wanda' group, is worth growing. They all prefer a cool rather than a hot position and they do appreciate and repay quite rich soil.

There is yet another group of hybrids, all of which are good garden plants. Here again I swerve from any attempt at detailed descriptions. The group name is *P. × pubescens*, which I once described as more a cry of despair than a reasoned attempt to identify any particular plant. The plants concerned are mostly hybrids between *P.auricula* and *P.latifolia*. Merely as an example I quote that splendid old plant, *P. × p.*'Mrs. J. H. Wilson', raised many years ago in what is now the Wisley Garden of the Royal Horticultural Society.

Two rather nice American species which make occasional rather shy appearances in British gardens are *P.parryi* and *P.ellisiae*. The former has narrow, lightly toothed leaves which grow as upright rosettes and the ten-inch stems carry umbels of tubular, bright purple yellow-eyed flowers; the latter shows shorter, rather fleshy foliage and mauve flowers, each petal marked with a deep purple blotch.

14 Sedums and Sempervivums

Somehow or other sedums and sempervivums always seem to go together, like bread and butter, pins and needles, or salt and pepper, and so they shall associate in this chapter. As this is not a botanical book I have not given the origins of generic names. I omitted them with some regret, for they are all interesting and some are amusing. I like, for instance, the meaning of *Sedum*, which comes from *sedo*, to sit. The name was given by the ancients to certain succulent plants from the manner in which some species grow on rocks. The meaning of *Sempervivum* is more obvious, coming from *semper*, always, and *vivus*, living. Where their common name of House Leek came from I am not sure, but it could be because *S.tectorum* was commonly grown on house roofs as a guard against lightning and may have caused roofs to leak. Sedums, too, have a common name, and are collectively referred to as Stonecrops. The meaning of this vernacular name I have yet to discover.

Some of the happiest days of my life were spent in becoming familiar with the trails and byways in the Maritime Alps and, particularly memorable, were the long days spent in the Miniera Valley; remote and seldom visited and with a wealth of alpine flowers to be discovered. Now, I believe, you can get there by car but I had to travel afoot—and enjoyed it. Never have I seen *Sempervivum arachnoideum* in finer form than it was to be seen there in vast numbers, outlining the cracks and crevices in partly shattered rocks. There was also a particularly distinct form of *S.montanum*, which I brought into cultivation, but which sadly seems to have disappeared. Its neatly rosetted leaves had conspicuously dark tips and the flowers were truly red, instead of the red-purple of the type.

Take note that I am ignoring the division of some species into the genus *Jovibarba* and employing the older, and better-known name. One of these is *S.allionii*, also from the Maritime Alps, whose very globular rosettes are composed of incurved, distinctly yellow-green leaves, sometimes nicely tipped with pink. Its flowers are sparsely produced and yellow. As with nearly all sempervivums, the rosettes are more gratifying than the blossoms.

When Wilhelm Schact, a plantsman of international repute, was head gardener to the King of Bulgaria, he was instrumental in introducing a number of the good alpines to be found on Bulgaria's mountains to British gardens. Handsome *S.ciliosum* is confined almost entirely to Bulgaria in its distribution and, like other species, isolates distinct variants to different localities—even to different mountains. Typically its rosettes are rounded, with incurved leaves, grey-green in colour, but the finest manifestation of the species is *S.c.borisii*, which covers its leaves so generously with white hairs as to appear almost pure white. From Mount Mali Hat comes a form with tightly closed rosettes of plum-coloured leaves. Many of these variants are identified in gardens only by the name of the mountain from which they originated.

There is no difficulty in identifying *S.grandiflorum* if you encounter it in the European Alps. Not only is it immediately recognizable by its curious lopsided rosettes of hairy, sticky leaves, but it emits a very definite smell of goats! The yellow flowers are spotted with purple on the base of each petal. It joins up with several other species in nature and is responsible for some of the hybrids which create so much confusion in this taxonomically difficult genus. There was an occasion when spending a night in an alpine hut with several companions that I spread out my day's collection on a table. Among the loot were several clumps of *S.grandiflorum* and, after an hour or so in the warmth of the hut the goaty smell became so obvious that I was politely asked to take them outside.

The best known of all must be *S.tectorum*; an old companion of man, the Greeks and the Romans knew it, and it was illustrated in the manuscript of the *Materia Medica*, written by Dioscorides in the sixth century. It, too, has been a prolific parent as well as being infinitely variable. I remember that my father, who loved sempervivums and was an authority on their nomenclature, once tried to sort out the *tectorum* tangle, but invariably 'came out by the same door that in he went'.

One very distinct species, about which there need never be doubt, is *S.wulfenii*, found in the Swiss and Austrian Alps. Its glaucous, hard and fleshy leaves close to an unmistakable conical central bud. It has worthwhile flowers too, with yellow petals crimson-lined at the base.

The primary purpose of an expedition I once made into the Atlas Mountains of North Africa was to see one or two of the local treasures, such as *Narcissus viridiflorus*, *N.watieri*, *Asphodelus acaulis* and *Ranunculus calandrinioides*. All these I found and I was also delighted to make the acquaintance of the only species, *Sempervivum atlanticum*, native to those regions. Although not completely hardy, it is likely to survive in a hot, dry situation and is, of course, perfectly happy if grown in a pot or pan under cold glass. Its asymmetrical rosettes have a curiously lop-sided appearance. The light green leaves are lightly stained with red. The fact that it seldom flowers is unimportant for the lax stems carry only a few undistinguished pink blossoms.

Although strongly tempted to plunge into the stramash of the *Semperviva* and discuss in detail the plethora of kinds, I must resist and move on to the sedums. If sempervivums interest you, you have only to see them and choose those which you find most attractive. There are some very handsome hybrids, mostly American-raised which have recently been introduced, with resplendent and richly coloured rosettes, often of great size. If you are curious about the Atlas plants mentioned above, you will find them in the next chapter, which promises to be a considerable miscellany.

It cannot be denied that there are black sheep among the sedums. I have already disclosed the demerits of *S.acre* and *S.album*; plant them if you must, but beware, you have been warned. Those of you who may have visited the Wisley Garden during 1981 could have seen in the Trial Grounds a very representative selection of sedums under trial, running the gamut from the tiny, creeping kinds to the giants more appropriate to the herbaceous border. These taller kinds do not, of course, fall within the scope of this book, although I may not be able to resist including a few favourites which are not too large for a sizeable rock garden. Most of the tender ones will also be excluded, although one or two very nice Mexicans may find their way in, purely because I like them and am content to give them alpine house protection, which is all that they need.

Annuals in the accepted sense, do not find a place on any rock garden of mine. I was once commissioned to construct a very large rock garden with Westmorland limestone, with waterfalls and pools galore by a wealthy industrialist. As far as I could discover his sole reason for the project was so that he would have a bigger and better one than his neighbour. When it came to planting time I was told that the gardeners would see to that. My agony can be appreciated when, on a later visit, I found that it had been entirely planted with bedding plants and annuals as well as massed scarlet geraniums. Not an alpine plant could be found and, when I remonstrated, I was told that he couldn't be bothered with those fiddling little things. There was a sequel, for the same person, a year or two later, asked me to build another rock garden in his London garden. I refused, and gave my reasons, which did not, I fear, lead to a friendly relationship, but, after all, what is the use of having principles if you don't abide by them?

That little outburst does not mean that I dislike annuals. I am very fond of them and use them extensively—in the proper context—and there are just a few which cause no offence and, indeed, find their proper place on a rock garden or in its environment. One of these is dainty little *Sedum caeruleum* from Corsica and other mediterranean islands. It is almost unobserved until it explodes into clouds of tiny, starry blue flowers on stems no more than three inches high. In a sunny spot it will self-sow in a modest manner, or, if it is not required again in that particular spot, the seeds can be gathered and sown *in situ* elsewhere. It is, as far as I know, the only hardy *Sedum* with blue flowers.

If you travel off the beaten track in our western counties, you may well come upon *S.anglicum*, a true native and by no means to be despised as a rock garden plant. As with all members of our much threatened native flora, it should not be collected, but is obtainable from most alpine nurseries. Very small and neat, its leaves are fleshy and green and prettily tinted with red. Give it spartan conditions in full sun and it will decorate itself further with myriads of short-stemmed heads of starry pink flowers.

From the coldness of Siberia comes *S.populifolium*, which doesn't look at all like any of its relations. On erect, woody branches, up to eighteen inches in height, are thick leaves, shaped like those of a poplar. Even without flowers it acts as an attractive dwarf shrub but it adds the bonus of many clusters of hawthorn-scented soft pink flowers. It is one of the trick plants we, perhaps rather naughtily, include in identification tests for students.

If you are averse to snakes you will probably not develop any great love for *S.anacampseros*, for it spreads at ground level from a central rootstock long, brown, reptilian stems clad with thick blue-grey leaves. Each stem ends in a flattish head of purple-pink flowers, which are actually more attractive than they sound. The lovelorn may find derivation of its name interesting, it comes from *anakampseros*, the Greek name for a herb which was said to bring back love when touched!

One of the Mexican species which I forgive for not being entirely hardy is *S.cupressoides*. It grows in the form of neat and tidy tufts of cypress-like growths, over which are bright heads of yellow flowers. Even less hardy, but safe in the alpine house, is *S.oaxacanum*, also from Mexico. On its branching, almost prostrate stems are fleshy leaves, green and bronze, often overlapping like scales. On each branch tip is a small cluster of yellow flowers—a very popular colour in the sedum family.

There are certain plants for which no factual description is likely to

Sedum populifolium

inspire desire, and *S.crassipes* (*asiaticum*) is one of these. It hails from the Orient and is herbaceous and when spring calls it to renewed life it erects upright, foot-high stems dressed with flat, toothed, bright green leaves and each stem is crowned with a head of crowded creamy-white flowers in late summer. No catalogue description will sell it, but it seldom fails to arouse admiration when it is seen. Another herbaceous species, this time from Tibet, is *S.hobsonii* (*praegerianum*). It really is rather a poppet, extending from a central crown of narrow, shining green leaves, radiating prostrate stems ending in clusters of urn-shaped rose-pink flowers. It ought to be hardy, but shows some aversion to a wet and cold winter in the open. I like it so much that I yield to its obvious desire for winter shelter and grow it in the alpine house.

Traditionally, sedums are sun-lovers, happy in hot and dry places but *S.humifusum*, another Mexican, joins the one or two odd men out, and likes moist soil and a cool position. An enchanting minute plant, it makes mossy tufts of tiny leaves, tinted red in winter, and stars its cushions with surprisingly large yellow flowers. I have grown it outside and it seems reasonably contented in a shady corner of a stone trough, but I also find that it benefits from being lifted and divided fairly often. If left alone too long it begins to look shabby and careworn. *S.pulchellum*, like *S.humifusum*, departs from family tradition and insists upon a moist situation. It will take all the sunshine it can get, but must have moist soil into which to thrust its vigorous roots. Given these conditions it spreads into a mat of reddish, widely sprawling stems densely clothed in narrow green leaves. The rose-pink flowers are produced in starfish-shaped heads from mid-summer onward.

Very pleasing, and decidely 'unsedum-like' in appearance is *S.primuloides*, from far Yunnan (it is yet another plant which appears in our identification tests and usually trips up the unwary). Over its mats of dark green, fleshy leaves, in late summer, it surprises you with large. white, bell-shaped flowers borne on very short stems.

Our good old friend *S.roseum*, or Rose Root, a good British native, must now be sought botanically as *Rhodiola rosea*, but I retain the name which I have known from childhood. An interesting plant, it forms a thick and fleshy rootstock, which rests unadorned by foliage during the winter. In spring many erect leafy stems erupt, ending in heads of greenish-yellow flowers. Even more spectacular is the variety *heterodontum*, in which the stems and leaves are purple and the flowers rusty-red in colour.

The rosettes of *S.sempervivoides* are so like those of a *Sempervivum* that it is usually mistaken for a member of that genus. It is monocarpic and each rosette that flowers will die, but it is generous in supplying lots of seeds from which a new generation can easily be raised and it is a good enough plant to justify the effort. In their second year the seedlings thrust upward, from the centre of the symmetrical rosette, a pagoda-shaped column topped by a head of scarlet flowers.

It is very obvious that I am bypassing most of the better-known sedums which are so familiar and appear in so many gardens that it is pointless to devote valuable space to their praise. My hope is that I may interest you in some of the less well-known kinds which are so rewarding, but apt to be overlooked in these days of economic stress, when it is the regrettable policy of many producers to grow more and more of less and less. It is fortunate for gardeners that there are a few specialized nurserymen who insist upon maintaining representative collections of plants with which the mass producers cannot be bothered.

You may have to search through many catalogues before finding *S.tatarinowii*, but it is well worth the effort, for this Chinese species will never fail to please. Dormant in the winter, it emits in spring annual stems set with blunt, fleshy, grey-green leaves, generously toothed on their margins. On six-inch stems it displays bold corymbs of white, pink-flushed flowers. It is hardy enough to attempt in the open but is more often treated as an alpine house plant.

From Turkestan, the home of so many good plants, comes *S.semenovii*, a foot-high plant whose leafy stems terminate in bottle-brush racemes of white flowers. It is a rarity in gardens, but good enough to justify the patience which may be needed to discover a supplier. I have no doubt that Dr. Peter Davis, who commenced his career as a student on my nursery, and has since devoted his life to producing a monumental Flora of Turkey, has not neglected to praise it.

15 Miscellanea

Many who see it for the first time find it difficult to accept that *Ranunculus calandrinioides* is related to the buttercups which lay a carpet of summer gold on our meadows. To discover it in the wild involves a journey to the Atlas Mountains of North Africa. The spartan diet which I have so frequently counselled for alpines will not be appreciated by this greedy plant. Its thong-like, deeply delving roots are eager for nourishment and rapidly absorb and exhaust the nutriments in the soil. When it is grown in pots it is essential to shake the roots free of soil during the winter resting period and re-pot into new compost. I find that it is very appreciative of a hefty dollop of well-decayed farmyard manure in the bottom of the pot or pan.

A very early riser, it begins to make new growth in December and the wide, broadly lance-shaped grey leaves are soon accompanied by fat buds which expand into huge, saucer-shaped flowers. These are basically white, but are frequently flushed with pink and, among seedlings, it is not uncommon to discover forms whose petals are wholly rose-pink. There may also be, among the seedlings, forms with narrow petals which do not form a shapely flower; these should be discarded and not used as breeding stock. Although quite hardy, *R.calandrinioides* is usually grown in the alpine house: its petals have the consistency of tissue paper and if flowering in the open during January and February, are all too easily damaged by the elements.

It was when looking for this handsome buttercup in the Atlas Mountains that I also sought another inhabitant of those regions, the quaintly green-flowered *Narcissus viridiflorus*. This was at a time when I was spending a penurious and footloose period based on a lodging in the Gorbio Valley behind Menton. In order to undertake anything more than local travel, I had to find some way of financing myself. I had scraped acquaintance with the captain of a small trading boat which plied between Nice and Corsica, usually carrying cattle and goats. In return for an occasional night spent 'hitting it up' in the less salubrious areas near the port, he would ship me as a deck hand whenever I wanted to visit my beloved Corsica. This meant spending a night on deck mixed up with the definitely odorous cattle but I counted it a small price to pay,

1. *Verbascum* × 'Letitia'

2. *Lewisia* hybrids

3. *Geum reptans*

4. *Gentiana saxosa*

5. Rock Garden

6. *Weldenia candida*

7. *Saxifraga moschata* 'Cloth of Gold'

8. *Sedum caeruleum*

9. *Phlox* 'Millstream'

10. *Dianthus alpinus*

11. *Saxifraga cochlearis* in stone sink

12. Alpine flowers and paving stones

especially as, directly we approached within a few miles of the island, I could lean out and drink in the aromatic scent of the *maquis* which drifted on the warm night air far out to sea.

On one of these Bacchanalian occasions I met the skipper of a trading vessel which wandered in a haphazard fashion round the Mediterranean, usually with a cargo of wine and a few passengers. He was a gigantic Swede, with an unquenchable thirst and an appetite to match. When he learned that I was desperately anxious to travel in search of plants, he thought this was uproariously amusing and, when his guffaws had finally subsided, offered me a job, whenever I wanted it, as assistant steward. This enabled me to become acquainted with many fascinating places. My duties on board (unpaid, of course), were practically non-existent, and my good friend the captain had no objection to my abandoning ship at one port and rejoining at another, often several weeks later.

One result was that I was able to spend several periods plant hunting in the lower and higher Atlas Mountains. I did discover the *Ranunculus* but for a long time the green-flowered *Narcissus* eluded me, which was frustrating, because I had been given very precise directions to areas where it was abundant. I eventually discovered, to my chagrin, that my own stupidity was the cause of failure. *N.viridiflorus* grows amid other herbage and, when not in flower is quite invisible and even when blossoming, its green petals are so well camouflaged that they are all too easily overlooked. Once I had detected one I began to pick them out more easily.

Tiny *Narcissus watieri*, who smiles up at you so cheerfully with rounded, snow-white flowers neatly displayed on four-inch stems is more readily located. It is just one of a whole group of miniature narcissi which can be dibbled between other plants in sinks and troughs where they will blossom in company with the earliest saxifrages. My own special favourite in this context is *N.asturiensis* (*minimus*). It is a pity that *minimus* has been abandoned, for it is the smallest of all the narcissi with truly daffodil-shaped flowers. On three-inch stems it carries flowers of pure gold with a tiny but definite trumpet.

No well-planned garden should lack its quota of very early flowers which brave with apparent composure the trials of snow and frost. Along with a galaxy of snowdrops come the snowflakes, *Leucojum vernum*, whose pendant green-tipped lampshade flowers of purest white bring solace after the long winter, and its yellow-tipped companion, *L.v.carpathicum*. Another, less common but outstandingly beautiful snowflake is *L.wagneri*, whose large flowers, carried in pairs on nine-inch stems ensure a daily pilgrimage to the corner of the garden which it decorates.

One more excitement from the Atlas mountains is *Asphodelus acaulis*. There are several tall and handsome asphodels to be found throughout the Alps, but this is the Lilliputian of the race. After its winter rest it produces loose clusters of long, narrow leaves, which are centred by almost stemless clusters of funnel-shaped pink flowers. If you grow it in the open it will appreciate a warm and sheltered position and, during its period of sleep, may even appreciate being given the protection of a cloche, or a covering of straw or dried bracken. More often it is grown in deep pots which will accommodate its lusty and vigorous roots.

Inevitably among the memories of places, people and plants, are regretful thoughts of places not yet visited. My ambition to explore the Drakensburg Mountains of Lesotho (old Basutoland) has yet to be fulfilled—and may never be realized, for it would be quite impossible to encompass my desired travel programme within the years remaining to me. However, I can enjoy in my own and other gardens some of the plants which I may never see growing in their native environments. One does not really expect plants from South Africa to be hardy in Britain, but there are a few alpines which have accepted our hazardous climate quite happily.

It was the intrepid Mrs. Milford who first brought to our gardens from the Drakensburgs, *Rhodohypoxis baurii*, a plant to which I accord slightly reluctant admiration. Few share my reluctance to give whole-hearted affection to a plant which has so many virtues, and perhaps I am over-critical. Shapeliness of flower ranks high in my appreciation of any plant, and the blossoms of *Rhodohypoxis* are shapeless bundles of petals, admittedly colourful but lacking grace. From their resting state tiny, cormlike roots emerge, early in the year, little clusters of narrow, hairy leaves and these are almost immediately accompanied by myriads of short stems topped by the bundles of petals. These are deep pink in the typical plant, but it is infinitely variable and since its introduction numerous named clones have been selected and named with a colour range from the typical pink, through deepening shades to crimson and some nice albinos. The particular virtue which I do fully admire is that the flowering period extends from early spring through the summer and well into the autumn months.

A very good plant, also from the Drakensburg Mountains, caused a lot of confusion when it was first introduced, not too many years ago. It came labelled *Euryops evansii*, and was quickly seized upon, propagated

Rhodohypoxis baurii

and distributed under that name. Only later was it discovered that the identification had been wrong and that it was correctly *E.acraeus*. It still exists in some catalogues under the erroneous name. As a novelty, and from South Africa, it was thought to be not too hardy, and was usually confined to the alpine house. It soon became evident that such care was not approved of and it only became really happy when it was taken outside and given a sunny position, where it makes a shapely, rather domed bush of grey stems and silver leaves over which hover the yellow composite flowers. It is quite easily propagated from cuttings but I have sought in vain for seeds. The curious thing is, that it has self-sown in several positions, notably on a large block of tufa rock although whatever I have sown has never germinated.

I like antirrhinums (who doesn't?), but the thought of a race of dwarfs said to be 'suitable for rock gardens' is pure anathema to me. I can still find myself, if no one is looking, gently pressing the sides of antirrhinum flowers to make the funny 'bunny-mouths', but I do not want any of the conventional ones on a rock garden.

There are, however, one or two species very appropriate to the rock garden, among which must be included the pretty trailer, long known as *A.asarina*, now referred to *Asarina procumbens*. It, too, hails from a sunny climate, being native to southern France, but, unlike its Spanish cousin, it likes to grow in a cool, semi-shaded spot. A sprawling trailer, its lengthy stems bear hairy, grey-green leaves and are bedecked along their length with large white Snapdragon flowers, gently tinted with yellow and red. It is not a tidy plant and is seen at its best when it can hang down from a crevice.

From hot hillsides in central Spain comes *A.hispanicum*, which I prefer to grow in its sub-species *glutinosum*, a neat foot-high bush of entangled woody stems. The leaves are noticeably sticky to the touch and the soft yellow flowers are carried in loose racemes. On the broad 'palate' of each flower are narrow red stripes. It is a plant to enjoy, but it will not do well for you unless you provide it with a position that will at least remind it of its homeland. Another Spaniard, and rather similar in appearance to *A.hispanicum glutinosum* is *A.molle*, also an avid sun-lover, covering its low bushes with white and yellow flowers.

One cannot think of the Pyrenees without recalling lovely *Ramonda myconi*, which haunts wide seams and crevices on so many cliffs. To me

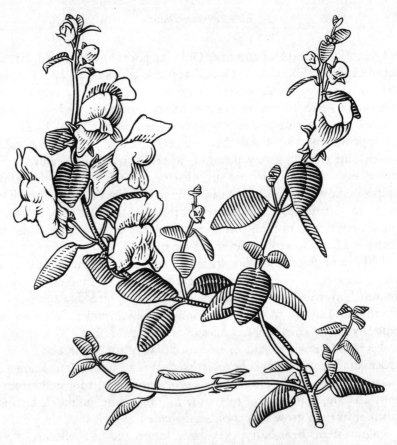

Antirrhinum hispanicum glutinosum

it will always be *Ramondia pyrenaica*, under which name I planted it on my very first rock garden, built with rocks filched from my father's nursery, but names, like times, have a way of changing. The generic name of this splendid plant honours the memory of Louis Francis Ramond, Baron de Carbonnière, who travelled and botanized extensively in the Pyrenees during the eighteenth and nineteenth centuries. Its wide, corrugated and toothed leaves form flat rosettes which hug closely the rocks among which it chooses to dwell. On the four-inch stems may be one or several rounded, wide-petalled flowers, purple-blue in colour, but there are variants with pink or white petals. Always try to find a cool, north-facing crevice for it.

If you take a very long step from the Pyrenees to the Balkans you will find *R.serbica* and *R.nathaliae*. There is a strong family resemblance between the three, but *R.nathaliae* edges its glossy green leaves with dark hairs, and the flowers of *R.serbica* are cup-shaped rather than flat. There has been recorded a *R.permixta*, reputed to be a hybrid between *R.myconi* and *R.serbica* but it is doubtful if it still exists.

During my early years of training on the then famous Six Hills Nursery in Stevenage, I remember vividly, soon after I had been promoted from washing pots and being the general nursery stooge, I was allowed to take a turn at the potting bench. The first plants I helped to pot were the very first large quantities of *Gentiana sino-ornata*, then an eagerly sought novelty. Now, nearly sixty years later, it is grown by the thousand and remains one of the best sellers, in spite of the fact that it demands lime-free soil. It is, in fact, just about the most lime-intolerant

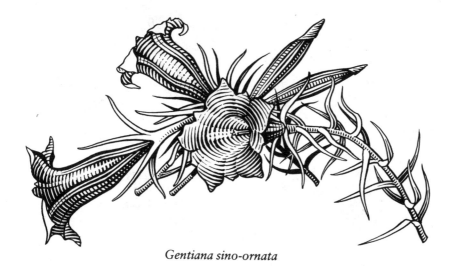

Gentiana sino-ornata

plant that I know and will turn yellow if there is the least suspicion of lime in the soil or water. Give it an open position in moisture-retentive soil and it will give you a solid sheet of azure flowers from early September on into the winter. I have sometimes been able to pick a few flowers on Christmas day, but that was admittedly exceptional. After two years the plants will have matted together and they should then be lifted in March, divided and replanted in new soil. When lifted they will fall into many separate thong-like roots and two or three of these should be bunched together and planted as one.

When I was first given some plants of *Diascia cordata*, I was no more than dubiously grateful, for I knew the genus to consist of South African annual and perennial herbs, not many of which were hardy. In fact I almost discarded them, which would have been a mistake, for it has proved to be an extremely desirable plant, making a splendid display during the summer. From its more or less prostrate tufts rise leafy foot-high stems, each one carrying a short raceme of terracotta-pink flowers. It is free and long flowering and perennial and is a very definite acquisition. There is now a hybrid between it and the annual *D.bar-*

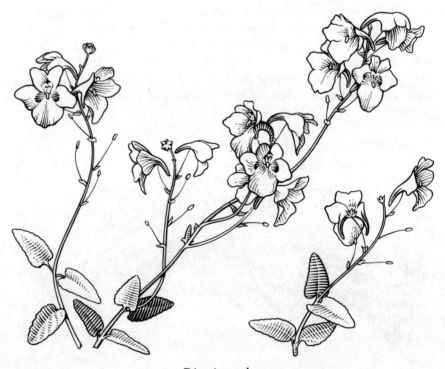

Diascia cordata

berae, which is equally floriferous, slightly taller and has flowers of salmon-pink. As might be imagined from its provenance, it is a confirmed sun-lover and is content in any soil that is well drained and well nourished.

There is a strong temptation, which I suppose I must resist, to devote considerable space in defence of alliums, a family whose pervasive family odour has earned for it an underserved bad name. Admittedly the all too familiar smell of onions is present in almost all of them, but it is seldom evident unless they are roughly handled and in none of the garden kinds that I know of is it as tear-producing as in the well-known occupant of the vegetable garden.

This is yet another of the many genera which my strongly developed collector's instinct has induced me to seek. There is some confusion in their taxonomy and, along with other lovers of the genus, I await with eagerness a revision of the family which I believe is being prepared by Dr. W. Stearn, to whom we are all indebted for the too occasional crumbs of his vast plant knowledge which he spreads before us. Permit me, then, to tempt you with descriptions of a few which are good rock garden plants, and even one or two which, although definitely invasive, pay a splendid rent for the space they will occupy, given the chance.

My first acquaintance with *Allium narcissiflorum* (*pedemontanum*) was made on the lower slopes of mountains in northern Italy. I was very young then, and my plant knowledge was fragmentary and, although entranced by the pendant wine-red flowers, I had no idea what it was—until I picked some of the flowers and immediately detected the familiar and characteristic smell of onions. Some of the fibre-covered rhizomes which I collected lived with me for many years, and, of course, it is an old inhabitant of our gardens and one which I treasure. The bell-shaped blossoms are carried in pendant umbels on six-inch stems.

There are weedy ones of course—every large family has a skeleton or two in its cupboard—and I have already warned you about *A.moly* and *A.triquetrum*. A special pet is *A.beesianum*, from China, on whose erect, nine-inch stems may be seen clusters of bright blue flowers without even a hint of the purple which suffuses so many so-called blue flowers. Then there is *A.ostrowskianum* from Turkestan, one of the nicest and most dwarf-like. From its small round bulbs rise tufts of narrow leaves and four-inch stems bearing many-flowered umbels of wide-petalled, wine-red blossoms.

Although it is really too tall for a rock garden, I cannot bear to lack *A.siculum* (*dioscoridis*); I believe botanists now prefer to refer it to the separate genus *Nectaroscordum*. Its thick, strong stems rise to a height of three feet or more and are crowned by an imposing umbel of large, bell-shaped flowers, almost square in shape. The flowers are a curious shade of blue-green or jade and each petal has a maroon stripe. It is a most unusual and strikingly lovely plant which I am surprised is not more widely known and grown, for it is easy to please in any good soil and an open sunny position. I like to grow it among more leafy plants in a border so that the long, tall and bare stems are partially concealed.

The same treatment is accorded to *Galtonia* (*Hyacinthus*) *candicans*, a bold and bulbous plant that displays its large, white, bell-shaped flowers atop high bare stems which are best hidden. Even more to my taste is its smaller relation, *G.princeps*, with soft green flowers—but then I have a liking for plants with green flowers, which is why I have such a fondness for the primrose which has transformed the petals of its flowers into green leaflets. To many this is an abomination but I find it attractive. Like E. A. Bowles I have a penchant for the oddities of plant life. He was so enamoured of them that they were gathered together in an area of his garden known as the Lunatic Asylum.

Also an eccentric is the Spiral Rush, *Juncus effusus* 'Spiralis', which I owe to Mr. Bowles, with his constant generosity he dug up a plant and gave it to me when I was a mere lad. It has lived with me ever since and is a never failing source of amusement—especially to children. It can claim no beauty whatsoever, but the long, cylindrical green leaves twist and coil into the exact shape of a corkscrew. It lives in a cool corner in companionship with that other curiosity which I have already written of, *Arisarum proboscideum*.

How exasperating plants can be. I see that my last remaining specimen of *Raoulia eximia* has given up the ghost, which saddened but did not surprise me, for this precious New Zealander has never taken kindly to cultivation and presents a constant challenge to those who will pick up the gauntlet and pit their skills against its waywardness. It never fails to evoke another memory of my youth when, with my father, I visited A. K. Bulley and his wonderful garden at Ness, in the Wirrall. His head gardener at that time was a Mr. Hope, a superb plantsman with a somewhat astringent character. He was our guide and it was soon made evident that I was expected to remain quietly in the background, on the principle that children should be seen but not heard. All went well until we walked through a cold greenhouse. When we came to an array of pots filled with splendidly healthy plants of *Raoulia exima* I could no longer contain myself and shouted with excitement. Hope turned to me and asked 'Do you know what it is'? When I replied that it must be *Raoulia eximia* from New Zealand (it was not labelled), his entire attitude changed and I was accepted as one of the club.

On the several occasions thereafter that I went to Ness I was greeted with the greatest kindness and made very welcome. Hope died some years ago, well into his nineties and I was told that he worked in the garden almost to the time of his departure to whatever Valhalla accepts dedicated gardeners. Incidentally, it was his employer, A. K. Bulley, who annoyed botanists by scattering seeds of exotic alpines in Snowdonia. I believe some of the more irate spent a lot of time in following years pulling out those that they could find of his introductions to the British Flora. It was Bulley too, who was responsible for firmly establishing the great nursery of Bees Limited at Liverpool, which survives and flourishes to this day—we are all familiar with the seed packets marked 'Bees Seeds that Grow'.

There are other, more amenable species of *Raoulia*. The best known is *R.australis*, whose flat carpets of silver rosettes make such pleasant coverings for small alpine bulbs. Then there is *R.lutescens*, even smaller, a mere silver-grey film on the soil, changing to soft gold when the myriads of tiny stemless flowers cover it in the spring. A more recent introduction came to our gardens as *R.hookeri* and has become well liked and popular under that name. Only today I learn that it is not *R.hookeri* at all, but *R.parkii*, a bothersome alteration which will take some time to become familiar. It is like a slightly enlarged and even more silvery *R.australis*. Much less exciting, but nevertheless an easy and useful carpeter is the green *R.glabra*, which becomes white when sheeted with clusters of tiny flowers. *R.eximia* has some equally enticing relations, such as *R.buchananii* and *R.mammilaris* but they are even more intolerant and, even if obtainable, should only be attempted by courageous and optimistic gardeners.

Even though trilliums are not strictly speaking alpine plants, they fall very comfortably within the category of plants which rock gardeners like to grow. They are ideal plants for peat beds, or cool nooks in the rock garden, or between shading shrubs. It is unfortunate that they are likely to become even more difficult to obtain than they are at present, for most of the stocks held by nurserymen are from wild collected plants and conservation demands that the wholesale robbing of natural colonies should cease. This applies particularly to the American species. They are not easily or quickly increased in cultivation and supplies have depended largely upon imported plants. I have vivid memories of seeing a magnificent stand of *Trillium grandiflorum* being ruthlessly devastated. The sight of hundreds bundled up, all destined for export, determined me to be very modest in my future purchases.

The one species which is commonly available and is also one of the best for garden purposes is *T.grandiflorum*. Like all other trilliums its leaves and other parts are all in threes. A herald of spring, it makes bold clumps of broad leaves on quite tall stems and produces large flowers which are pure white at first but often adopt soft pink tints as they age. There is also a rare but supremely beautiful form in which the flowers are completely double, with a multiplication of petals. Although in general I prefer single flowers, I cannot deny the loveliness of the double *Trillium*.

There are, of course, a lot more desirable species, some from North America and others from the Orient and, just occasionally, a few of them appear in catalogues. If you hanker after them, and are fortunate enough to obtain a plant or two, I will give away a trade secret and tell you how to make more—albeit slowly. If, when the leaves have died away in the autumn, and the plant is resting in its thick, almost tuberous root, you carefully uncover the crown and, with a very sharp knife, make tiny nicks around the circumference, then cover the crown again with soil, by the spring it is probable that from each little nick that you have cut, will rise a shoot which can be severed and grown on as an individual. It is only by this method, and by sowing the seeds which are occasionally and scantily produced, that the plant can be increased. Anything which is done to prevent the decimation of wild colonies is admirable, and it behoves us to increase and distribute the species which are already in gardens.

The sad story of the threatened trilliums can be repeated in the case of all the hardly cypripediums, which, too, are endangered. No satisfactory method has yet been discovered by which they can be propagated in quantity and we remain dependent upon plants collected from the wild. I have already mentioned *C.calceolus* which now exists as a British native by a very few isolated and jealously guarded plants. One of the most beautiful is the North American *C.reginae* (*spectabilis*), whose sepals and petals are white, often rose-flushed and with a bold, inflated rose-pink pouch. In the past this was imported in great quantities but I learn with happiness that it is now a protected plant and any collecting from the wild is illegal and should be discouraged. Established plants of any of these desirable plants can be carefully divided, but attempts to raise them from the seeds they produce in such abundance have, so far, met with no success. They have been germinated on agar in flasks but attempts to grow them on from the seedling stage have failed. Who knows, perhaps the tissue culture methods, now being widely practised on the Continent, may solve the problem for those able to provide the necessary laboratory conditions.

No place, time or circumstance that I can recall provide the reality of complete peace and contentment to be found in the solitude of high mountains. Ones ego is scaled down to a proper level, consistent with the majesty of the mountains. Appreciation of beauty is quickened and one is able to look with due reverence at the exquisite alpine flowers. I recall literally kneeling in worship before silver-leaved mats of *Potentilla nitida*, studded with almost stemless rich pink flowers, glorifying the screes in which it loves to grow. In gardens it is apt to be less liberal unless it is given a spartan diet. Variable in the intensity of flower colour, there are forms with almost white flowers. Others, selected in captivity, such as 'Rubra' and, particularly 'Lissadell', have blossoms of a rich and glowing deep pink.

The genus *Potentilla* is a valuable and important family, offering a diversity of form and colour. There are the invaluable and multifarious forms of *P.fruticosa*, ranging from hummocky bushes to yard-high shrubs and providing their white, yellow or rosy red flowers throughout the summer months, although they are mostly too tall for the rock garden. A much neglected species which deserves wider recognition is *P.alba*, a sun-lover from central and southern Europe. Its habit of spreading into wide, ground-hugging mats of dark green leaves makes it

Potentilla nitida

a useful ground-cover plant. The foliage forms an excellent contrast to the large white flowers, shaped like those of a single rose, reminding us of the family relationship to the roses. It is very much a Cinderella and needs a fairy godmother to lift it from its neglected state.

Ever since I saw the golden sheets of *P.aurea* decorating rocky alpine meadows I have had a special fondness for this easy and showy species. It asks for nothing but a sunny spot and any well-drained soil. Its leaves are divided in to leaflets and the rich yellow flowers are carried in loose clusters and great profusion. It has a form with semi-double flowers and another, *P.a.chrysocraspeda*, whose blossoms are vividly orange-yellow. Like others of its genus, *P.aurea* occupies a good deal of space, for which it pays a very handsome rent.

Were I to compose a list of the good garden plants which have come to us from Japan it would be a lengthy one, and one which would certainly not be excluded is *P.megalantha*. For a long time it was listed in catalogues as *P.fragiformis*, which is a different species, not, as far as I know, in cultivation and far less beautiful, so that we need not regret its absence. The leaves of *P.megalantha* are large, rounded and lobed and softly hairy, forming low tufts and mounds, over which are displayed the large and boldly handsome yellow flowers.

All these low-growing potentillas are ideal plants for associating with other alpines in the alpine meadow, which is just a conglomeration of plants of a somewhat similar character. The alpine meadow was another of Clarence Elliott's splendid ideas. I have always liked it because it enables one to grow alpines in the manner to which they are accustomed. The tendency in a constructed rock garden is to create a series of isolated 'pockets', in each of which we set one particular plant, where it has to grow in solitary splendour. I am convinced that most alpines prefer to grow in close association with their neighbours and I believe that such association may be actually beneficial.

In gardens, of course, it is not possible to adhere too closely to nature and adaption is inevitable but an alpine meadow is easily contrived on a fairly large, open area, either flat or gently sloping, with a few isolated rocks here and there, which not only relieve the flatness, but act as useful stepping stones. It will not be a tidy garden and may not appeal to those to whom neatness is a necessity but it can be great fun and a lot of plants which sulk in solitude will relish the companionship of others.

To launch here into a long and detailed descriptive list of plants appropriate to an alpine meadow would make dull reading. I will, among the lists of plants for special purposes to be found at the end of the book, include a selection of plants which I have found to adapt happily to such conditions. They must all be good survivors, able to cope with the cut and thrust competition of aggressive neighbours, which will inevitably be more forceful in soft garden conditions than in the harsher austerity of their native haunts.

In case it is felt that I have been unkind to those who like a well-ordered and tidy garden I confess to a preference for gardens in which plants can riot about to their hearts content. I remember visiting a very large garden, full of interesting plants. It should have filled me with envy and admiration, but I was unutterably bored, for each plant exactly filled its allotted space and there was not one weed to be seen. It was joyous to return to my own wilderness, and to read once again that Reginald Arkell wrote about the over-tidy garden— permit me to quote:

> Miss Mary Martindale worked on and on,
> Polishing her garden until it shone;
> She wouldn't let young children smell her roses,
> Unless she knew they had wiped their noses.
> And yet, somehow, her garden never earned
> Those cries of ecstasy for which she yearned.
>
> People admired her garden, it is true:
> No GENTIANS had ever been so blue;
> No garden paths were ever quite so neat;
> You felt they were too fine for human feet.
> The tennis lawn was cut and nicely rolled,
> And yet, somehow, her garden left you cold.
>
> This worried poor Miss Martindale a lot,
> What was it that her garden hadn't got?
> She asked if I could tell her, so I said:
> Your garden lacks a modicum of weeds;
> I'll send along some dandelion seeds.

(*Green Fingers Again*, Herbert Jenkins Ltd, 1942)

My affection for tiny alpine plants by no means blinds me to the nobility of the larger plants. I have a great affection for thistles of all kinds, especially those with the architectural qualities of, for example, the giant *Onopordon acanthium*, whose stately stems adorned with silver-grey leaves and bold heads of purple flowers tower to a height of six feet or more. This I always find a place for, and round its feet I plant a few of the thistle with the unbelievable name *Silybum marianum*, otherwise known as Blessed Thistle, Holy Thistle or Our Lady's Milk

Thistle. It is a biennial, with leaves marvellously patterned in green and silver and short-stemmed heads of rich purple flowers.

There is another thistle for the rock garden too, *Carlina acaulis*, which has been grown in our gardens since the seventeenth century. The prostrate clusters of pinnate, spiny leaves are centred by almost stemless whitish flower heads. It is also known as the Weather-glass: its flower heads, if dried and tied in bunches and hung outside, will expand with the advent of dry weather, and close if rain is threatened. If you have room for it, *C.acanthifolia* is magnificent, able to make a wide, flat rosette eighteen inches in diameter with a huge shaving brush of little brownish-red flowerlets as its centrepiece—but it is space consuming.

It would be impossible for me to say with truth that there is any plant which I actually dislike, but I have less than warm affection for some flowers which have multiplied their petals to the exclusion of grace and elegance; among these are the double daisies used as bedding plants. With one possible exception they should never be planted on a rock garden. The one which, somewhat shamefacedly, I do accept as a possibility, is *Bellis* 'Dresden China', whose neat little pink pompons are

Carlina acaulis

so appealing that I cannot resist its daintiness. It has a pure white counterpart, to which I extend the same tolerance.

A few daisies are, however, acceptable. Growing in mountain pastures you may find *Bellidiastrum michelii* (*Aster bellidiastrum*) which resembles a slightly enlarged version of our common lawn daisy and tints the ray florets of its inch-wide flowers with delicate pink. To the horror of those whose lawns are sacred sanctuaries reserved for nothing but grass, I admit and admire daisies on my lawn. There was an occasion when an Indian potentate was being given VIP treatment which included a tour of great British Gardens. At the banquet which concluded his visit he was asked what he had most admired in our gardens. His reply, which shattered his erudite audience was, 'I liked the daisies on your lawns'. The sequel was that he left an order with one of our great seedsmen for a large quantity of daisy seed to be sent to him in India.

Despite its lack of any startling beauty I have a considerable affection

Bellidiastrum michelii

for *Bellium minutum*, which was once described in his catalogue by a witty nurseryman, as 'Little Mary'. It comes from the Levant and makes a completely prostrate mat of minute leaves which it studs with white daisies on inch-high stems. It is a nice plant to insert in the cracks between paving stones. Then there is a charming daisy from North Africa, *Bellis rotundifolia* 'Caerulescens', whose flowers are similar to those of our common daisy, but the ray florets, or petals, are broader and fewer and tinted to a soft blue colour. *B.sylvestris* hails from southern France and is yet again like our daisy, but taller and the tips of its white petals are crimson. These, then, are a few of the admissible daisies. None of them is a traffic stopper, but they are all likeable with a gentle and simple appeal.

My aversion to the use of traditional annuals on the rock garden has already been made abundantly clear, but I have never been able to resist the charm of delicate little *Ionopsidium acaule*. It comes from Portugal and is never more than a couple of inches in height. On these short stems it crowds clusters of small lilac flowers. I like to sow a pinch or two in a sunny spot among other plants which will not smother it, and it is also useful for sowing in the narrow chinks between paving stones. Children in particular will enjoy it because it grows quickly and is soon in flower. There is nothing more encouraging to the budding gardener than rapid results. For children's gardens I would always supply packets of seed of this, and Virginian Stock and radishes.

Plants which flower all the summer through are always appreciated but we do not commonly expect bulbs to fall in this category; *Ipheion uniflorum*, however, is seldom without blossoms. I have some colonies of it in a narrow, sunny border at the foot of a wall and there have been flowers open in ten months of the year. It is best grown in the cultivar known as 'Wisley Blue', which bears inch-wide clear blue flowers on four-inch stems above the tufts of narrow green leaves.

On my way into London every spring I pass two gardens which offer a brilliant display of the trio which I call 'The three A's'—*Arabis*, *Alyssum* and *Aubrieta*—and I wonder why there has been this concentration for just one short period. Seen later in the year the gardens are totally without colour and everything has been sacrificed for wide spring sheets of white, yellow, pink, purple and red.

By no means ought these three genera to be neglected, but they should be used in moderation and with discretion. Once their initial display is over they have little to offer. The dozen or so species of *Aubrieta* are widely distributed in the wild but these are not the ones which light up our gardens with their scintillating colours. Aubrietas in

Ipheion uniflorum

the garden are represented by a wide range of selected variants of
A.deltoides and probably some hybrids between these and other species.

The named cultivars are increased vegetatively for they do not breed
true to type from seed. Any alpine catalogue will offer lists of kinds from
which a selection can be made, in colours ranging from pink, through
deeper shades to bright red and also blues, mauves and purples;
however, there is not a good white-flowered *Aubrieta*. Various mixed
strains of *Aubrieta* seed can also be found and they will provide a carpet
of mixed colours. Avid sun and lime-lovers, they are magnificent wall
plants, hanging from crevices in great shields of vivid colour. They will
be long lived too, if they are trimmed over with garden shears or scissors
after they have finished flowering. Should this simple chore be neglected
they tend to become loose and straggly and may perish after a few years.

The common *Arabis*, which has been cultivated since the late
eighteenth century and was known as *A.albida* is now more correctly
A.caucasica. It too is a splendid wall plant, and in any open, sunny place
is invaluable for giving spring colour. It also benefits, as aubrietas do,

from a good haircut after blossoming. The colour range is from white to rich pink—almost red—and there is one good albino which is fully double. There are other species of Arabis, gems for the alpine house, of which more later.

The last of my three 'A's' is *Alyssum*. When I was a small boy I delighted in sowing seeds of what was then known as *A.maritimum*, a dwarf, white-flowered annual which gave quick and showy results—just the plant for a child's garden. Now it has been renamed *Lobularia maritima*. All true alyssums have yellow flowers. The most commonly grown species is, of course, *Alyssum saxatile*, a lime-lover and sun-worshipper. Excellent in a sunny wall and for open sites on the rock garden. The type smothers its loose cushions of grey leaves with bright yellow flowers and there are forms, such as *A.s.citrinum* which is lemon-yellow, and 'Dudley Neville', whose blossoms are orange-buff in colour. All these should be used in moderation and cut back quite severely after flowering.

For more selected positions, but always in full sun, I cherish prostrate *A.montanum* and especially *A.troodii*, a tiny shrublet from Cyprus whose flowers are richly golden, and the ground-hugging *A.wulfenianum*. The nice, spiky hummock with white or soft pink flowers which is still often named *A.spinosum* is more properly named *Ptilotrichum spinosum*.

It may sound slightly ridiculous to speak of *Clematis* for the rock garden, but a beautiful picture can be created if there are largish rocks

Alyssum montanum

and boulders over which *C.alpina* can be allowed to scramble. It will climb in the traditional *Clematis* manner if given the opportunity and will take advantage of any adjacent shrub, into which it will ascend. It has rejoiced us in gardens since 1792, when it was first introduced and it is always a happy day for me when I encounter it in the European Alps (it also grows in Asia), draping rocky outcrops with its far-flung leafy stems, liberally adorned with flowers consisting of four powder-blue sepals centred by a cluster of creamy white petals.

The fence which defends the privacy of my garden from a rather busy road is generously draped with the related *C.macropetala*, which was introduced from either China or Siberia early in this century. Of more robust habit than *C.alpina* and with larger flowers, it really is a very handsome plant. The sepals of its blossoms are powder-blue and the centre of each flower is filled with petal-like segments, the outer ones blue and the inner ones white. In spite of its vigour I also give it the freedom of an area where it can scramble over and between large rocks and boulders. I am tempted to copy an association I saw in an Irish garden, where it had been encouraged to thread its way through the branches of a huge bush of *Kalmia latifolia*. The two lived together very amicably

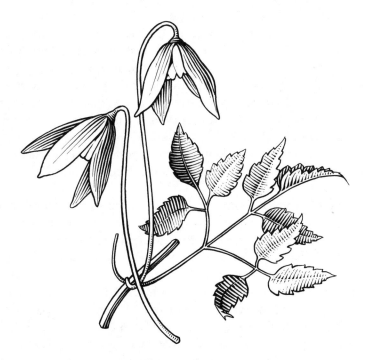

Clematis alpina

and the coexistence of the blue and white flowers of the clematis with the rich pink chalices of the *Kalmia* created a memorable picture.

In that same Irish garden was a marvellous colony of *Phlox* 'Chattahoochee', a recent introduction from North America and supposedly a natural hybrid between *P.divaricata* and *P.pilosa*. I was particularly impressed because it has so far turned a churlish face towards any of my efforts to please it. I gathered a few crumbs of comfort from the fact that others, too, were finding it rather temperamental. That was several years ago and I am happier now that it seems to have accepted captivity—although it is not yet a plant that you can plant and forget. It demands, and deserves, a little extra care and attention. Not particularly dwarf, it has erect and leafy twelve to fifteen-inch stems crowned with loose heads of neatly rounded, inch-wide flowers of deep violet with a purple eye. It obviously found the soft climate and humidity of Ireland very much to its liking and when I created for it an environment as nearly similar as I could, there was an immediate and favourable response.

Having so far rather shamefully neglected such an important family, apart from my dalliance with *P.hoodii* on Calgary golf course, some amends should be made. Another quite recent introduction from America is *P.*'Millsteam'. It, too, is a hybrid which happened in the garden of Lincoln Foster, doyen of American alpine gardeners, whose splendid book *Rock Gardening* (published in America in 1979) is a constant help to me when seeking information about alpines in American gardens. The parentage of *P.*'Millstream' is uncertain, although it is assumed that one of its parents was *P.amoena*. A pretty and accommodating plant, it is dwarfer than *P.*'Chattahoochee', not exceeding six inches in height. The large pink flowers have a white eye, centred by a red star. It is fast becoming a very popular plant and counted a valuable addition to the many phloxes which add so much colour to our rock gardens.

In limited areas of California and Oregon grows *P.adsurgens*, which is thought by those who have succeeded with it to be one of the most beautiful of all alpine phloxes. It is definitely happier in acid soil and appreciates a modicum of shade. It has never really given of its best for me, but my nearest approaches to success have been in a north-facing peat bed, sheltered from cold east winds. Commonsense would seem to dictate that, if a plant really disapproves of what you have to offer, it should be abandoned, but our gardens would be the poorer if we all adopted that policy. I relish the challenge of trying to please any plant which obviously has a very definite opinion of its own as to the conditions in which it can flourish. No effort should be spared to induce *P.adsurgens* to decorate its loose mats of spreading branches with handsome blossoms. The five rounded petals of its large flowers are coloured in shades of pink and peach, and each petal is pencilled with a central stripe of deeper colour. As so often happens with a species there is a form, named 'Waggonwheel' which has larger flowers of richer colour. I do not know if it was discovered in the wild or is a garden selection. It by no means thrusts the type into obscurity, and there is room for both.

No basic planting of any rock garden would be complete without a selection from the many named clones and hybrids of *P.subulata*. It is of considerable historical interest to note that, in 1745, in a letter from John Bartram addressed to one Peter Collinson, the plant was referred to as 'The fine creeping Lychnis'. At that time Linnaeus had not yet made clear the distinctness of Phlox from Lychnis and Collinson named it *Lychnis sempervirens flore rubra*. In 1919 Reginald Farrer wrote: 'The day that saw the introduction, more than a century since, of *P.subulata*, ought indeed to be kept as a horticultural festival.' Widely distributed in North America, *P.subulata* is infinitely variable. I have seen it growing in great colonies and could pick out many quite distinct forms, both in habit and colour of the flowers. Generally speaking it is a cushion-forming plant, forming dense pads and hummocks, on which rest the multitudes of blossoms. It would be quite impossible to select one plant and say 'that is typical *P.subulata*'. It must be regarded as a blanket name covering a whole range of desirable plants.

In gardens during the many decades that *P.subulata* has been cultivated there have been innumerable selections which have been given clonal names. Undoubtedly some of these are of hybrid origin, arising from marriages with *P.douglasii* and perhaps other species too. Any good alpine catalogue will offer you a selection ranging from those with white flowers, through shades of pink to deep red and also blues and purples. Inevitably, over the years, new variants have been raised and named and have flourished for a while and then disappeared or have been superseded. This is unavoidable when a particular plant has to be increased vegetatively by cuttings or division. One is continually propagating the same plant which eventually perishes from sheer old age, a fact which we have to accept with resignation, although the loss of such excellent varieties as, for example, *P.s* 'Vivid' is wholly regrettable. It was a distinct and splendid plant, rather upright in habit, with very bright pink flowers. There are plants under this name, but all of those that I have obtained have been imposters.

There is much confusion in gardens concerning a plant which appears in different gardens and at different times as *P.mesoleuca*, or *P.triovulata* or *P.nana ensifolia*. I am far from clear in my own mind as to which is which and what is what. Dr. Wherry, in his exhaustive monograph on the genus, states that the plant grown in British gardens as *P.mesoleuca* is not that species, but *P.triovulata*. Whatever the truth may be the plant we have is a very beautiful one, but is also one demanding some care and attention. I have never been successful with it in the open and always harbour it in an unheated alpine house. It is a stoloniferous plant and spreads by underground roots, popping up here and there with rather straggling, semi-woody stems, sparsely clothed with narrow leaves. It is not a tidy plant by any means but the flowers are gorgeous—large, perfectly rounded and of a delicious clear pink colour. Grow it in wide, fairly shallow pans, in light, sandy soil and hope for the best. It may delight or disappoint you.

With one exception (a species which is not, I believe, in cultivation) all phloxes are of American origin and we have good reason to be grateful to those who have introduced to us so many good garden plants. Another which also suffers from a plethora of names, is *P.stolonifera*. It can be found in gardens and catalogues as *P.reptans* and *P.procumbens*. It has been more or less supplanted in gardens by two selected forms, *P.s.* 'Blue Ridge' and *P.s.* 'Pink Ridge'. Both grow as rather loose mats from which rise nine or twelve-inch stems ending in panicles of quite large flowers, one a good rich blue and the other pink. There is also a desirable, but rather rare form with pure white flowers.

P.douglasii, like *P.subulata*, is not only variable in itself, but has intermarried with other species, resulting in a number of named clones or hybrids, all compact and cushion-forming—usually more densely hummocky than *P.subulata*, but equally floriferous in a wide range of colours. Also not to be spared from your garden is *P.divaricata* (*canadensis*), especially in the form named *laphamii*, which displays on foot-high stems heads of violet-blue, dark-eyed flowers. It is a trifle large for very small rock gardens but makes a good 'front-of-the-border' plant.

A name change which I regretted more than most was when *Anomatheca cruenta* became *Lapeyrousia laxa*. The name by which I had known it so long translated more or less into 'Bloody Windbag' and that added a touch of amusement to a very charming dwarf bulbous plant. It was as popular with the clergy as was *Saxifraga erioblasta*. Yet another surprisingly hardy South African, it flowers throughout the summer months. From its tiny bulbs rise flat fans of iris-like leaves, and, on four to nine-inch stems are many inch-wide red flowers, marked with deeper colour in the throat. It is easily raised from seed and among the seedlings there are usually a few with white flowers. In nature I believe it is often found growing in rather moist conditions, but in gardens it is quite unfussy as long as its position is open and sunny. It colonizes nicely and self-seeds in moderation.

Whatever you do, do not, unless you happen to be a dedicated botanist or taxonomist, become involved in the genus *Hieraceum*. These are the hawkweeds and, in the *Flora Europaea* there are listed some 2500 names. F. J. Hanbury, whose marvellous natural rock garden at Brockhurst, East Grinstead, is still missed, wrote a very large volume on the genus. It is a race of weeds and, although I unashamedly admit that my own garden contains a number of plants which my friends dismiss with contempt as weeds, there is only one *Hieraceum* that I willingly admit. *H.aurantiacum* is wild in Central Europe, but it has escaped from gardens and become naturalized here and there in Britain, and has acquired the curious common name of 'Grim the Collier'. Weed though it is I like the heads of fiery orange-scarlet flowers and allow it to occupy odd corners here and there. I have always liked the description of *H.pannosum*, which inhabits limestone crevices in the Balkans, but does not seem to be in cultivation. It should make tight clusters of silver-haired leaves adorned with large yellow flower heads.

A plant of which my wife is especially fond is the Winter Aconite, *Eranthis hyemalis*. Always willing to please I made repeated attempts to establish it in my slightly acid soil by planting dry bulbs. Failure attended every effort until the day when I mentioned my problem to a wise old head gardener, who told me that I should obtain plants 'in the green', after they had finished flowering. He generously dug up for me several large clumps. This was the end of failure and the colony thus established is now self-seeding and spreading. It is one of the most cheerful harbingers of spring, along with the snowdrops and snowflakes. Encouraged by this success, I am using the same method to please the form of *E.tubergeniana* named, 'Guinea Gold', which has bronzed leaves and larger flowers on taller stems. Brian Mathew, in his excellent book on dwarf bulbs, has solved an *Eranthis* problem for me. I have never been able to distinguish any pronounced difference between *E.hyemalis* and *E.cilicica* and I am delighted to learn that they are synonymous.

The first time that I saw *Cortusa matthioli* growing plentifully in an alpine coppice, I was sure that it was a *Primula*, a genus to which it is indeed closely related. Never a common plant, it is locally abundant throughout the mountains of Europe and is also to be found in northern Asia. It has an equable temperament and grows contentedly in a cool, lightly shaded place in humus-rich soil and will soon spread into welcome tufts of soft, crinkled, lobed and hairy leaves, from which rise six-inch stems carrying a shower of pendant rose-magenta bells.

How I wish that someone would go to Turkestan and bring back *C.semenovii*. It has smooth leaves and yellow flowers and sounds highly desirable, but is not, as far as I can discover, at present in cultivation. If I am wrong, and anyone has it, or knows where it is being grown, I would be more than grateful for the information.

Should you happen to have an area in your garden, which is shaded and moist and with soil in which few plants will grow, then *Soleirolia soleirolii* is just the plant for you, but avoid it like the plague elsewhere, for it can be a pernicious weed. It is sometimes named *Helxine*. It is, both genetically and specifically named in honour of Joseph Francois

Cortusa matthioli

Soleirol, who appears to have been responsible for its introduction from Corsica. Oddly enough, in spite of many visits to the island, I never saw it growing there. In an appropriate position it will clothe ground which would otherwise be bare with a flat carpet of tiny, rounded, glossily green leaves. I once had to take to pieces an entire rock garden, of which it had taken possession, in order to eradicate it.

In spite of having been grown here since 1694, *Spigelia marilandica* has never achieved much popularity. Perhaps this is partly due to Reginald Farrer's description of it in *The English Rock Garden*, where he dismisses it as a 'mimp'—one of his favourite condemnatory adjectives—with flowers like those of a dingy *Gentian*. Admittedly it is not a plant of startling beauty, but I have always had a fondness for it, and it never fails to arouse interest when the foot-high stems carry terminal clusters of erect, rather tubular flowers, red on the outside and yellow within. It does seem to miss the warmer climate of its native Maryland (U.S.A.) and should occupy a sheltered position or be grown in the alpine house.

Scant attention has, so far, been given to the deservedly loved and popular cyclamens. Such is the diversity of their season of flowering that it is possible to have a *Cyclamen* in blossom at almost any time of the year. Most of them are hardy and will colonize happily, but a minority need winter protection. One of the most handsome of these is *C.graecum*, but even this will survive out of doors in a chosen position. I remember seeing it growing in the garden of Sir Frederic Stern at Highdown, on the Sussex coast. The tubers had been tucked underneath stones in the rock garden, made in a chalk quarry, and came through every winter without harm. The leaf shape and marking in *C.graecum* is infinitely variable and always superb. The flowers too, vary from soft rose to deep pink, but there are always two plum-purple blotches at the base of the petals, from which run pink veins almost to the tips of the petals. It inhabits the mainland of Greece, with variants on many of the islands.

For a continuity of blossom you could begin with *C.repandum* in the spring (already described in an earlier chapter), followed by *C.purpuras-cens (europaeum)* whose fragrant flowers of rose-pink carmine appear in the summer, to be followed in the autumn by *C.hederifolium (neapolitanum)*. *C.coum* should really be regarded as a blanket name covering a diversity of plants which are a continuing problem to the taxonomist. The group has a wide distribution through eastern Europe, the Caucasus, Asia Minor and Iran, each region having its own version. They are all delightful and flower during late winter and spring.

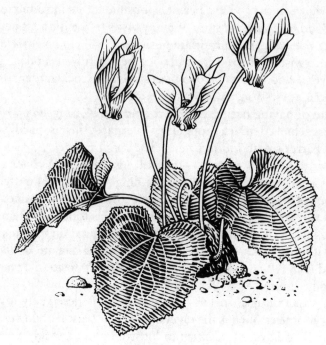

Cyclamen graecum

Confined to the Lebanon, where it is now extremely rare, is *C.libanoticum*. Definitely not hardy, it is perhaps the most beautiful of all. The large, lobed leaves are nicely patterned and beetroot-red on the undersides. In February and March the flowers appear with broad petals of clear rose-pink. There is a garden in Dorset where it grows in the open and self-seeds, but this is exceptional and not to be attempted unless your garden is sheltered and able to cope with half-hardy plants. It is safe enough in an unheated alpine house.

Even more uncommon, with a very limited distribution in Libya, is *C.rohlfsianum*. This too, is not hardy enough to be grown outside. In nature it inhabits rocky crevices and receives a complete summer baking and should be kept really dry during its resting period. The pink flowers, with pointed and slightly twisted petals, appear in the autumn. It will make an enormous corky-skinned tuber which has growing points here and there over the surface. It can be increased by cutting the tubers into pieces, each with one of these growing points, an unusual facility in cyclamens.

A matter of never failing interest—and considerable frustration—to alpine gardeners is the cussedness of *Gentiana acaulis*, which will flower magnificently it one situation, and never display a blossom in another, sometimes only a few yards away. I remember a nursery in Hertfordshire whose entrance drive was bordered on each side by a solid edging of *G.acaulis*. One side was blue with flowers each year, on the other side hardly a flower was ever seen.

Some years ago, when visiting the Botanic Gardens in Munich, I made a side trip to the Weihenstephener Experimental Gardens, then in the charge of Dr. Hansen. He, too, was intrigued by this unexplained characteristic and had gathered together plants from many sources and was growing them in a diversity of soils and situations. In later correspondence Dr. Hansen told me that, after several years, he abandoned the experiment; he could come to no definite conclusions, or discover any viable reason for this curious behaviour. The only answer, which seems ridiculous, is to move your gentians if they do not flower, even if only a yard at a time, and eventually you will find a place where they will produce and delight you with their glorious trumpets.

It was during my footloose years spent at the feet of the Maritime Alps that I first made the acquaintance in the wild of *Globularia cordifolia*. It was already a familiar friend in my father's nursery but there is always a tremendous thrill in meeting a well-known plant in its native habitat for the first time. The woody stems are crowded into entangled compact hummocks and set with small, leathery, dark green leaves gently notched at their tips. On short stems are balls of many tiny blue flowers. It will remember the hot and dry mountainsides on which it grew and relishes a sunny spot, liking to spread its stems over adjacent stones.

There are other nice globularias too. *G.repens* (*nana*) from Southwest Europe is like a condensed *G.cordifolia*, smaller in all its parts, and with similar requirements—a confirmed sun-lover. Rather bolder is *G.trichosantha*, which comes from the Balkans. Its broader, dark green leaves are thrice notched at the tips and the prominent heads of bright blue flowers are borne on nine-inch stems. *G.meridionalis* (*bellidifolia*) is also European but spreads into Asia as well. In most respects it is much like *G.cordifolia*, but the leaves are without the terminal notch. From the sun-baked mountains of Greece comes *G.stygia*, which is the smallest of all. Just a tangled film of woody stems and dark, tiny leaves on which rest blue powder-puffs of flowers.

Every garden has its quota of gravestones, representing plants which have been loved and lost. One of mine is the monument to *Globularia spinosa*, which I grew for a number of years with only modest success until its demise; since when I have been unable to replace it. It grows in

Spain and I have had small pieces sent to me by friends who found it
there, but it is a woody-rooted plant which resents disturbance and
should only be collected as seed. It is not the most beautiful plant you
ever saw, but I was fascinated by its iron hard tufts of holly-like leaves
and could ignore the rather dowdy-blue flower heads on lanky stems.

Another Spaniard which I have managed to keep alive through many
hard winters is curious little *Vella spinosa*, a crucifer which forms a
rounded bush of rigid branchlets, becoming spiky as they age. Plants are
acquired by all sorts of roundabout routes. My original plant of
V.spinosa was given to me by Joel Spingarn, when I visited his
wonderful collection of conifers on Long Island. It travelled with me in
America for several weeks, immured in a plastic bag but showed no
resentment and that original plant is still alive. It is another plant which
will cause no cries of excitement, but is a pleasant sight when the
bushlets are smothered with pale yellow flowers. I have not tried it in the
open but I believe, if I had the courage to plant it in a hot dry place, that
it would survive.

There was a time when, if you looked at the exhibits of alpine plants
at the Chelsea Flower Show, you would be certain to see displayed the
glorious purple trumpets of *Wahlenbergia serpyllifolia* 'Major'. This
exceptionally fine form of the type was launched a great many years ago
and, because it has to be propagated by cuttings, has gradually lost its
vigour and is now a rare plant. The weakly plants of it which are
sometimes to be had, stand little chance of survival and I fear that this is
one good rock garden plant which has to be written off and will live only
in the memories of those who once counted it among the best alpine
plants. It has lost, not only its health, but its name, for it is now correctly
included in the genus *Edraianthus*. There has always been confusion
between the two genera, but there is one easily distinguished difference
between them: the flowers of *Wahlenbergia* are carried singly, whereas
those of *Edraianthus* are in clusters.

What a delight it is, when walking in boggy areas of Britain, to see
gleaming from herbage at your feet the pale blue stars of *Wahlenbergia
hederacea*. Very different to the commanding beauty of *W.serpyllifolia*,
it is a shy, frail plant, once included in the genus *Campanula*. Grow it in
a moist, cool spot and it will spread about contentedly and it does
appreciate small companions with whom it can mingle its prostrate
stems. It is always a pleasure to welcome a newcomer and *Wahlenbergia
gloriosa*, a recent introduction from the Kosciusko Mountains of
Australia is fast becoming a favourite and as it becomes better known
and widely distributed, will be desired by everyone who sees it. It grows

in the form of a leafy bush, some nine to twelve inches high and its erect stems terminate in large richly purple flowers. Its absolute hardiness has yet to be proven, but it has just survived a particularly vicious winter with me in the open and shows only minor signs of distress.

Whenever I pass a specimen of the gigantic *Gunnera manicata* (or the slightly smaller *chilensis*) I think with amusement of the species which I grow and which are so very, very different. The frame of a small garden will not compass *G.manicata* whose immense, rhubarb-like leaves can measure a metre or more in diameter, but for the rock gardener there are some completely dwarf, almost mat-forming species which, without being spectacular, are great fun. Any of the following will amuse you: *G.magellanica*, from South America and *G.arenaria* and *G.dentata*, both from New Zealand. It must be realized, however, that if left unprotected through a very cold winter, they can suffer. Even giant *G.manicata* has its great leaves folded down over the robust crowns as a winter blanket.

With one exception all the plants we have long known as lithospermums are now either lithodoras or moltkias. Our good old friend *L.prostratum* 'Heavenly Blue' is now *Lithodora diffusa* 'H.B.'. The genus has undergone a thorough taxonomic shake-up, but old dogs do not learn new tricks easily and we who are approaching our final decades will, I am sure, continue to use the familiar names. Our very good old friend 'Heavenly Blue' is another victim of old age. It has, for so many, many generations been increased by cuttings that its vigour is fading. Fortunately it has been more or less superseded by a selected clone named 'Grace Ward'. A lusty plant, it has all the merits of the older clone but also shares its aversion to lime. This is curious, for I have seen the type plant growing wild on limestone rocks. Given a sunny position and lime-free soil, no plant will provide a more gorgeous sheet of azure flowers.

When I first saw the yellow-flowered *L.canescens* growing in North America I was enchanted and did not rest until I had secured a few plants. I am not sure into which genus it has now been shunted, but in any case it has persistently refused to do more for me than to make a few straggly branches, terminating occasionally in clusters of orange-yellow flowers. In fact, I have finally admitted defeat until someone can tell me how to make it flourish, as I dearly wish it would.

Much more satisfying has been the behaviour of the Pyrenean *L.oleifolium* a wanderer by means of running, underground stems, which emit scattered tufts of rounded leaves clothed in a pelt of fine grey hairs and cymes of flowers, sometimes pink in bud, but expanding into flowers of clear light blue. The habit of following pink buds by blue flowers is a common characteristic of many of Boraginaceae, the family to which *Lithospermum* belongs.

Let no one persuade you to plant our native *L.purpureo-caeruleum* among choicer neighbours, for it is an inveterate spreader, throwing its leafy, prostrate stems a yard or more in every direction. I find it useful when it is used to cover the ground between and beneath shrubs with a summer carpet of green leaves and bright blue flowers. It is not evergreen and the long bare stems are unsightly and should be cut back to base before the spring. It, too, has suffered taxonomically, and is now supposed to bear the cumbersome name *Buglossoides purpureo-caerulea*.

I almost fear to embark upon the genus *Corydalis*, for they are very particualr favourites of mine and I am sure to be tempted to continue singing their praises *ad nauseam*. They are too important to be ignored and I will try to restrain my enthusiasm to a few special pets. A very special treasure is *C.transsilvanica*, perhaps a sub-species of *C.solida*. From a large, curiously shaped, almost square tuber, it emits clusters of cleft leaves and short, erect racemes of terracotta-pink flowers. If it is good enough to provide a few seeds and you sow these, the resulting plants may have flowers ranging from the characteristic colour to mauves and purples. I first made its acquaintance many years ago when one tuber was given to my father by Sir William Lawrence. All our efforts to increase it failed. It retained its one tuber and gave no seeds until one spring, when shaking it free of soil before repotting, the one tuber was found to have divided into two. From then on there was an annual fifty per cent increase and finally, it also began to set viable seed. It remains a great rarity to be eagerly acquired, whatever its often terrifying price may be.

Ther are no problems with *C.wilsonii*, which came to us from China in the early years of this century. From deeply delving roots rise clusters of grey, fern-like foliage amidst which rise foot-high stems bearing racemes of canary-yellow flowers. I think of it as rather a Cinderella which is not appreciated as fully as it deserves to be for it possesses all the virtues we demand from a good garden plant. The foliage is attractive, the flowers are beautiful and it is easy to grow; what more could one ask?

In the flower-filled high valleys of Kashmir grows startlingly lovely *C.cashmiriana*. It is a frail plant with low tufts of blue-green, deeply divided leaves from which rise four to six-inch stems carrying a few flowers of glacier-blue. That is the form in general cultivation; in the

Corydalis wilsonii

wild it is said to occur with yellow or white flowers. It is slightly
capricious, succeeding here and failing there for no apparent reason. In
general I think it is far happier grown in humus-rich soil and a cool
position out of doors than it is when cosseted in an alpine house. I shall
never forget the sight of a square yard of it in flower in the garden of
Keillour Castle in Scotland. Like other Asian plants it does seem to have
a preference for the humid atmosphere of northern Britain.

Yet another Cinderella is *C.nobilis*, which comes from cold Siberia
and is understandably hardy. It has thick and fleshy roots and produces
a few deeply dissected leaves and nine-inch stems carrying spherical
racemes of yellow flowers with dark marking at the tips of the petals. It
will live and increase very happily in gritty, but not impoverished soil
and a sunny position.

Our native *Geranium sanguineum*, sometimes named (quite without
offence) the Bloody Cranesbill, is overlarge for most rock gardens. Its
local variant, *G.s.lancastriense*, however, qualifies for inclusion in any
select list of indispensable rock garden plants. The widespread mats of

Geranium sanguineum lancastriense

leafy stems form a green backcloth for the innumerable wide, saucer shaped flowers of salmon-pink. It is one of those easy and decorative plants which every garden should have. Even if there is no rock garden for it to inhabit, it can be grown in cracks between paving stones, in walls, or even as an edging to a flower bed.

There is special welcome in all gardener's hearts for plants which begin to flower even before the rigours of winter have passed and help to alleviate the grief we may be feeling for some winter-slaughtered treasure. *Omphalodes verna* has inhabited our gardens since the early years of the seventeenth century and has never outgrown its welcome. As the snowdrops fade it produces tufts of fresh green leaves over which are many short stems bearing clusters of cheerful blue flowers. It is not a sun-lover and likes best to be grown in light shade, where it will colonize contentedly. It has also a rather nice form with pure white blossoms.

Usually a trifle later and slightly taller, is *O.cappadocica*—still sometimes found under the name *O.cornifolia*. The bright blue flowers are carried in showers over the heart-shaped green leaves. We have good reason to be grateful to the members of the Borage family, so many of which have flowers of unsullied blue, a colour not too common. A particular treasure is *O.luciliae,* an aristocrat from cliffs in Greece. Not a plant to receive cavalier treatment, it should be provided with lime-containing soil and a sunny chink between stones in which to develop its rather pendant stems, clad with glabrous, blue-grey leaves and loose racemes of sky-blue flowers. It is not usually regarded as one of the easiest plants to please and can confound the experts. I remember once being invited to visit a garden belonging to an eccentric 'Lady of the Manor', which I found to be immaculately tidy and completely uninteresting—until I came to the kitchen garden. This was divided into a number of symmetrical beds, each one of which was bordered by edgings of *O.luciliae*! I do believe that we are sometimes over zealous in our attempts to please a plant which has the reputation of being 'difficult'. A little wholesome neglect is sometimes the recipe for success. I remember a particular, reputedly very 'difficult' plant with which we struggled for a number of years but which resisted all our blandishments. Finally losing patience I consigned it to the rubbish heap, where, some months later, it was found to have established very happily.

Every now and then a plant makes a brief appearance, and then disappears. I was intrigued some years ago by *Arnica nana* which was exhibited at one of the Alpine Garden Society's exhibitions. It was much admired but now seems to have lapsed into obscurity. I know nothing of its provenance and would like to have news of it, for it was a nice, dwarf, golden-flowered plant. The members of this small genus are found in Europe and North America, and the European *A.montana* is the most handsome. Confined to lime-free areas in alpine pastures, it makes rosettes of oval, hairy leaves and, on quite tall stems, carries large flowers of rich gold colour. It is, of course, the plant from which the medicinal tincture of arnica is made. For those with alkaline soil an alternative is *A.alpina* from North America which displays no aversion to lime. It is not quite so boldly handsome as *A.montana* but is good enough to be accepted as a substitute. A pleasing association in an alpine meadow is to grow arnicas in companionship with the bearded bellflower, *Campanula barbata.* They grow very amicably together and provide a nice mingling of soft blue and yellow flowers.

There are certain aromatic plants for which cats have an absolute passion and *Teucrium subspinosum* is a nice, dwarf, spiny shrublet which I have had to abandon, for it is destroyed by our cats rolling on it and eating it. Only a few inches in height, its thin twiggy branches become hard and spiny and on them are tiny, grey, aromatic leaves. In summer the whole bushlet is spangled with small pink flowers, but, unless I surround it with a cat-proof barricade it is always decimated.

The common Catmint, *Nepeta* × *faasssenii* is also popular with cats. We once were ruled over by a Siamese, for whom we had to buy a new *Nepeta* every year because she kept it permanently eaten to the ground.

We keep cats to combat the mice, and we have a very sophisticated breed of mice who we are convinced, are able to read our catalogue and select the rarest and most expensive varieties of *Crocus*, for those are the ones which they burrow down to and consume before moving on to the commoner kinds. I am devastated to discover that they have now developed a taste for the bulbs of *Nomocharis* and have destroyed the few colonies I managed to grow.

These bulbs with such enchantingly beautiful flowers do not grow as well in the south as they do in the humid north. I so well remember my first visit to the treasure-filled garden in Scotland of Andrew Harley. As I drove into the drive I was halted by a small gentleman energetically using a hoe on the drive surface. He introduced himself as the owner of the garden and apologized for the obstruction, saying 'I was hoeing out the damned *Nomocharis*, which will seed themselves all over the place'. For a long time after that I did not even try to grow them, but inevitably eventually succumbed to the irresistible urge to try to persuade them that it wasn't as bad as all that down here in Sussex. Now I shall have to start all over again.

By no stretch of the imagination could the Edelweiss, *Leontopodium alpinum* be described as a beautiful flower and yet it has so captured the imagination of those who love and grow alpine plants that it is symbolic of mountain flowers. In parts of Switzerland it is known as the Bridal Flower and it is traditional for a bridegroom to risk life and limb by gathering flowers of the Edelweiss for his bride to be. That such gallantry is unnecessary seems not to matter, for the plant grows plentifully on open alpine pastures. It is almost as traditional that *L.alpinum* should be planted on every rock garden. Not that I object, for I am very fond of it despite its lack of flamboyant beauty. From low tufts of narrow grey leaves rise erect stems ending in a head of tiny florets, the outer ones female and the inner ones male. These are surrounded by silver-haired bracts. If anyone tells you that it is difficult to grow, do not believe them. It thrives in any good soil and a sunny position.

There is another Edelweiss, *L.haplophylloides* this time from the Himalayas. It is similarly unimposing in appearance, but the whole plant is strongly lemon-scented. Of yet another I hardly dare write, for it is only dubiously in cultivation, which is unfortunate, for it is a real beauty. It is a form of *L.alpinum* named *crassense* and it was introduced from Eastern Europe by my father many years ago. Only an inch or two

Leontopodium alpinum

in height, its foliage is intensely silver and the flower head is large and glistening white. I know that it still exists in the Munich Botanic Garden, and it may be in the gardens of a few amateurs, but it is certainly not in general cultivation.

How sad it is that so many good plants are brought into cultivation, stay with us for a while, and then drift into obscurity. It behoves everyone who gardens to seek out and preserve any of them that can be discovered. It is to be hoped that the newly formed National Council for the Protection of Plants and Gardens will serve a useful purpose in this service of conservation, so necessary in these days when nurseries are producing more and more of less and less, and the rarities, not likely to be in great demand, are abandoned in favour of plants which can be easily propagated and popularized.

High in the mountains of Iran can be found aged plants of *Gypsophila aretioides*. I remember in particular one enormous cushion measuring many feet in diameter which must have been centuries old. It was iron-hard and when I stood on it, wearing nailed climbing boots, no impression at all was made on the packed rosettes of tiny green leaves.

There is an even more condensed form to be found in the Caucasus. This was introduced to cultivation by my father, many years ago and is now a treasured inhabitant of many alpine houses. Both the type and its condensed Caucasian form are easy to grow, but they are very, very slow. My own largest specimen now measures nine inches in diameter and is more than twenty years old. In gardens it tends to be shy flowering, usually offering only a spattering of the stemless white flowers but it is such a fascinating hummock that it may be excused this small fault.

Other, perhaps more commonplace, but very worthy gypsophilas exist, mostly as forms of *G.repens*, of which *fratensis* and 'Rosea' are especially good, both of trailing habit and with pink flowers. 'Monstrosa' is more robust and will cascade from a crevice with sheets of white flowers. *G.cerastioides* is a neatness from the Himalayas which is almost cushion-forming with close tufts of soft leaves and white flowers veined with pink.

One might well wonder to see a holly commended as a rock garden shrub, but there is an endearing pygmy, *Ilex crenata* 'Mariesii' which will never outgrow its welcome, however small the rock garden. It even qualifies as a shrublet for a sink or trough garden. The type is Japanese, but I have been unable to trace the provenance of this clone beyond the fact that it is said to have been distributed originally by the famous firm of Veitch about 1879. When, in 1947, to the sorrow of his many friends, Dr. Paul Giuseppi died, his great collection of alpine plants was auctioned and a great many of his rarest specimens still exist in the gardens of those who bought them at the sale. One of my own purchases was a foot-high plant of *I.crenata* 'Mariesii' and this I still possess and, in the intervening years it has added little more than a foot to its stature. Of rigidly erect habit, its woody stems are closely covered with small, round, leathery dark green leaves. The inconspicuous flowers are often followed by glossy black berries.

My father counted Paul Giuseppi one of his closest friends, and they travelled widely together. A small man, of tremendous and ebullient energy, he was an amusing companion. His fiery temperament ensured that there was never a dull moment in his company and occasionally produced some slightly embarrassing situations when he was confronted by officialdom when moving from one country to another. He was a doyen of alpine growers and the gap left by his death has not been filled, and probably never will, for there could not be two Paul Giuseppis.

Even when March comes in like a lion, its stormiest, wettest day is brightened for me when I see the first signs of life on funny little

Hacquetia (*Dondia*) *epipactis*, a curious little umbellifer and the only species of its genus. From its winter rest below ground it emerges with tiny tufts of three-foliate leaves and heads of golden flowers set on a circle of green leaves. It looks just like a small fried egg on a green platter. It comes from the European Alps and likes to grow in a cool, lightly shaded position or to have a northerly aspect.

A worthy companion to the Gods who dwell on Mount Olympus is the fabulous *Jankaea heldreichii*. A close relative of the ramondas, it has the same flattish rosettes of leaves, but they are coated with a pelt of silver hairs and the short stems carry several bell-shaped flowers of crystalline-blue. The gods must love it too, and cast a spell upon those who wrest it from the cliffs on which it grows, for it is not easy to please in gardens and the occasional successes are regarded as great triumphs. Treasure it in the alpine house, or, if you dare, wedge it into a narrow cleft between rocks.

A wave of excitement is sweeping through the higher echelons of alpine gardeners at the reappearance of an almost mythical bigeneric hybrid between *Jankaea* and *Ramonda*. It was created, many years ago, by a Mr. Van der Dem, and distributed by the famous Correvon nursery in Geneva. It seemed to have been lost but is again being grown in this country by one or two skilled enthusiasts. It has been cursed by the rather clumsy name *Jankaemonda vanderdemii*. We hold our breath and hope that it can be increased and distributed.

It is always a pleasure to find a place in the garden for a few of our own native plants, being careful, of course, always to choose those which are available as nursery or garden grown stock so that there is no danger of depleting the ever shrinking native flora. Few of these are alpines in the true sense of the word but there are some which fall comfortably into the pattern of rock gardening. As a ground-coverer for a cool, even slightly moist position I delight in a spreading mat of *Lysimachia nummularia* 'Aurea'. This is the golden-leaved form of our wild Creeping Jenny. The small yellow flowers are of no great importance, but the colourful foliage brings radiance into a shady area.

Another friendly little wanderer is *Maianthemum bifolium*. Only dubiously a native, it has so successfully established itself here and there that it really qualifies to be accepted as a British plant. Its white roots spread vigorously in all directions and from them in the spring rise twin heart-shaped bright green leaves and four-inch stems bearing plumes of fluffy white flowers. Its mobility should be borne in mind and a generous amount of space allotted. It relishes the same conditions as the *Lysimachia* and has no liking for a hot and sunny situation.

There are people who seem to have a special relationship with plants. They can break all the rules and achieve success. Such a one was Frederick Millard, from whom I learned a great deal when as a young man I was just beginning to walk along the path of dedicated gardening. His particular delight was to grow plants which others found difficult and some of his results were quite astonishing. He took no heed of text-book gardening and followed no conventional methods. He would grow shade-lovers in the sun and took a perverse pleasure in side-stepping traditional methods; such was his affinity with plants that he usually got away with it. He did, of course, have failures, we all do and they do no more than to spur us on to further efforts. Whereas we all provided *Epigaea repens* with a cool, lightly shaded position, Millard planted it in full sun and I remember a group of pundits being shocked by a yard-wide mat of it. My own efforts to persuade it to grow in such unlikely conditions met with complete failure. What was it that that man had and we had not? Browsing through a list of the plants in his garden published in 1934, I read of *Uniola latifolia, Zephyranthes ochroleuca, Werneria pygmaea, Podolepsis acuminata, Polygala paucifolia, Rhexia mariana, Helonias erythrospermum, Leptodactylon nicholsii,* and many other treasures. Where could one find those today?

Among the few plants with which I have a sort of love-hate relationship, is that pernickety little shrub *Trochocarpa thymifolia*. Like a lot of other good plants it comes from Tasmania, and like other Antipodean plants it is not absolutely hardy, although even here it is capricious. I have known plants in the open, with no protection, survive really severe winters, and yet be badly damaged after a comparatively mild winter. The rigid, erect, woody stems are thickly clad with tiny, pointed, hard, dark green leaves. In the spring the growing tips are pink and at the same time the flower buds appear, looking like small bunches of minute red grapes. These eventually expand into red, yellow-edged, bell-shaped flowers. It is an enticing and exciting plant and, if you do not care to risk it in the open, it is quite happy grown in a pot or pan in the alpine house.

There are euphorbias to suit all tastes, for the members of this huge genus range from annual herbs to stout herbaceous perennials, trees, shrubs and even succulents. Few of them are suitable for rock gardens and I have already issued a warning to be cautious with *Euphorbia cyparissias*. The only other species that qualifies is *E.myrsinites*, a quite spectacular plant from Southern Europe. To be seen at its best it should be allowed to trail over the face of a sunny wall. From its deeply delving roots spring long, snake-like branches clothed in closely packed spirals of fleshy, scale-like leaves. Every stem ends in a cluster of yellow bracts and flowers. It demands a lot of space but does not spread far afield like *E.cyparissias.* Like all euphorbias it exudes a milky sap when damaged and this can cause blisters on sensitive skins.

Few seem to sing the praises of tiny little annual *Ionopsidium acaule,* which is a shame. I first fell in love with it when I saw it growing in Southern Portugal many years ago. It was introduced in 1845 and has maintained a tenuous hold in cultivation but is too seldom included in seed lists. A tiny plant, never more than two inches high, it gives a long summer display of crowded lilac flowers. It is permissible in a sunny pocket on the rock garden but I prefer to sow it in the crannies between paving stones and enjoy the colourful ribbons it so easily and generously provides. It is a good plant for a child's garden for it gives quick results and will be in flower only a few weeks after sowing.

Thoughts of Portugal remind me of a plant which has never taken kindly to gardens. At the southern tip of Portugal, on Cape St. Vincent, grows *Polygala microphylla*—or that was what it was named when I was first enchanted by its beauty. Now, I believe, it is correctly *Brachytropis microphylla.* I have made repeated attempts to persuade it that life in an English garden is bearable but have never kept it for more than a year or two. Conditions in its native habitat induced the thought that a somewhat spartan diet would be acceptable, for it grew in hot, dry places in sandy, gritty soil. When this was spurned I gave it a richer

Euphorbia myrsinites

compost, but to no avail. Whenever I can obtain a few seeds I keep on trying, for it is too good a plant to be abandoned. Its bushes, of no more than a few inches in height are composed of hard, woody stems which are concealed in summer beneath myriads of flowers of vivid gentian-blue. Sometime, somehow, we must discover the secret of growing it.

It must already be apparent that plants which flower very early in the year have a special place in my affections and one whose claims cannot be ignored is the Japanese *Polygonum tenuicaule*. It surprises me that such an easily grown harbinger of spring is not more widely known. Any not too hot corner will please it and induce it to spread into low tufts, decorated with cylindrical racemes of small white flowers, as soon as the snowdrops and snowflakes have faded. It is no peacock, but has a comely attractiveness.

Plantago major, the common and ubiquitous plantain which we endeavour to remove from our lawns, or wherever else it seeds itself, has at least one aristocratic relation and the family should not be damned because of one misbehaving member. *P.nivalis* is a well-behaved neatness with rosettes of narrow leaves densely felted with silver hairs. No plantain has flowers with any pretence to beauty, but the almost black flower-heads of *P.nivalis* are effective against the silver foliage. *P.argentea*, too, is worth growing and can be described as a rather less neat and tidy version of *P.nivalis*. Either can be planted with confidence, for they are modest in their habits and do not spread their progeny in all directions.

Just for fun, but certainly not on the rock garden, I like to grow a few plants of the Rose Plantain, which is probably a form of *P.media*. Instead of flowers it carries at the tip of what should be the flower stems a neat rosette of small green leaves—in array as orderly as a Victorian posy—but beware of an imposter, a mutant of *P.major*, which does the same thing in a much less neat and orderly manner. A present long ago from E. A. Bowles's collection of lunatic plants, was the red-leaved plantain which forms a robust rosette of leaves of beetroot-red. It is coarse, but amusing and colourful. Admittedly it is no more beautiful than a beetroot, but who wants to grow a beetroot in the flower border?

Life would be a lot easier for those of us who like to keep our taxonomy reasonably up to date, if botanists would come to a decision and stick to it. The plant I used to grow as *Jeffersonia dubia* gave me great pleasure, as well it might, for it is a plant with very lovely flowers. Then I was told it should be *Plagiorrhegma dubia*, but, no sooner had I altered all my labels, when back it went into the genus *Jeffersonia*. I promise myself to ignore any future shuffling from genus to genus.

J.dubia, curiously belonging to Berberidaceae hails from Manchurian woodlands, and rests during the winter as a rather woody root, from which rise on wiry stems rounded, grey-green leaves. On similar thin wiry stems are solitary, cup-shaped blue flowers. It likes gritty, but humus-rich soil and, if you wish to gather the seeds they must be watched for: the flowers as they fade, tend to be hidden by the elongating leaf stems. There is another, North American species, *J.diphylla*, which has had an equally uneasy taxonomic existence, having been named, at various times, *J.binata* and *Podophyllum diphyllum*. Perhaps not quite such an aristocrat as *J.dubia*, it is a pleasant occupant of a cool, lightly shaded position with round leaves deeply cleft into two lobes, and solitary, quite large white flowers.

My few plants of *Sarcopoterium (Poterium) spinosum*, evoke rueful memories of the day when, climbing on one of Sardinia's hot dry mountains, I stepped on a loose stone and fell, rolling several yards before I came to rest on a cushion of this viciously spiky shrublet. When I extricated myself from a decidedly uncomfortable resting place I saw that there were ripe seeds, which I collected. My present plants consist of the resultant seedlings. Never really happy in the open in British gardens, it makes an interesting alpine house specimen, especially when the thorny, wiry, iron-hard stems produce solitary crimson flowers in the leaf axils. I fear it is yet another of the plants which does not interest nurserymen who feel they must concentrate upon plants which are easy to propagate and sure to be in demand. The survival of the species depends upon the dedication of a few specialist nurseries and the interest of amateur gardeners, upon whom we rely more and more for the preservation of rare plants. It is vitally important that anyone fortunate enough to possess a rarity should increase it and distribute it into as many hands as possible. Too often I have known a single specimen of a choice plant to be jealously guarded and gloated over—only to die and disappear.

Colour in the last months of the year is as important as it is in the beginning. If ever I am confronted with a searingly hot and dry position I colonize it with *Zauschneria californica*. Elsewhere it may make lush growth, flower less abundantly and possibly perish in the winter. Known in its native America as the Californian Fuchsia, it provides a splash of vivid colour in tune with the warm tints of autumn. The floppy, twiggy bushes of wiry stems and grey leaves are concealed beneath countless tubular scarlet flowers. It has an albino form which interests but does not enthral me.

Although the richest and most abundant alpine flora is found on limestone formations, there are glorious exceptions, and one of these is *Geum reptans*. To discover it you must explore Europe's non-calcareous mountains. There, on the high shingles, growing in what would seem to be a very spartan diet indeed, are the loose rosettes of pinnatifid leaves from which spring lengthy, red, strawberry runners, terminating in small clusters of leaves which eventually take root and spread the colony. Borne singly, on six-inch stems are enormous rounded flowers with overlapping petals and of the richest imaginable golden colour. It is precariously in cultivation but too often succumbs as a result of an over-generous diet.

It is all too easy to overfeed high alpine plants which are accustomed to seek far and wide for sustenance and, for that purpose, develop root systems disproportionate to the growth above the ground. Given a rich diet, too easily assimilated, they grow fat and lush and uncharacteristic and perish from sheer over indulgence. Give *Geum reptans* a compost which is at least fifty per cent stone chippings—lime-free, of course—and you may hope for success.

Less demanding is *G.montanum*, found at lower elevations in the mountains. Less of an aristocrat, it is easily pleased and rewarding. Its dense tufts of rounded and softly hairy leaves emit erect, short stems carrying large, rounded yellow flowers. To be sought, and cherished if found, is a form, *G.m.* 'Maximum' which was once found in the Eastern Alps. The variant is of special magnificence, having taller stems and larger flowers, and has a special significance for me: it was first discovered by my father. Sadly, I have lost it and would be overjoyed to learn of its whereabouts. Many plants of it were distributed from my nursery and it surely must still exist in someone's garden.

When business or pleasure takes me to Cornwall I never tire of exploring those splendid Cornish hedges—really walls which have become so densely clothed with vegetation that no stone is visible. In them you may find the dainty white, green-striped flowers of *Allium triquetrum* and sometimes, a great treasure, blue-flowered forms of *Anemone nemorosa*. As you near the coast the walls sometimes have bare tops and there may be dense sheets of *Sedum anglicum*, and mats of entangled leafy stems aglow with stemless pink flowers. This is *Glaux maritima*, a daintiness which is perfectly admissible in the rock garden, or tucked into a corner of a trough or sink garden. It is a monotypic genus and, apart from its British maritime stations, can be found in many northern temperate regions. It is another example of a plant which can be spoiled by a too generous compost. In rich soil it will become loose and much less attractive than when starved into a characteristic compact habit. It will not be found in any garden centre and few catalogues list it, but a few seeds gathered when they ripen in mid to late summer, will provide plenty of young plants.

If you can find a few pieces of half-rotten, punky wood, save them to place in the bottom of a large pot or pan and then seek a plant of *Lysionotus pauciflorus* and set it, in humus-rich soil, over the decaying wood. This rare Japanese sub-shrub is a saprophite and its roots will eagerly seek the mouldering wood. On its erect, woody, foot-high stems are narrow, dark green leaves, from the axils of which spring handsome pendant tubular flowers, as much as two inches long, of lilac colour veined with darker tints. I have tried to establish it in a peat bed, but without much success and now confine it to an unheated alpine house.

Plant associations from the decorative angle have been widely written about and discussed, but less is known of association from the angle of compatibility. As I have said in previous chapters, I am convinced that many plants benefit from a close association with others, and not necessarily of the same species, genus or even family. As far as I know there has been no organized research into this theory and my own opinions are based only on observation over many years and a comparison between the manner in which plants grow in nature and that in which we cultivate them. I have seen, for example, how well certain plants grew when they were planted in an alpine lawn, cheek by jowl with all sorts of neighbours, whereas when planted in solitary state in a pocket of the rock garden they were obviously much less pleased with life. Can it be that there is some symbiosis between plants making them dependent, perhaps not for existence, but for their well-being, upon a close association between their roots and those of others? We know that such symbiosis exists in fungi and lichens and I see no reason why it should not extend, to some extent, into the area of flowering plants.

This is all guesswork, based only on observation with no proven facts and I believe that there is a useful field of research for someone or some organization equipped to collect data and make experiments. There are all sorts of bits of fragmentary knowledge and theory which should be gathered together. I was recently asked why it was that heather cuttings rooted more successfully in soil in which heathers had grown than when given the standard treatment and inserted in sand. I could only give the rather feeble answer that it was probably due to the presence of some mycelium in the soil.

As I approach the final pages of this book I become more and more conscious of the many plants which I have omitted. To include all those about which I could happily enthuse would demand a multi-volume book. I can only now, in the space remaining to me, dig once more into that deep rag-bag of memories and bring forth the neglected ones which most urgently demand praise. The entire family of anemones for example cries out for mention and, in particular, that section of the genus which is now included in *Pulsatilla*. On the Chiltern chalk hills can be found our own Pasque Flower, *P.vulgaris*; it is now accepted as a native but was probably originally introduced by the Romans. The species is widely distributed in Europe in a number of distinct forms and flowers varying in colour from white through shades of blue and purple to pink and almost red. The blossoms rise on twelve-inch stems over sturdy tufts of finely-cut leaves. Our own is a midget, growing in turf and from its few carrot-like leaves rise, on very short stems, flowers rather like those of a purple crocus. Like all of its kind it relishes full sun and soil containing lime. From seeds collected in the Chilterns I have, over the years, grown many hundreds of it, but have never seen any colour variation.

One of the glories of European alpine meadows is stately *P.alpina* which emits from its bold clumps of ferny foilage tall stems crowned with large, snow-white flowers. It has a sub-species with yellow flowers which is commonly found growing on granitic formations but in gardens it will accept at least a modest alkalinity. All the plants in this genus object strongly to root disturbance. Once established they should be left alone. Several times I have lifted and transplanted large specimens and have always regretted doing so.

It was in the mountains of north-west America that I first encountered, and fell deeply in love with *P.occidentalis*. Alas, my love has never been reciprocated and my many attempts to grow it have invariably ended in failure. Undaunted, I still ask kind friends to send me seeds in the hope that it may eventually forget its homesickness and delight me with its handsome flowers, whose petals are white on the inside and suffused with purple-blue on the reverse. It flaunts equal beauty when it displays great heads of long-awned, tawny silken seeds. At this moment I have some two-year-old seedlings which look more promising than anything so far achieved and I have my fingers crossed!

Pulsatilla vernalis has been acclaimed, and with justice, one of the most beautiful of all alpine flowers. Found here and there in the Alps of Europe, it appears as a low tuft of carroty leaves, both these and the stems aglow with golden-bronze hairs. The upturned, goblet-shaped flowers are opal-white and irridescent within, with a central tassel of golden stamens. On the outside the flowers shimmer in a mist of silky,

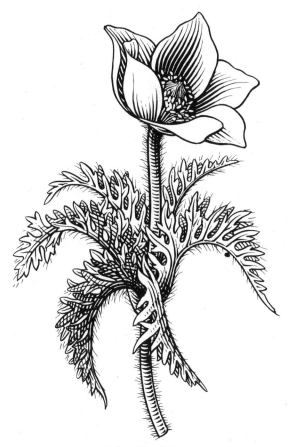

Pulsatilla alpina

gold and violet hairs. Truly a gem of the first order and one to be acquired and enjoyed. It is long-lived and not difficult to grow in a sunny place and gritty soil. Once firmly established it should never be moved—like all of its genus it deeply resents root disturbance. It fully deserves to be designated a GGP (Good Garden Plant) which, I freely admit, some of the 'miffs' and 'mimps' I have enthused about, certainly do not.

It is on hot, sun-baked Mediterranean hillsides that you must seek *Putoria calabrica*, a tiny shrub too seldom seen in gardens. Its generic name derives from the Latin *putor*, a strong smell, and it does, if roughly handled, emit a rather unpleasant odour. Avoid bruising its stems and leaves and enjoy the purple flowers, followed by the juicy red berries decorating its prostrate leafy stems clinging to the rocks among which it likes to grow. It really is rather a Cinderella and I would like to see it more widely known and grown. It will never be a garden centre plant and must be sought in the catalogues of specialist nurserymen who still grow the off-beat plants with which the mass producers cannot be bothered.

Over many years I have slowly come to the conviction that many plants are killed by kindness and are fussed and cosseted to death. The latest evidence of this I discovered when I gave the members of the genus *Pygmea* V.I.P. treatment, never letting them see the light of day except when filtered through the glass of an alpine house. These are high alpine cushion plants from New Zealand and I read in a book which I wrote myself some years ago, that they must be regarded as alpine house plants and given the same treatment as that allotted to Aretian androsaces and other cushion plants.

My pygmeas certainly lived, but only just and it was not until I saw healthy pads of *P.pulvinaris* growing on an open scree in a Scottish garden, that I learned my lesson. All my plants were immediately taken into the open and planted in stone sinks, to their obvious contentment. They have now passed through several winters without any protection at all and are rewarding me by smothering their tiny cushions with myriads of stemless white flowers. They do demand very perfect drainage in gritty soil

How nice it would be if the pyrolas would take more kindly to cultivation than they do. There are a dozen or so species, to be found in Asia, North America and Europe, including three British species. Of one of these, *P.rotundifolia*, a jealously guarded tiny colony, still exists in open forest land only a few miles from where I write in West Sussex. They are, however, frequently found in the north where they find the cool and humid conditions more to their liking. There should be a fourth native, but *P.uniflora* as was has now been moved to the genus *Moneses*. I will not tempt you with praise of its dainty beauty, for it really is almost ungrowable.

16 Final Thoughts and Memories

If those who have bravely read as far as this have obtained even a tiny percentage of the pleasure it has given me to write this wandering and discursive book, I shall be well pleased, largely because the writing has evoked so many memories of an equally wandering and discursive life. Many of these memories reach back into the distant past, but only today, as I was looking at a plant of *Camphorosma perennis*, I lived again the time spread over several years when I accepted a commission to construct an enormous rock garden in Iran. It was a fascinating project, of which it may amuse you to read a brief résumé.

Some years before the final eruption of revolution in Iran, the Shah and one of his sisters decided that it was time Iran possessed an International Botanic Garden. Their final decision was taken after reading a book *The Great Botanic Gardens of the World*, written by Edward Hyams. A large site was secured, at the very foot of the Elburz Mountains, part of the range which sweeps across the high plateau of Iran. It was on the hot, dry side of the mountains and was bare of all vegetation. It was then discovered that Iran, not horticulturally orientated, could not provide the expertise needed to create such a garden and approaches were made to organizations in England, seeking help and advice. A part of the project which was deemed to be of major importance, was to construct a rock garden on a vast scale; it was to be 'The largest and finest rock garden in the world'!

At the suggestion of Edward Hyams, whom I knew well, and whose advice had also been sought, I was asked to view the site and report on its potentiality and, if it seemed feasible, to be responsible for the creation of the rock garden. When I was eventually taken to the site my first reaction was that such a project was completely impossible on an absolute desert without a blade of grass or a plant with foliage and a most inhospitable soil. I knew that the summer temperatures would be very high and that there was a minimal rainfall, although sub-zero temperatures could be expected in the winter, but when I turned and saw the superb backcloth of mountains I thought again, and as I was told that if I undertook the task I could have anything that was needed, regardless of cost, I embarked upon what was to be an amazing project.

We went into the mountains with bulldozers, lorries and cranes and brought to the garden thousands of tons of marvellous rocks of immense size, many weighing twenty or thirty tons. Soil was imported and peat transported from overseas, for there is no peat in Iran, and vast quantities of compost were prepared. Thereafter, during the folowing four years massive rock formations were constructed, with cascades falling seventy feet into a large lake—which also had to be created and water supplied by artesian wells.

My constant worry, of course, was the fear that alpine plants would not appreciate the desert climate, even though the garden was at an elevation of around three thousand feet. To my considerable astonishment few of the many thousands of plants used showed any resentment. We were, of course, able to provide constant irrigation and did, in fact, create a mini-climate.

To return to the plant which induced these memories. At the time I was there Professor Per Wendelbo from Sweden was spending a sabbatical period training young Iranian students as botanists, and making many excursions into the mountains. One of the plants discovered and introduced was the grey-leaved cushion plant, *Camphorosma perennis*. Although its flowers are quite unimportant, it makes enticing huddles of densely crowded stems and tiny grey leaves and is an admirable subject for a sunny scree with an austere diet.

Happily my great rock garden was completed just before the political and social upheaval, although a great deal of other development remained unfinished. One can only hope that this great project will, one day, be completed. Many experts, from many countries, took part in its initiation and it would be tragic if all the effort were to be wasted, and the Ariamehr Garden did not take its place among the great Botanic Gardens of the world.

Although bulbs as such have played only a minor part in this book of memories and affections, I cannot omit a hybrid bulbous iris with which I have a sort of love-hate relationship. The cross was made by that great gardener E. B. Anderson in his garden in Gloucestershire. It was supposedly a hybrid between *Iris danfordiae* and *I.histrioides major*, but some opinions are expressed that the seed parent was not *I.danfordiae*, but *I.winogradowii*. The truth will never be known, but, whatever the parentage may have been it produced a child which has provoked much comment. It is admired by some and disliked by others. I stand half-way between: granting it full marks for handsome, bold flowers with wide falls and standards, I cannot, however, summon any great enthusiasm for its strange colouring, which is a melange of white, lavender-blue and dark purple. The falls are streaked and spotted with colour and the throat of the flower is yellow. It rather reminds me of a painter's palette in which the colours have run together. I admit to a preference for more decisive colouring. It is in cultivation under the name of either *I.* 'Katharine', or *I.* 'Katharine Hodgkin'.

Iris 'Katharine Hodgkin'

A special fondness for origanums has induced me over the years to gather together as many as I could of the twenty-four or more known species, mostly natives of Mediterranean regions. I was bothered when botanists moved most of them to the genus *Amaracus*, and relieved when they changed their minds and restored them to *Origanum*. One which I am particularly partial to is *O.rotundifolium*, which came to us from Turkey. It likes to grow in hot, dry places where, from a hard and woody rootstock rise profusions of thin, wiry, arching stems clothed in pairs of rounded, stem-clasping grey leaves. Every stem ends in a drooping inflorescence with soft pink flowers which are massed in

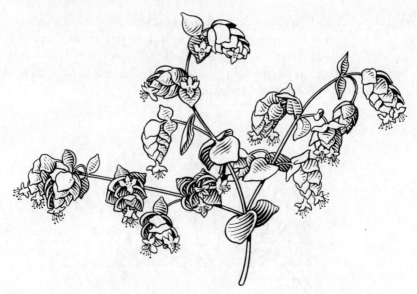

Origanum rotundifolium

whorls. Below each whorl of blossom is a pair of wide, apple-green bracts. A most admirable and desirable plant.

O.amanum should not be omitted from any book whose theme is alpine plants, for it is a beauty, although rare and probably not easy to come by. Discovered and introduced from Anatolia by Dr. P. Davis, the author of a monumental flora of Turkey, it has not been with us all that long, and has achieved instant popularity. Its habit is to form a neat bushlet of arching, wiry stems, set with attractive pale green leaves and displaying numerous clusters of long-tubed lilac-pink flowers subtended by pink bracts. If you are so fortunate as to locate a source, it will thank you for a hot and dry position if grown in the open, but it is sufficient of an aristocrat to justify a place in the alpine house.

One of the many glories of the high alpine meadows in Europe is the St. Bruno's Lily, *Paradisea liliastrum*. There, with neighbours such as *Lilium martagon, Campanula rhomboidalis*, some astrantias and tall geraniums, it raises its tall stems, from which hang several pure white trumpet-shaped flowers. Farrer described it in his inimitable style as being like a clean deed in a rough wild world. In the garden I like to associate it with plants of similar height in a sort of alpine pasture, rather than grow it as an isolated specimen. Sadly, I find that slugs like it as much as I do, but for a different reason: they find it extremely palatable.

Paradisea liliastrum

I have already apologized to the anemones for the neglect they have so far received on these pages. A large family of great diversity varying from tubers to alpine plants and to tall herbaceous plants, I can give it scant justice and confine myself to mention of a few special favourites, without which I would feel any garden to be poorly inhabited. With them were at one time included the hepaticas, and of these I have already enthused.

Both *Anemone apennina* and *A.blanda* grow, like our beloved native Wood Anemone, *A.nemorosa*, from tuberous, woody rhizomes. These are often stored and sold as dry bulbs which they do not particularly like. They are better planted as fresh as possible after lifting. Both species are mountain dwellers and like cool, shady conditions. They exist in many selected named forms with flowers varying in colour from white through pinks to red and several shades of blue. I like them all, but have a special affection for the deep blue flowers of *A.blanda* 'Atrocaerulea'.

Anemones rank high among the plants which, for me, provoke memories of empyrean and ecstatic days spent in distant lands. I shall never forget my first sight of myriads of the soft blue flowers of *A.trifolia* carpeting the ground at Misurina. A memory which I can seldom provoke is that of the excitement of seeing the first white, blue-backed flowers of *A.occidentalis* emerging from the last of the melting snows in the Rocky Mountains of north-west America. I know that it is now correctly a *Pulsatilla* and not an *Anemone*, and it will not grow for me or yield to any of my persuasions, but it is an unforgettable sight in the wild—and no less beautiful when the blossoms are followed by the Struwelpeter heads of long-awned silvery seeds.

One need travel no further than our own woodlands to enjoy the beauty of our native *A.nemorosa*. We call it the Windflower, the name having supposedly been derived from the Greek *anemos*, wind, but this has been debunked by a great authority, who tells us that anemone is a corrupted Greek word borrowed from the Semitic and referring to the slain Adonis, or Naaman, whose scattered blood produced the blood-red *A.coronaria*.

Any plant with flowers of perfect shape is always sure of a welcome from me and this is just one of the reasons why I find the Snowdrop Anemone, *A.sylvestris*, so bewitching. A native of Europe, and extending into Turkestan, it runs moderately from the root (never enough to be a nuisance) and emits tufts of hairy, deeply cut leaves. On foot-high stems it carries loose heads of gently drooping, cup-shaped fragrant white flowers. There is a double-flowered form, which I dislike, and a splendid selection named 'Spring Beauty', whose flowers are larger but have lost nothing of their grace.

At the risk of being thought undemocratic I insist that there are aristocrats and commoners among plants, as there are in humans. The commoners are not to be despised and I have much affection for many of them. Definitely not in the upper echelon but worthy of a place in any garden is *A.magellanica*. Native to Chile and Patagonia it asks for no special care and is a pleasant sight when adorned with many heads of cream-white flowers on nine-inch stems. There is a major form which differs only in having flowers twice the size of those of the type.

Among the other floral delights in the high valleys of far Kashmir may be found the so-called Blue Buttercup, *Anemone obtusiloba*. Although known in cultivation for many years it has never become common in gardens, but is a 'must' if it can be obtained. From its tufts of lobed and softly hairy leaves radiate spreading stems carrying many rounded flowers of pure soft blue. In nature there are forms with white, cream or violet flowers but few, if any of these variants seem to have crept into cultivation. We need not grieve too deeply, for the blue is certainly the most desirable, and that we have, even if sparingly.

Should you find yourself near Misurina in Italy, spare a while if the time is spring, to wander into the woodlands and seek dainty *A.trifolia*. In leaf it resembles our native *A.nemorosa* but the flowers are a soft, clear blue. It very prettily inhabits cool places in the garden.

There are not many anemones with yellow flowers, but the blossoms of *A.palmata* are of an irresistible shining gold. Properly a native of North Africa, it does stray into southern Europe and may be found occasionally in Portugal and Spain. The leaves are quite unmistakable, thick and round with a few blunt marginal lobes. Splendidly rounded golden flowers are carried on short, leafless stems. Although in nature it seems to prefer dry, often quite arid conditions, it is very tolerant in gardens, as long as the drainage is good—I have even seen clumps of it adorning the front row of a border.

Common in European alpine woodlands and spreading far away into the Caucasus is *A.ranunculoides*, which likes us so well that it escaped from gardens and naturalized itself here and there. A frail plant, it creeps gently around and bears showers of small yellow flowers on branching stems. It would not, as an American friend of mine once said of a plant he found uninspiring, 'stop any traffic', but it is nevertheless a gently charming plant which I could ill spare from my garden.

Paved terraces and patios can have their severity relieved by tucking into the crannies and nooks between stones small plants which will spread into low tufts. One such is a mule of uncertain parentage, *Thymus* 'Doone Valley'! Slightly more robust than the ever popular forms of *T.serpyllum*, it flecks its tiny olive-green leaves with gold. The crimson buds expand into lavender flowers carried in small rounded heads.

For an area of paving that is shaded there is no better inhabitant than the tiny Corsican Mint, *Mentha requienii*. A mere film of minute bright green leaves, it is intensely aromatic and has no objection to being trodden on occasionally. The green tufts change in colour during summer when they are smothered with myriads of little purple flowers. How well I remember the intense peppermint smell (as I walked over carpets of it in shaded Corsican canyons) mingling with the fragrance of the *maquis* growing on the hotter upper slopes. Mrs. Archer did well to name her fascinating book about Corsica *The Fragrant Isle*. Another very aromatic plant to be found on Corsica is *Thymus herba-barona* whose mats of tiny dark green leaves emit a pungent aroma of caraway seeds.

It was with genuine pleasure that I made the acquaintance of *Pratia pedunculata* when it received its well-deserved Award of Merit in 1980. A comparative newcomer to Britain, it hails from Australian mountains. There is always justifiable doubt as to the hardiness in this country of plants from Australia, but this delightful introduction has passed through several quite severe winters and came to no harm. The habit of this charmer is to grow as a prostrate mat of entangled frail stems clothed in tiny rounded soft green leaves. The pad will eventually become foot-wide and the foliage disappears for weeks on end beneath untold numbers of small, exquisitely pale blue flowers. Indeed, the plants which I cherish are seldom without blossom the whole summer through. It is happy in a gritty scree in full sun, and also makes a delightful specimen pan for the alpine house. I rank it very high among recent introductions.

Should you seek in the Royal Horticultural Society's *Dictionary of Gardening* for a description of *Eryngium glaciale* you will see that it is described as being from three to six feet high. This does not agree with my long experience of the plant, or with its description in Wilkomm and Lange's *Flora of Spain*, where its stature is correctly given as about six inches. I have grown it, off and on, for many years, but regretably more off than on, for I have not found it easy and it is certainly difficult to propagate. Throughout my life there have been plants that I have been desperately anxious to grow, but which have resisted all my efforts to please them and this likeable miniature *Eryngium* is just one of these. Coming from hot Spanish hillsides it cannot be expected to relish an average British winter, but even when I cosset it in an alpine house it merely exists, tantalizing me with a mere glimpse of how admirable it could be. Its rigid, firmly woody stems are erect and clothed with grey leaves and quite definitely thorny spines. The globose heads of soft blue, sometimes almost white flowers are surrounded by a crown of silvery-grey thorns. Try to get it and, if successful, I hope it behaves better with you than it does with me.

It is North African and definitely not hardy, but I so dearly love *Convolvulus mauritanicus* that I do not shrink from the chore of sheltering a few plants under glass during the winter in case disaster strikes outside. I give it here under its well-known name, although it is now more correctly *C.sabatius*. It is certainly not an alpine plant and my greatest success has been when I tucked a plant between paving stones in a warm and sheltered corner. It spreads into a lush carpet of trailing, leafy stems and is totally obscured during the summer beneath a wealth of large, rounded blue flowers. It can be set in a wall or even in a rocky crevice on the rock garden, although it is, to me, slightly out of context there. I have also seen it used to good effect in hanging baskets where it makes a welcome change from blue *Lobelia* and ivy-leaved pelargoniums.

The nearer I get to the end of this book, the more bothered I become about the innumerable plants I have left unpraised. Bent this morning in admiration over some plants of *Hypericum cuneatum* I decided that one or two of the best of these decorative and useful plants must be given mention. *H.cuneatum* is native to Syria and Asia Minor, and like so many of these sun-worshipping plants it loves to grow where it is assured of plenty of warm sunlight. Never more than a few inches in height, its thin red stems are very brittle, so it is best to grow it where it is not exposed to high winds. I keep in in the alpine house and there enjoy its neat, wavy-edged leaves which are bespattered with dark markings, and its racemes of bright yellow flowers.

Much less of an aristocrat, but invaluable nevertheless, is *H.olympicum* (to be found in some catalogues as *H.polyphyllum*). It qualifies to be included in any list of the hundred best alpines—indeed, were I to be asked to name the ten best, easily grown all round alpines, *H.olympicum* would surely be there. Widely distributed in southern Europe, Syria and Asia Minor, it will flourish in any soil and full sun, making low, mounded leafy bushes totally obscured when in blossom by the large, richly golden flowers.

For those to whom small is beautiful, *H.yakushimanum* will surely appeal. It comes from the island of Yakushima, famous for many miniature plants and also the home of the fabulous *Rhododendron yakushimanum* which has no place in this book but is one of the most beautiful of all dwarf rhododendrons. The *Hypericum* grows in creeping carpets, flat on the ground. Its frail stems carry tiny leaves and small starry yellow flowers, which are succeeded by red seedpods. It is quite charming, but frail and should not be placed where it can be smothered by more vigorous plants.

It was in 1955 that Mrs. Tweedie brought to us from Patagonia *Oxalis laciniata* and it immediately captured all hearts. With a habit of growth similar to *O.enneaphylla* it makes chains of tiny tubers. The green leaves are cut into segments and margined with purple. On very short stems are the large, trumpet-shaped flowers which vary in colour from almost white to rich and glowing purple. It liked us so well that it looked around for a mate, which it found in Mrs. Hecker's garden and hybridized with *O.enneaphylla*, producing a lovely child which has been named *Oxalis* 'Ione Hecker'. The foliage is like that of *O.enneaphylla* but the flowers are large, beautifully rounded and violet-blue in colour.

O.magellanica covers the ground with a flat mat of dark green leaves, enlivened by stemless, rounded pearl-white flowers. Admittedly it is a spreader, but it is so frail that it is harmless and there could be no more pleasant occupant of a cool and lightly shaded place. It will grow out in full light, but is obviously more happy in a less open situation.

There are many very lovely oxalises, but the family also nurtures some pestiferous weeds. One in particular which should be avoided unless it can be given large areas in which to colonize is *O.pescapria*, a name which has replaced its older one of *O.cernua*. Originally a native of Bermuda, I believe, it has naturalized in the warmer parts of Europe. I have seen, and admired, great sheets of its golden flowers around the Mediterranean, but lovely though it is, it is kinematic to an unsafe degree.

A long time ago I saw *Oxyria digyna* growing on the rocky slopes of a mountain in Scotland. It was autumn and the tufts of fleshy leaves had adopted rich red tints and the flat seed pods were a rich bronzy-red. The seeds were ripe and I gathered a few and planted the subsequent seedlings on a small rock garden. All was well for the first year but then disaster struck. The wretched plant seeded itself madly in every direction. The seedlings had long, strong and tough roots, from which the tops broke if you tried to pull them out. Eventually the entire rock garden had to be taken to pieces and rebuilt and resoiled. So, be warned. It is one of the very few plants that I have firmly decided not to grow! The tale of woe was not even then complete, for I had given plants to a neighbour, which nearly destroyed a long friendship, and he has never really forgiven me, even occasionally throwing a boxful of *Oxyria* seedlings over the hedge into my garden.

Botanists can be classified in two groups, the 'lumpers' and the 'splitters'. It is with the latter that I become most annoyed, for they delight in splitting one genus into several to the eternal confusion of we the gardeners. The American botanists are particularly addicted to this game. For example, they have divided the genus *Oenothera* into such distinct genera as *Anogra*, *Megapterum* and *Meriolix*—and there are others.

What they have done with my pet *Oenothera acaulis* I do not know, or wish to know. Perhaps they feel that, as the genus is entirely

American in its distribution they have a right to divide it up. *O.acaulis* comes from Chile, and, as its synonym *taraxacifolia* suggests, has leaves exactly like those of a dandelion, which puts it at risk at the hands of careless or ignorant weeders. In the midst of its tufts of lush foliage are centred stemless clusters of large flowers, which can be white or yellow.

So many times has its name been changed that I scarcely know from day to day how to address the plant I know as *Sonchus spinosus*. It has also been known as *Acanthosonchus cervicornis* and is now correctly, I am told, *Launaea cervicornis*. It comes from Spain's hot hillsides and is a tangled huddle of thorny stems with a few narrow, toothed, grey-green leaves and, in high summer, many small yellow flowers. Unless you can provide it with an environment similar to that which it is accustomed to, it is best given alpine house treatment and a fairly spartan diet. If fed too liberally it will grow out of character. It apparently lives to a great age: a plant of mine, now about two thirds the size of a football, has been in its pot for many years. It has never been repotted but is given a feed of bonemeal once a year.

It will be increasingly obvious to you as you read that this final chapter is, in the main, a final gathering together of plants and recollections which have been neglected on earlier pages. The constant endeavour to avoid producing yet another catalogue of plants inevitably creates omissions which come constantly to mind as my thoughts wend their erratic way back through the many years which intervene between now and my childhood on an alpine plant nursery.

In the mountains of south-west France I was always delighted to encounter *Teucrium pyrenaicum*; not a common plant there, but much more frequent in the Spanish mountains. I do not grudge it the considerable area it occupies on a sunny raised bed, where it has spread into a yard-wide mat, only a few inches in height, of woody stems generously clothed in rounded, softly hairy leaves. Rising just above this handsome carpet are heads of hooded cream and lavender flowers. A throughly nice plant, presenting no problems and decorative even when not in flower.

One would hardly expect to find a jasmine on a rock garden, but there is an enticing dwarf, *Jasminum parkeri*, discovered by R. N. Parker in the Himalayas in 1919 and introduced to Britain three years later. It was given a well-deserved Award of Merit in 1933. It tends to form a domed mat of closely entwined woody branches and amidst the leafy twigs are many yellow flowers, which grow singly or in pairs either terminally or from the leaf axils. Given the opportunity it will fall from a high point in a curtain over a rock face. There is a magnificent specimen to be seen on the rock garden in Kew Garden. It has given me much pleasure for forty years or more and has proved thoroughly hardy. It even struggled through the unforgettable winter of 1961–2, emerging damaged but undaunted.

Having recently been given a generous gift of some enormous clumps of *Gentiana acaulis*, I was reminded of a Mr. May, who lived in Caterham, on the Surrey hills, whose garden I often visited with my father. May was a delightful, but eccentric and rather intolerant man and had no patience with the many visitors who asked to see his well-known garden. Eventually he planted a rare shrub on each side of his front door. When visitors knocked and asked if they might see the garden, if they commented on either of the shrubs, they were 'in', if they did not, they were 'out'. He grew and flowered *Gentiana acaulis* better than I have ever seen it. Foot-wide borders of it, many yards in length, became ribbons of blue. He was as generous as he was eccentric and we never left his garden without a box full of treasures.

Those wonderful characters among gardeners seem to be a dying race; I remember so many of them. When, as a boy, I spent some years in the Wisley Garden, I became acquainted with one John Cornhill, who lived in a state of squalor—not because he was poor, but because he liked it that way. He was a bachelor, cared for by a cousin, Lizzie Towers, who was as unorthodox as he was. When one visited, rubbish was swept off chairs and we were told 'park your carcass'. John had lived in France for much of his life, and dressed like a French peasant. His existence was completely primitive and the only sanitary arrangements consisted of an earth closet 'down the garden path'. It was John's custom to cut out items he thought of interest from papers and magazines and to paste them on the walls of the closet. The local vicar on his way to church one Sunday needed to answer a call of nature and as he knew John, called and asked if he might visit the closet. When he emerged he said to John: 'I have discovered material for at least three sermons from your wall decorations.'

The large garden was, as might be imagined, always in a state of complete chaos, but among the weeds were a great many noteworthy plants. He had a special love for *Cyclamen* which rioted everywhere. I was once there while he was clearing an area beneath trees, and lifting tubers of *C.hederifolium* which measured a genuine fifteen inches in diameter. John said that he had planted them as seedlings forty years previously. That was truly a man and a garden to remember. Alas, the garden is now buried beneath the houses and roads of a building estate.

Few plants can equal *Tropaeolum polyphyllum* for tumbling down the face of a sunny wall, or glissading down the front of a large rock and for sheer effulgent beauty. The large tuberous roots of this Chilean plant should be planted deep in well-drained soil. Twelve inches of depth is not too much and from this they will delve even deeper. I was once given permission to dig up *T.polyphyllum* from a derelict garden and was still discovering tubers at a depth of three feet. From these unshapely roots rise, in late spring, slender stems clothed in leaves of intense silveryness and from the leaf axils of the terminal half of the stem spring countless richly golden nasturtium flowers. It is really spectacular when in blossom and has a unique beauty all of its own.

The liking that one can have for a quite unlovely plant is a very personal thing. When I compare notes with gardening friends I find that some of them too, have an affection for plants which most people would pass without a glance, or, if they did have their attention drawn to it, would be uncomplimentary. The plant that aroused this particular thought is growing in the corner of one of my stone troughs. It is *Herniaria glabra*. With a very wide distribution it can be found in Britain, many parts of Europe, Asia and North Africa. Its name derives from *hernia*, a rupture, for which it was once supposed to be a cure. It does no more than make a flat mat of minute green leaves. The flowers are quite inconspicuous. Somehow or other, despite its lack of conventional beauty, it strikes some chord and I am very happy with it and give it an appreciative look whenever I pass it.

Another of these non-U plants with which I find myself in sympathy is *Bartsia alpina*, an occasional native of British mountains where I have seen it growing, and admired it in a modest way. It is not a plant to associate with more distinguished rarities but in a cool, slightly moist position I admire its tufts of purplish leaves and short, stiff spikes of purple flowers between purple bracts. Farrer says that it has the taint of a parasite and is difficult to keep, but I have found that the plants I have raised from wild collected seed always flourished and proved long-lived. It's close relative, *B.spicata*, from the Pyrenees differs only in being slightly larger in all its parts.

When I first made the acquaintance of *Talinum okanoganense* in the Okanogan Mountains of the State of Washington, I thought that it would be a particularly pleasant inhabitant of an alpine house and, many years later, find no reason to amend that opinion. Closely related to *Lewisia*, it relishes similar treatment and especially appreciates a drying off period after it has flowered. When it goes to rest for the winter it can look very dead, but do not be alarmed, it resuscitates happily in the spring. It is completely prostrate, its fleshy stems, adorned with needle-shaped grey-green leaves, rest flat on the gritty soil in which it likes to grow. On these mats lie stemless saucer-shaped flowers of satin-white, each blossom with a prominent central cluster of stamens. It is easily raised from seed but these must be sown immediately they are ripe to ensure a good germination, and, be warned, the seeds fall even before they are fully ripe.

Should anyone be visiting the island of Guadalupe, they should there seek *Talinum guadalupense,* where it grows in the narrowest fissures of black volcanic rocks. I have not seen it, and doubt if it is in cultivation, but its enticing description says that it makes tufts of white, fleshy leaves and has panicles of lavender-blue flowers. Very definitely an acquisition to be desired.

My liking for the species *Tanacetum* was never more than half-hearted. In general they are grown for their foliage rather than for their flowers. They are grey-leaved and aromatic and pleasant enough in a hot, dry position. It was not until I met *T.densum amani* that I became really interested. From Asia Minor, it makes low mounds of finely dissected, intensely silver foliage and, for once, the blossoms have value, consisting of flat corymbs of bright yellow disk florets, surrounded by an involucre of wooly white bracts. A fine alpine house plant, it is well able to cope with outdoor conditions, given a sunny spot.

One of the principal reasons for a visit to Pikes Peak in Colorado was to see in the wild what I then knew as *Boykinia jamesii* but which has now been determined as *Telesonix jamesii.* Led by Mrs. Marriage, a talented American plantswoman, we spent two days on that splendid mountain and were able to admire myriads of what I persist in calling *Boykinia jamesii* in full flower. It spread in multitudes along narrow crannies and crevices. Over tufts of rather leathery, kidney-shaped leaves were six to nine-inch stems carrying racemes of carmine-crimson flowers. The plants I have grown have never equalled in the colour of their flowers those which enraptured me on Pikes Peak; they are a rather dusky, slightly dingy red. Every year I raise it from seed, hoping that some of the seedlings may be of the desired colouring. Maybe it needs the strong clear light of the mountains.

Not infrequently I am hauled over the coals for praising plants which are capable of becoming a nuisance. Only recently I received an indignant letter from someone to whom I had recommended *Borago laxiflora.* Admittedly it will seed itself freely, but, in the right place this is no disadvantage. My correspondent blamed me for the hours spent in pulling out unwanted seedlings. Maybe I am biased, for it always brings back vivid memories of Corsica, where it grows in the *maquis.* Loose tufts of coarsely hairy leaves and branching, foot-high stems carrying many gentian-blue flowers throughout the summer months. I grow it among dwarf heathers and other small shrubs, an association which pleases it and me. I also grow it together with *Alchemilla mollis*, another plant which has brought me much censure.

A plant which I constantly mourn is *Senecio websteri*. I first saw it growing by the side of the long trail leading to Hurricane Ridge in the Olympic Mountains of America. A number of plants were raised from seeds I brought home, but fell victim to a plague of rabbits in the days before myxomatosis. I had not had time to distribute it, as I always do with any new introduction to ensure its survival somewhere, and have not been able to replace it. A bold plant, perhaps over-large for a small rock garden but good for the front row of a flower bed, it makes robust tufts of wide, leathery leaves, deep green above and crimson beneath. On foot-high stems it carries large richly golden flowers. It is known as the Olympic Butterweed and, according to Abrams and Ferris in their *Flora of the Pacific States*, should be correctly named *S.newebsteri*. Should it exist in any British garden I would like to know.

Although it has been known since it was introduced from North India in 1796, too little notice has been taken of *Androsace rotundifolia* and only very recently have its merits been recognized when it was given an Award of Merit by the appropriate committee of the Royal Horticultural Society. Its mounded hummocks of circular to kidney-shaped leaves, slightly lobed at the margins, are surmounted by many-flowered umbels of good pink flowers. I am sure it would grow well enough in gritty soil in the open, but I have always given it alpine house treatment and now regularly apologize to it for not having appreciated what a good plant it is.

Plants are, for me, inevitably associated with people, and I still treasure a pretty *Campanula* for which I have never discovered a name. I keep it because it reminds me of Mark Fenwick, who gave it to me. When I visited him in Gloucestershire, he was already confined to a wheel chair, but what a chair it was! Attached to it was every possible kind of tool, and that indomitable man wheeled himself about the garden equipped to deal with many small gardening chores. When I admired the unknown *Campanula*, for which he, too, had no name, he gave me a trowel and said 'dig yourself up a piece'. Apart from the pleasant association, I like the *Campanula* itself, which is rather like a very dwarf, large-flowered form of *C.rotundifolia*—which is probably just what it is.

It is regrettable that the Victoria Medal of Honour, the highest award that the Royal Horticultural Society can make, cannot be given posthumously, for if anyone deserved it, it was Margery Fish, who grew a wonderful collection of plants in her Somerset garden, and wrote about them so charmingly in her many books, which I read and re-read with immense pleasure. They conjure up memories of my visits to her and her unbounded generosity. The essential accompaniment to any walk with her in her garden was a large trug basket and a lifting tool, and one always left with a wealth of goodies, many of which survive with me and give me endless pleasure.

What a lot of enticing plants are still growing in their native fastnesses but have not yet made their way into our gardens. For years I have had an insatiable desire to grow some of the species of *Nototriche* which are to be found at immense elevations in the Andes of South America, many of them in southern Peru. Seeds have been sent to me, but have never germinated but I believe that a few skilful members of the Alpine Garden Society have at least kept some of them alive for a year or two. We have obviously not yet discovered what they need to be made more tractable. Descriptions of their cushions of felted leaves and brilliantly coloured flowers which one can read in the Bulletins of the Alpine Garden Society make it more and more desirable that determined efforts should be made to persuade these high alpine Andeans that captivity need not be a signal for death.

Our native Sea Pink, *Armeria maritima*, which emblazons the cliff tops of Cornwall with its myriads of pink flower heads has also beautified our gardens in the form of several selections which smother their mossy tufts with flowers ranging from pure white to brilliant red. Those named *lauchiana* and 'Vindictive' are especially desirable and are good 'fillers' for a sunny spot on the rock garden, or, in a more plebeian manner, providing an edging to paths and borders. They serve a very useful purpose for those whose gardens are near the sea and perhaps exposed to salt spray, to which many plants object but to which the *Armeria* is well accustomed.

Our native *Parnassia palustris* I have already praised and it is always welcome to a place in my garden, but I remember being very excited by the beauty of *P. fimbriata* when I saw it in great numbers, growing in moist meadows in North America and British Columbia. Not unlike our own species in general appearance, it is slightly taller when in flower and the large white blossoms have every petal delightfully and elegantly fringed. It is not commonly in cultivation but should be snapped up at any opportunity.

There are far too many plants which have been grown but which have almost or entirely disappeared from gardens. Before writing this paragraph I looked through forty plant catalogues but in not one of them (including my own, I am ashamed to say), did I find listed *Jaborosa integrifolia*. Its rarity surprises me for it is not at all difficult to grow and has good garden value. A native of South America, it spreads modestly by means of underground stems, emitting here and there as it runs a few fleshy, oval green leaves and quite large, bell-shaped white flowers during the summer. My own colony succumbed during the winter of 1960–1, which destroyed so many plants we had thought to be hardy, and I have not yet been able to replace it.

When Harold Comber was finding and introducing so many fine shrubs and plants in the Andes during the 1920s, he sent home both plants and seeds of the amazing rosulate violas, several species of which are to be found there at great elevations. Until the typical *Viola* flowers are produced they look exactly like sempervivums, with similar symmetrical rosettes of pointed, fleshy leaves. Sadly, this importation failed but there have been subsequent sendings. I have myself raised some from seed but when they reached the size of sixpence, one by one they passed into whatever Valhalla is reserved for plants. Here, too, is a genus with which we must persist in our efforts to grow. If only they could be established they would be a nine days wonder in the alpine world.

I have great hopes that the newly formed National Council for the Conservation and Protection of Plants and Gardens (NCCPG for short) will achieve, as one of its objects, the discovery and propagation of some of the missing rarities. Many may linger in some obscure garden— perchance a garden made and planted in the past and now neglected. Anyone who possesses a plant which they suspect is rare and is not seen elsewhere would render a great service by sending details of it to The Director, RHS Garden, Wisley, Woking, Surrey. Its name should be given if known, or, failing that, a specimen for identification. I have myself, when visiting gardens, especially in Ireland, discovered a number of plants which were thought to be out of cultivation. One of these was the unlovely but amusing primrose whose petals had become green leaves and this, I am happy to say, is now firmly back in our gardens. Only the collector of oddities will desire it, but they are just the ones who continually seek for rarities.

Another very old plant which is now rare is the form of the common lily of the valley whose leaves are handsomely striated with golden lines. It is beautifully illustrated in E. J. Lowe's splendid book entitled *Beautiful Leaved Plants*, written in 1861. It may occasionally revert to plain green leaves, but this appears to be only a temporary phase, the variegated foliage reappearing in the following year.

For many years, specifically to please my wife, who loves it dearly, I tried to establish the common Lily of the Valley, in its finest manifestation 'Fortin's Giant', in my garden, without much success. Finally, following its normal habit of wandering far and wide, it discovered a position it liked better than anything I had offered, and became aggressively vigorous and is now engaged in battle with a colony of Woodruff—once *Asperula odorata*, but now *Galium odoratum*. I watch with no little interest to discover which will be the victor. The Woodruff must survive, if not there, then in another place, for it is still a pleasant custom to dry it, as our grandmothers did, and put it into little muslin bags among the sheets in the airing cupboard.

Crepis incana is an aristocrat in a rather weedy race. An inhabitant of rocky places in southern Greece, it is hardy, perennial and decorative. From its deeply delving woody roots rise rosettes of narrow, grey, notched leaves and stiff and branching stems on which can be seen myriads of soft pink Hawk's-beard flowers, which persist for weeks on end during the summer. Its only cavil is a resentment of being moved once firmly established. If you want it elsewhere or wish for more, the seeds it sets freely germinate well.

Pretty little *Dicentra peregrina* has been the delight, and only too often, the despair of alpine gardeners for many years. It comes from Japan and has never really secured a firm roothold in our gardens. Mrs. Anley once told me, after a visit she had made to Japan, that she had seen it growing in several gardens, in a mixture half of which was small broken pieces of coal. This I tried, but with no more success than had attended the many other special composts I had tried. *Dicentra* still died on me. Maybe we have fussed too much. I have no material with which to experiment now, but the next time I have I shall give it much less V.I.P. treatment. I have found with other tricky plants that a little wholesome neglect can work wonders. Perhaps, like the pygmeas, it would rather be in the open air than in an alpine house? Anyway, be that as it may, to successfully grow this delightful little plant would bring joy to the heart of any enthusiast. Its intensely silver leaves rest in little clusters at ground level and the pink, lyre-shaped flowers are carried demurely on three-inch stems. There is also a rare form with pure white flowers, each as lovely as the other.

Once included among the phyteumas, *Petromarula pinnata* is an attractive dweller in the crevices of Cretan rocks, where it enjoys the company of *Daphne sericea* and *Ebenus creticus*, whose flower heads are like those of a large pink clover. *Petromarula* makes bold rosettes of pinnate, deeply slashed leaves from which rise tall candelabra carrying hundreds of small, star-shaped mauve-blue flowers. To expect it to face an average English winter without protection is asking a bit much. Wedge it between pieces of rock in large pots or pans and grow it in the alpine house—or in an unheated greenhouse. Its choice of habitat is evident in its name: *petros* is Greek for rock and the Cretan vernacular name for it is 'rock lettuce'.

Also from Crete, where it is an inveterate crevice haunter, is that pretty harebell, *Campanula calaminthifolia*. Although a perennial, it is short-lived and after two or three years will literally flower itself to death. Fortunately it is liberal in the production of seeds. From its tap root rise prostrate rosettes of hairy, radiating stems clothed in ash-grey leaves. Both terminally and in the leaf axils appear many very attractive soft blue flowers. A frail plant—perhaps too frail for an outdoor existence, it is of sufficient quality to deserve V.I.P. treatment in an alpine house.

When I began my horticultural career as a humble pot-washer on the famous Six Hills Nursery in Stevenage, a mecca for lovers of alpine plants, I became acquainted with Helena Moules, a large lady of commanding character, of whom I was initially terrified. When I came to know her better we discovered a mutual interest in and love for small plants and I spent much time in her garden. She lived in a tiny house, behind which was a surprisingly large garden, that had been entirely devoted to a series of rock gardens, in which she grew to perfection the plants she loved so dearly. Such contacts encouraged and fostered the love for alpines which has persisted and increased throughout my life.

Nursery life was tough in those days: we worked from six a.m. until six p.m. My father was at that time in partnership with Clarence Elliott and, as the son of one of the bosses, starting at the very bottom of the ladder, I was given all the dirty jobs. There were times when I sickened of being the nursery stooge and might well have abandoned the whole idea of becoming a nurseryman, had it not been for the constant encouragement of Helena Moules, and, outside the day's work, with which my father did not interfere, his constant sharing of the great knowledge he possessed.

When at last I was promoted and allowed actually to handle plants, all was well and I never thereafter faltered in my determination to learn all that there was to know about the facinating children of the hills. Now that I am old I know that complete knowledge is impossible but the never ending search for it is utterly absorbing.

In spite of all the trials and tribulations those were wonderful days, but not free from near disasters. I was eventually given charge of the sun frames, which were the original mist propagators. Frames were set out in full sun and filled with cuttings. Every half hour, when the sun was shining, the frame light had to be lifted and the cuttings sprayed with water. One very hot day I forgot my duty for several hours. This neglect resulted in the total loss of thousands of cuttings. Needless to say I was promptly demoted and went back to crocking pots for a period. The nursery foreman at that time was Frank Barker, a forthright Yorkshire-man, a fine plantsman and a magnificent propagator. From him I learned a great deal. I still read and re-read his excellent book *The Cream of Alpines*, sadly the only book he had time to write before his untimely death.

A plant which I vividly remember from those Six Hill days is *Aquilegia glandulosa*, which grew there in greater magnificence than I have ever seen it elsewhere. A species from the Altai it is now seldom seen in its true form. A guide to its verity may be seen even before it is a growing plant, for its seeds are dull, whereas the seeds of all other aquilegias that I know are glossy and shiny. From tufts of bold foliage rise fifteen-inch stems carrying large flowers of blue and white. How well I remember the sensation that was caused when more than a hundred large plants in full flower were exhibited at Chelsea Show. Thousands were sold against a stock of several hundreds. You cannot divide an *Aquilegia* and seed is the only method of propagation. It took three years to supply all those orders.

My father eventually left Clarence Elliott and, with Gavin Jones, started a nursery in the neighbouring town of Letchworth; I, of course, went along. The site for the new nursery was a bare and open field, in one corner of which bubbled up a spring of water. I think this finalized the decision to buy the land and a rock garden with pools to accept the running stream was created. This functioned perfectly for several years, until the local Council, seeking the cause of a water deficiency, discovered that our 'spring' was, in fact, a leak in the water main!

During my many flights into cloud-cuckoo-land, when I have tried to please such notoriously problem plants as *Pyxidanthera barbulata*, *Eritrichium nanum*, *Ranunculus glacialis*—oh, and many more—I have come to several conclusions, one of which is that some plants resent being grown in loneliness, without companions of other genera. In our rock gardens we do tend to devote 'pockets' to individual plants, whereas in nature they are accustomed to live in lose companionship with others. The nearest I ever got to success with *Pyxidanthera* was when I set a few tufts, kindly sent to me from the Pine Barrens by an American friend, in a peat bed accompanied by dwarf cassiopes, some wandering gaultherias (*G.praestans* for example) and other plants of a similar character. They were none of them plants which the Pixy Moss would encounter in its native habitat, but they appeared to be compatible and got along very well together—although the *Pyxidanthera* did eventually succumb. It did, however, endure much longer than it had ever done before.

Cool north-facing crevices in the rock garden or in a wall, so appropriate to ramondas, are equally appreciated by haberleas, which are of rather similar appearance but with their hairy leaves in loose rosettes rather than laid flat as in *Ramonda*. They display rather tubular flowers of lavender colour on short stems. The two closely related species are *H.ferdinandi-coburgi* and *H.rhodopensis*, the former is possibly only a form of the latter, slightly larger and with gold frecklings in the throats of the flowers. There is also a handsome albino, *H.virginalis* whose blossoms are snow white. Haberleas are native to the Balkans and have been grown in our gardens for at least one hundred years.

Seekers after rarities will always be intrigued by dainty *Sarcocapnos crassifolia*, which belongs to the sub-family Fumariaceae of the much larger family Papaveraceae, along with such genera as *Corydalis* and *Dicentra*. It can be found in both Spain and Morocco, usually inhabiting shaded crevices at considerable elevations. It has a tenuous hold on cultivation as yet, not having been with us all that long, but it is by no means difficult and should get into more general circulation before too long. Both leaves and stems are fleshy, grey and glabrous. The soft pink flowers are carried on very slender racemes. The whole plant does not exceed six inches in height. The rather frail and fleshy growth suggests that it would be wise to give it alpine house treatment until we know more of its likes and dislikes. Should you have any choice, the form from Spain, which I have not seen, is said to have larger flowers and is sometimes given the varietal name of *speciosa*.

Ricotia davisiana falls in rather the same category, but not in the same family, for it is a crucifer. It was found in Crete by Dr. Peter Davis, who began his horticultural career on my nursery and is now one of our foremost botanists. It, too, should be thought of as a plant for the alpine house and grown in gritty soil not devoid of humus. Its woody base produces brittle, fleshy stems with equally fleshy blue-grey leaves. The stems terminate in small rounded heads of pink flowers. Only a few inches in height it makes a notable specimen plant. It has been known to flower with such abandon that it hastens its own demise, but it provides plenty of seed from which young plants are easily raised, or non-flowering shoots will make cuttings. It is only right and proper that collections of alpine plants should contain representatives of some of these off-beat plants, perhaps not easy to secure, but well worth hunting for.

High in the Rocky Mountains of Canada, where I first saw *Romanzoffia sitchensis* growing, it is known as Mist Maidens. It is very reminiscent of a dwarf *Saxifrage* but actually belongs to a quite different family, being a member of Hydrophyllaceae. The genus is named in honour of Prince Nicholas Romanzoff, who generously financed a round-the-world expedition during 1816–17. As soon as the spring sun has enough power to set free the flowers, you may see this dainty plant, illumining the dark rocky crannies in which it likes to grow with rounded flowers, pure glistening white and the texture of velvet, resting on low pads of rounded and gently scalloped leaves. Not difficult to grow, it prefers a not-too-hot position in very gritty soil which is also well supplied with humus. There is another species, *R.unalashkensis*, which comes from the Aleutian Islands and is similar in appearance, with waxy white flowers in profusion.

On an earlier page I have already enthused about our native Mountain Avens, *Dryas octopetala*, but I have lavished no praise on *D.drummondii*, which is another inhabitant of the Canadian Rockies. The omission was partly due to the fact that I have always found it a rather disappointing plant. The fact that the petals of its flowers are golden yellow conjures up the vision of a plant to be treasured. In fact the flowers do not expand sufficiently to disclose more than the tips of the yellow petals, but there is a bonus in the form of splendid plumose seed heads. It has also hybridized with *D.octopetala* and the child of this marriage is *D. × suendermannii*, whose cream flowers open widely, making it a definitely worthwhile plant.

Whenever my thoughts go back, as they often do, to days spent on the hot slopes of the Maritime Alps where they sweep down to the blue Mediterranean Sea, I conjure up visions of the curious, rush-like *Aphyllanthes monspeliensis*, which grew in profusion in hard, dry, sun-baked soil. When not in flower it could be passed by, for its tufts of green stems would pass for a rush—until it blossoms. At the tip of the stems, amid chaffy bracts, are good flowers of clear gentian-blue. It belongs to Liliaceae and is the only species in its genus. So many blue-flowered plants have albinos that I spent many hours in search of a white *Aphyllanthes*, but without success, nor can I discover that one has ever been recorded. As might be expected from its habitat, it should be favoured with a hot, dry position, in soil which is sparse rather than rich.

One of the best examples of the confusion which can occur when botanical 'splitters' and 'lumpers' get to work can be found when trying to sort out where *Didissandra* should belong. There has been much confusion between this genus and *Oreocharis, Briggsia, Ancylostemon, Roettlera* and *Tremacron*. They all belong to Gesneriaceae, to which also belong such familiar plants as ramondas, gloxinias and saint-paulias. I have engaged in tussles with several of them, under all sorts of names but the only one with which I am currently having some little success is *D.grandis*, which is to be found growing on shady rocks in Yunnan. Its rosettes of ramonda-like leaves give forth umbels of very attractive, tubular violet-blue flowers in the spring—if you are lucky. No one that I know of has succeeded with it in the open, but it is well worth giving it a trial in peaty soil in the alpine house, during the hottest summer months plunging its pot in a shady place out of doors, or in a cold frame if you use one in conjunction with your alpine house.

Although *Athamanta cretensis*, as one would expect from its specific epithet, grows on Crete, I have not seen it in the wild, nevertheless I grow it and like it for the sake of its cushiony mounds of silver filigree foliage. To be really appreciated it needs to be planted in a hot and dry position, exposed to all possible sunlight. Its clusters of cream-white flowers are not exciting, but they are fragrant in an aromatic sort of way which recalls the fragrance of the sun-baked *maquis*.

Another genus with which you never quite know where you are taxonomically, is the genus I learned to know and to be interested in as *Azorella*. Most authorities seem to have decided that they are more correctly identified in the genus *Bolax*. Not a family laying claim to any floral beauty, they do make the most fascinating hummocky, iron-hard cushion plants and will handsomely adorn a sunny scree. The only one likely to be encountered in nursery catalogues—and that not very often—is *B.gummifera*, (you might find it also listed as *B.glebaria* or *Azorella caespitosa*, under both of which names it has masqueraded). It comes from the Falkland Islands and is also to be found in Magellan and Chile. Its mounds are composed of tightly packed rosettes of hard, leathery green leaves. The minute yellow flowers are carried in stemless umbels in the centres of the rosettes. Long-lived and very slow growing it can eventually make a specimen the size of a pillow.

A long time ago I decided that Australia was one country I felt no urge to visit, but a number of recent introductions of alpines from some of the high mountains, notably in the Kosciusko, have made me wish that I had not made such an arbitary decision. A recently published book has whetted my appetite even more. Entitled *Kosciusko Alpine Flora* and written by a team of enthusiasts, it vividly describes and splendidly illustrates the plants to be found there. Judging by the few which have already come to us we have a very good chance of growing them. Just one of the most spectacular, picked out at random, is *Ranunculus anemoneus* which carries splendidly large, rounded white flowers, above an elegant frilled bract. Another, perhaps less spectacular, but a charmer nevertheless, is *Brachycome nivalis*, a neat and tidy tuft of soft foliage surmounted by blue or white daisy-shaped flowers. This shows every sign of liking our conditions. The plants I raised from seed three years ago are proving hardy and perennial and are free and long flowering.

Exasperating though it can be I cannot help liking *Eomecon chionanthum*. It belongs to the poppy family and is the only species in its genus. Introduced from its native China late in the nineteenth century, it has taken such a liking to our gardens that it can become a nuisance because of its insistence upon sending underground runners in all directions, erupting here and there with succulent stems on which are large, rounded leaves. The flower stems, usually a foot or less in height, bear rounded, pure white flowers, each with a yellow centre. I became so annoyed with its wandering habits that I finally planted it together with that other vagrant, *Houttuynia cordata*, in both the single and double-flowered forms, and left them to fight it out. They appear to have come to an amicable understanding, live happily together, and repel any plant which attempts to invade their territory. There is a lot to be said for associating some of the more aggressive plants which, if set among more stay-at-home subjects can become a positive pest, but given others of a similar character as companions, will create a gorgeous medley and do no harm.

No one could wage a more ruthless war than I do on the common Bellbine, *Calystegia sepium*, but its great white funnel flowers are so beautiful that I sometimes weaken and, when it is scrambling through a vigorous shrub to which it could do no harm, I allow it to remain, against my better judgement. It is amusing to read in Clapham, Tutin and Warburg's *British Flora*, 'Sometimes a weed but fairly easily eradicated' at the end of the description. Whoever wrote those words had obviously never had to struggle with ground of which it had taken firm possession. The tiniest portion of its spaghetti roots remaining will soon be a thriving plant.

With the Sea Bindweed, *Calystegia soldanella* I would be quite prepared to have a friendly relationship—if it would grow with me, which it will not, in spite of all my blandishments. A plant of the sea shore, it creeps about at ground level and has fine trumpet-shaped flowers of soft pink or soft purple. My most recent attempt is to grow it, together with the Sea Holly, *Eryngium maritimum*, in a bed of pure sea sand and there are indications that this might be successful.

A cross, which all gardeners have to bear, is that just a few of the plants they most desire to grow, will not yield to whatever care and attention is given to them. I have never been able to accept the advice, often given to me, that the wise gardener grows only those plants which are most likely to succeed in the environment available. Such a complacent attitude would rob me of the excitement induced by an occasional triumph. A lot has been written in these pages concerning partial or total failures but I am quite unrepentant. I know that many of my readers are as eager as I am to accept the challenge offered by 'difficult' plants, and will admire and applaud the success of those who succeed where we have failed.

The plant which really inspired that paragraph is the annoying but enchanting little crucifer from the high screes of New Zealand, *Notothlaspi rosulatum*. As far as I know it has never been grown in this country for more than a very short time. I have myself almost, but not quite, admitted defeat and am prepared, when I can obtain seeds, to have another go. I have repeatedly germinated the seeds and have even grown them on until they were neat rosettes the size of a sixpenny piece, at which point they determinedly, and one by one, died.

On the top of a fleshy tap-root sits a flat, symmetrical rosette of leaves, serrated at their margins and densely felted with a pelt of fine grey hairs. From the exact centre of the rosette of leaves rises a short, tapered inflorescence on which, closely packed, are fragrant cream flowers. It is monocarpic and dies away, after it has flowered, so that one has to save the seeds and start all over again. It is perhaps not surprising that only the dedicated enthusiast will persist. I can offer no recipe for success, having tried everything, orthodox or unorthodox and in both acid and alkaline soils. My nearest approach to triumph was when the seedlings were planted in almost pure, lime-free grit with just a modicum of humus and a generous application of bonemeal. Germination offers no problems; it is afterwards that perplexity arises. In New Zealand they call it the Penwiper Plant. In moments of frustration I have been known to give it other names.

Among the faults of this book will be the omission of so many good alpine plants. The continual difficulty has been to decide what to exclude. Had I written of all the plants which delight me the book would have assumed the proportions of a multi-volume Victorian novel. After taking a short break from the typewriter and walking past a raised bed reserved for 'Specials', I find that an apology is also due to *Triptilion spinosum*, a very pretty composite from Chile, which is currently (mid-July) displaying elegant heads of blue flowers over clusters of lobed and pinnate leaves. I have known it and liked it for many years, in spite of the fact that it is not very long-lived—it can literally flower itself to death—but it is liberal in the provision of seeds and can be quickly replaced. Despite not being a difficult plant it remains curiously rare in cultivation and will not often be seen in many gardens, or in many nursery catalogues.

It only remains to say that 'these are some of my favourite things' and to hope that you may find as much pleasure in reading about them as I have found in the writing. Forgive the omissions and be tolerant of the errors.

Lists for differing soils, situations and environments

Plants for hot, dry positions in full sun

Acaena
Acantholimon, all kinds
Alyssum, all kinds
Cistus
Cytisus
Dorycnium hirsutum
Genista, all kinds
Helianthemum, especially all named
    varieties of H.nummularium
Helichrysum, all kinds
Hypericum, all kinds

Linum
Lithospermum 'Heavenly Blue',
    L.'Grace Ward'
Penstemon
Raoulia, especially R.australis,
    R.tenuifolia, R.glabra
Santolina, all kinds
Sedum, except S.pulchellum,
    S.humifusum
Sempervivum, all kinds
Zauschneria californica, all forms

Plants for poor soil and adverse conditions

Acaena
Ajuga
Alchemilla mollis
Antennaria, especially forms of
    A.dioica
Armeria maritima forms
Bergenia
Campanula poscharskyana
Cotula, all kinds
Epimedium
Erinus alpinus
Euphorbia myrsinites
Festuca
Genista pilosa
Geranium sanguineum forms
Gypsophila repens, all varieties

Helianthemum
Hieraceum, mostly weedy but useful
    for such positions
Montia parviflora
Pachysandra terminalis
Polygonum vaccinifolium
Potentilla tonguei
Sagina glabra forms
Saponaria ocymoides
Sedum album and forms, S.ewersii,
    S.spurium
Sempervivum
Thymus serpyllum forms
Veronica filiformis
Vinca minor forms

Plants needing moisture-holding soil and/or cool shade

Astilbe
Cyclamen
Dicentra
Gentiana, the autumn-flowering,
   lime-hating kinds
Hosta
Houstonia caerulea
Linnaea borealis
Lysimachia nummularia 'Aurea'
Meconopsis
Mentha requienii
Mimulus, all kinds

Nepeta hederacea 'Variegata'
Omphalodes cappadocica, O.verna
Oxalis acetosella 'Rosea'
Polygonatum
Primula, of the Candelabra section
Ranunculus ficaria forms, do not
   plant the type
Reineckia carnea
Tellima grandiflora
Tiarella cordifolia
Tricyrtis species
Trillium

Plants for dry shade

Ajuga
Brunnera macrophylla
Campanula portenschlagiana,
   C.poscharskyana
Chiastophyllum oppositifolium
Convallaria (Lily of the Valley)
Galax urceolata (G.aphylla)

Geranium phaeum
Lamium maculatum forms
Polygonum affine forms
Pulmonaria
Saxifraga × urbium (umbrosa) forms
Vinca minor forms

Plants of use and interest to flower arrangers

Acanthus, all species
Actaea spicata
Agapanthus
Ajuga reptans 'Multicolor'
Alchemilla mollis
Angelica archangelica
Anthemis cupaniana
Artemisia, various kinds
Arum italicum 'Pictum'
Ballota pseudodictamnus
Crocosmia, all kinds especially
   C.masonorum

Curtonus paniculata
Hosta
Leycesteria formosa
Mentha rotundifolia 'Variegata'
Molina caerulea 'Variegata'
Nerine bowdenii
Phygelius aequalis
Santolina, all kinds
Sarcococca, all kinds
Sedum maximum forms
Vinca major 'Variegata'

Plants for free-standing or retaining walls

Acantholimon, all kinds
Aethionema
Alchemilla mollis
Alyssum saxatile forms
Androsace lanuginosa
Anthemis cupaniana
Arabis caucasica (*albida*) forms
Arenaria ledebouriana
Armeria maritima forms
Artemisia
Asplenium trichomanes, A.ruta-muraria
Aubrieta
Campanula portenschlagiana, C.garganica, C.poscharskyana
Dianthus, many kinds
Dryas octopetala
Erinus alpinus

Erodium, all kinds
Euphorbia myrsinites
Genista lydia
Gypsophila repens forms
Helianthemum
Hypericum polyphyllum (*olympicum*)
Iberis sempervirens 'Snowflake'
Lewisia, except *L.tweedyi, L.brachycalyx, L.rediviva*
Phlox subulata, P.douglasii, all varieties
Polygonum vaccinifolium
Ramonda myconi (north aspect or cool position)
Saponaria ocymoides
Saxifraga
Sedum cauticolum
Zauschneria californica

Plants for rapid ground covering and planting between paving stones

Those especially suitable for paving are marked (P)

Acaena (P)
Achillea, dwarf kinds
Ajuga
Antennaria dioica forms (P)
Anthemis nobilis 'Treneague'
Arenaria balearica (cool position)
Armeria maritima forms (P)
Campanula cochlearifolia (P) *C.poscharskyana*
Cotula (P)
Crassula sedifolia (P)
Euphorbia robbiae
Genista pilosa
Geranium sanguineum lancastriense
Herniaria glabra (P)

Hypsella longiflora (P)
Lamium maculatum forms
Lotus corniculatus 'Plenus' (P)
Mazus reptans
Mentha requienii (P) cool position
Pachysandra terminalis
Paronychia nivea (P)
Potentila tonguei
Raoulia tenuicaulis (P)
Sagina glabra 'Aurea' (P)
Saxifraga aizoon forms (P)
Sedum floriferum
Thymus serpyllum forms (P)
Veronica filiformis

Plants for trough and sink gardens

Aethionema coridifolium 'Warley
     Rose'
Anacyclus depressus
Androsace, all cushion kinds,
     A.sempervivoides
Antennaria dioica forms
Armeria juniperifolia (caespitosa)
*Asperula gussonii, A.suberosa,
     A.nitida puberula*
Berberis irwinii 'Corallina Compacta'
Bolax glebaria
Campanula, all dwarfest kinds
Celmisia bellidioides
Crassula sedifolia
Cyclamen, all smaller kinds
Dianthus, small, cushion-forming
     kinds
Dryas octopetala 'Minor'
Edraianthus pumilio
*Erigeron aureus, E.trifidus,
     E.compositus*
Erinus alpinus forms
Erodium reichardii (chamaedrioides)
Genista villarsii
Gentiana verna angulosa
Geraniums, especially *G.cinereum,
     G.subcaulescens, G.argenteum* plus
     any of the really dwarf kinds
Gypsophila fratensis, G.repens forms
Hebe buchananii 'Minor'
Helichrysum coralloides, H.milfordae

Hypericum empetrifolium
     'Prostratum'
Hypsella longiflora
Iris, dwarf, bulbous kinds,
     I.chamaeiris forms
Lychnis alpina 'Rosea'
Mentha requienii
Mibora minima (verna)
Minuartia verna
Morisia monantha (hypogaea)
Phlox, all dwarf, cushion-forming
     forms of *P.subulata, P.douglasii,*
     plus any compact species
Polygala calcarea
Primula, any dwarf alpine kinds
*Ranunculus alpestris, R.crenatus,
     R.montanus* 'Molten Gold'
*Raoulia australis, R.glabra,
     R.tenuifolia*
Salix, any really dwarf alpine kinds
Saxifraga, a multitude from which to
     choose from the cushion-forming
     silver and encrusted kinds.
Scleranthus biflorus
Sedum, any non-spreading dwarf
     kinds, especially *S.cauticolum*
Sempervivella alba
Sempervivum, all kinds
*Spiraea (Petrophytum) caespitosum,
     S.hendersonii*
Viola yakushimana

Plants for peat beds and walls

Achlys triphylla
Anagallis tenella, especially 'Studland'
     form
Andromeda, any dwarf species
Anemone such as *A.apennina,
     A.blanda* and forms
Arcterica nana

Arctostaphylos, any dwarf, spreading
     species
Asarina procumbens
Asarum, any species
Asteranthera ovata
Astilbe glaberrima
Bruckenthalia spiculifolia

Bryanthus gmelinii
Calceolaria, such as *C.biflora*,
   C.tenella
Caltha introloba
Cardamine trifolia
Cassiope, all kinds
Chimaphila umbellata
Coptis asplenifolia, C.trifolia
Cornus (*Chamaepericlymenum*)
   canadensis, C.suecica
Cortusa matthioli
Dodecatheon, all kinds
Empetrum nigrum
Eomecon chionanthum
Ficus pumila
Galax urceolata
Galium odoratum (Woodruff)
Gaultheria, any of dwarf species
Gentiana, for those with chalky soil
   the peat bed may be the answer for
   growing the autumn-flowering,
   lime-hating kinds
Haberlea
Helonias bullata
Hepatica, all kinds
Houstonia caerulea
Houttuynia cordata
Isopyrum thalictrioides
Kalmiopsis leachiana
Laurentia tenella
Leiophyllum buxifolium
Leptarrhena amplexifolia
Linnaea borealis
Lithophragma parviflora
Lobelia linnaeoides
Loiseluria procumbens

Luetkea pectinata
Luzuriaga radicans
Lysionotus pauciflorus
Maianthemum bifolium
Mitchella repens
Mitella, all kinds
Oakesiella sessilifolia
Ourisia, all kinds
Parochetus communis
Pernettya tasmanica
Philesia magellanica (*buxifolia*)
Phyllodoce, all kinds
Phyllothamnus erectus
Polygala chamaebuxus
Polygonatum falcatum, P.hookeri
Primula, especially Asiatic species of
   the *petiolaris* section
Pyrola, all kinds
Ramonda myconi
Reineckia carnea
Roscoea, all kinds
Rubus arcticus
Sanguinaria canadensis
Sarmienta repens
Saxifraga fortunei
Shortia, all kinds
Sibthorpia europaea
Smilacina stellata
Stylophorum diphyllum
Tanakaea radicans
Tiarella, all kinds
Trientalis europaea
Trillium, all kinds
Tsusiophyllum tanakae
Vaccinium, all dwarf kinds

Plants suitable for growing in an alpine meadow

Acaena, all kinds
Arnica montana
Borago laxiflora
Buglossoides purpureocaeruleum
Bupthalmum salicifolium

Calamintha grandiflora
Campanula, the taller kinds
Ceratostigma plumbaginoides
Coronilla varia
Cotula, all kinds

Dentaria, all kinds
Dianthus, the taller kinds, but not border Pinks.
Diascia cordata
Epilobium glabellum
Erysimum linifolium
Erythronium meleagris
Festuca, the dwarfer kinds
Galium odoratum (Woodruff)
Gentiana asclepiadea, *G.septemfida*
Geranium dalmaticum, *G.renardii*, *G.sanguineum*
Geum borisii, *G.montanum*
Globularia trichosantha
Helianthemum, all kinds
Hieraceum aurantiacum
Hypericum olympicum
Iberis sempervivens 'Snowflake'
Inula ensifolia
Jasione heldreichii
Leontopodium alpinum
Libertia

Lychnis alpina
Millium effusum 'Aureum'
Phlox divaricata, *P.stolonifera*
Polemonium caeruleum
Polygonum affine, and forms
Potentilla megalantha, *P.tonguei*
Pulsatilla vulgaris
Rhodiola rosea
Scabiosa alpina
Sedum floriferum, and forms, *S.spurium*
Serratula seoanii
Silene schafta
Solidago brachystachys
Symphyandra wanneri
Teucrium chamaedrys
Thymus × *citriodorus*, and forms
Tunica saxifraga
Veronica cineria
Viola cornuta
Waldsteinia ternata
Wulfenia carinthiaca

These lists are neither arbitrary or absolute. There are many more from which to choose, but they indicate a selection of the best plants for the various positions and purposes. Not all of them will be found in the body of the book, however the great majority are obtainable from nurseries although there is a minority of rarities for which you may have to seek a specialist grower. A list of plants for the alpine house is not included. You will, of course grow there the real rarities, but many other plants qualify and help to maintain a year-long display. Throughout the book I have indicated those plants which need and deserve V.I.P. treatment.

Index

Numbers in italics denote illustrations.
Alternative plant names, arising from changing plant nomenclature, are given in brackets.